A WELSH ＿＿＿ＲＡＭＢＬＥ ALONG THE LLŶN COASTAL PATH

A Journey of Memories and Discoveries

ISBN: 978-1-84527-897-7

Published with the financial support of the Books Council of Wales.

Cover design: Eirian Evans

Published by Gwasg Carreg Gwalch 2021
12 Iard yr Orsaf, Llanrwst, Wales LL26 0EH
☎ 01492 642031
books@carreg-gwalch.cymru
website: www.carreg-gwalch.cymru

Published and printed in Wales

Jean Brandwood lives in Greater Manchester and is married with two sons in their 20s. Her career has mostly been in the NHS as an Occupational Therapist, working with children, young people and families with mental health difficulties and more recently with neurodiverse adults. She is passionate about all things Welsh, fell in love with Llŷn more than 30 years ago and began learning the language in 2012.

A Welsh Learner's Ramble Along the Llŷn Coastal Path

A Journey of Memories and Discoveries

Jean Brandwood

Thank you to:

Jim for sharing the journey with me and for always reaching out a hand just when I need it.

Tom and Simon for being you and for all the amazing memories.

My dear friend Letizia for convincing me that others may want to read this.

Diolch i:

Amanda, Brian, Elain ac Owain Lloyd am eich cyfeillgarwch.

Bobl Llŷn am eich croeso cynnes Cymreig.

Aran a Catrin Jones a phawb yn SSIW am y iaith hardd 'ma.

Myrddin ap Dafydd ac Eirian Evans (Gwasg Carreg Gwalch) am eich cyngor a'ch help efo popeth.

For Jim, Tom and Simon with all my love

Introduction

This is my story of a walk along the Llŷn Peninsula Coastal Path in North West Wales, with my husband Jim. It's a simple tale, with no acts of heroism and daring, unless being bitten by horse flies or scrambling down the steep bits on my bum counts for anything. We didn't beat any records with this walk either. Some of the guide books suggest it can be done in 'ten easy walks' and perhaps over the course of a week or two. We weren't in any hurry though and it took us just over three years and 42 walks to complete the journey! That did also include a long break halfway through due to being rudely interrupted by a global pandemic!

    This is a ramble in both senses of the word; a ramble along the coastal path between Porthmadog and Caernarfon, and plenty of rambling on about the people, places, flora and fauna that we discovered along our journey as well as some personal memories evoked from the many years that we've been visiting this very special area. Before you join me on the walk, I'd like to ramble on a little about how and why I came to love this very special part of Wales and then also about my passion for the language, **Cymraeg** (Welsh), which is still spoken as a first language by more than 70% of the population there.

"The first thing that particularly stood out for me about this text is the perspective; that is, it is written from the point of view of an author who is a little older, and who is quite open about having some limitations on her physical activity. This is very unusual in this genre, where most texts I have read are by young 'yompers' who complete trails in long segments. In contrast, this book breaks the walk down into more, shorter walks suitable for day trips, and considers stopping points in more detail. As a personal narrative it does this entirely pragmatically and it is incidental rather than focal to the text. Nonetheless, it's a missing perspective in the sector and will speak directly to a large audience who interact with the Llŷn in this way but who I feel are very under-represented in this area of publishing.

The second thing that stood out is the importance of the Welsh learners' angle and the inclusion of cultural themes, such as introducing Welsh language musicians and poets with clear personal love of the subject. This is another way the text extends beyond being a travelogue. Bearing in mind the current sensitivities around holidaymakers in rural Wales and their impact on local communities, my feeling is that this book not only introduces this topic well (e.g., some of the problems caused by second homes) but has a very positive role to play. It is in no way preachy on the issue, but as a non- resident of the area the author describes how she personally has chosen to navigate this: learning the language, investing in local community enterprises and so on. By outlining these positive steps and the immense benefit she has gained in taking them, it quietly provides a very positive example for the likely audience for this book."

Books Council of Wales reader

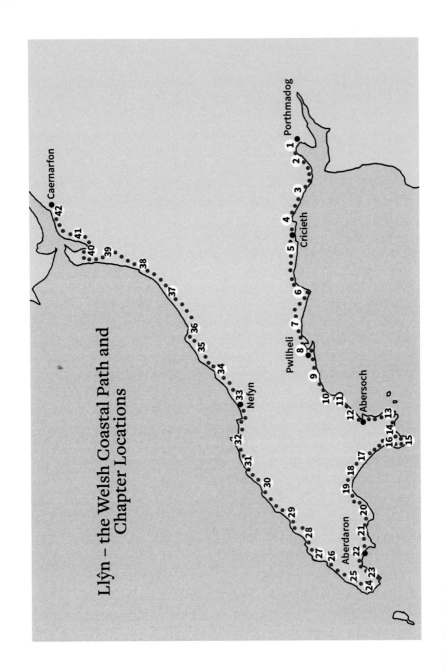

Llŷn – the Welsh Coastal Path and Chapter Locations

Caernarfon
42
41
40
39
38
37
36
35
34
33 Nefyn
32
31
30
29
28
27
26
25
24 23
22
21 20
19 18 17
16 14 13
15
12
11
10
9
8
7
6
5
4
3
2
1 Porthmadog
Cricieth
Pwllheli
Abersoch
Aberdaron

Contents

Love for Llŷn

The Llŷn Peninsula, often just known as Llŷn, was introduced to me in the Spring of 1991 by my then fiancé Jim and in the summer of that same year, we honeymooned together there, in the village of Edern, near its north coast. Llŷn extends 30 miles into the North Sea separating the bays of Caernarfon and Cardigan. It is sometimes referred to as Pen Llŷn, but Pen Llŷn actually means the head of Llŷn so really only includes the areas at the very tip of the Peninsula. In 1957, a part of Llŷn was designated as an Area of Outstanding Natural Beauty, one of only five such areas in Wales.

Jim was already familiar with Llŷn, having enjoyed holidays with his family there in his younger days, and he'd thought that I may also like it. As a child, I had travelled to North Wales on the train with my parents and two older brothers for our annual holiday, until Mr Beeching kindly closed our local station in 1969, but we had never ventured further west than Llanfairfechan, other than for a day trip to Portmeirion when I was 12. Jim was right of course; I immediately fell in love with this very special part of Wales and knew that I would need to return. I have a love of islands and my first impression was how island-like the peninsula felt. As it averages only eight miles across, the sea is rarely out of sight and breath-taking views are to be seen from the summit of even the smallest of hills, of which there are many. I soon began to realise that there was something else that made this part of the world so extraordinary; it was the people, who as a result of their strength and determination had managed to hold onto their heritage, culture and their beautiful language **Cymraeg** of which I'll speak of further.

From 1991 onwards, in addition to holidays elsewhere, Jim and I made at least one or two visits to Llŷn each year, staying with native Welsh speakers, when possible, in their chalets, caravans or cottages. Day trips and holidays have always been one of our main priorities, especially after the arrival of our sons Tom and Simon. Despite often being on a tight budget we have managed to give them a taste of many parts of the UK, between and including Land's End and John O' Groats. When the money stretched a little further, we travelled a little further, to Ireland, Holland, France or Belgium. But we always ensured that there was enough in the pot for at least one annual visit to 'The Peninsula,' as it became known to us all. The new kitchen continues to be on hold! Thanks to the generosity of our hosts, who never over charged for accommodation and always offered the best Welsh hospitality possible, our visits increased over the years and we made some wonderful lasting friendships.

If you were to draw a line on the map between Trefor on the north coast of the Peninsula and Cricieth on the south, everywhere to the west of that line is what defines 'The Peninsula' for me. We have visited and enjoyed many beautiful areas beyond this border, but it is there that we have made most of our treasured family memories, many of which came flooding back as we did this coastal walk. I still feel a strong sense of coming home as we pass the range of three hills called Yr Eifl on our arrival, and a feeling of sadness as I see them disappearing in our rear-view mirror as we leave. By the end of this book, you will be sick of hearing of Yr Eifl, as I will be mentioning them often, as they are my favourite hills and are in view for much of the walk. At this point I need to mention that Yr Eifl are known in English as The Rivals, because it is said that non-Welsh speakers thought it had a similar sound. **Yr** simply means the, but **Eifl** rhymes with naval and not with rival and means forks or strides. My favourite Welsh word is **Hiraeth**, which doesn't really have a straightforward English translation, but my understanding is that it means a combination of nostalgia, yearning and homesickness. I can certainly relate to this feeling when I'm not on 'The Peninsula,' even though I also love my home near Manchester. Over the years, as more happy memories have been made there, the yearning has become stronger.

Llŷn is usually the name used to refer to the whole of the Peninsula, but in recent years, I've discovered that there is a division and that the south eastern part, between Abererch and Porthmadog is known as Eifionydd. According to locals it is the river Erch that provides the boundary between Llŷn and Eifionydd and I've heard tales of gentle rivalry between the two areas. Each area has its own Welsh language monthly newspaper– *Y Ffynnon* (The Fountain) for Eifionydd and *Llanw Llŷn* (Llŷn Tide) for Llŷn. I remain neutral and buy them both! Throughout this book, for ease, I will refer to the whole of the peninsula as Llŷn, in the hope that I don't cause any offence. The well-known local musician and poet Twm Morys has written a poem, or doggerel as he described it, about the division of the peninsula and the rivalries between the people in the two areas. I'd heard him perform it on TV, on the Welsh language channel S4C and afterwards had searched for the verse in his published poetry books, but without success. A few years later we were part of a small audience for an intimate performance of music and chat at Caernarfon's art centre, Galeri, with Twm and his partner, Gwyneth Glyn, who is also a musician and poet. They invited everyone to come and speak to them in the bar following the gig. As we nervously approached, Gwyneth gave us a lovely welcome, as she remembered us from the audiences of several of her previous performances. This gave me the courage to ask Twm about his poem and where to find it in print. He very kindly took my email address and a couple of days later I received a copy of the poem in both Welsh and English. In addition to being the lead singer of the lively folk-rock group, Bob Delyn a'r Ebillion since the 1980s, Twm Morys is also known for being a master of **cynghanedd**: traditional patterns of word-music in Welsh poetry which uses a combination of rhyme and alliteration. **Cynghanedd** means chiming and has a melodious sound which is fascinating to listen to even if you are unable to understand the words. Twm is the son of Jan Morris who was famous as a travel writer and for having been the first person to report the successful conquering of Mount Everest by Hillary and Tenzing in 1953. Twm appears to have inherited his kindness from her. I have read Jan's books about Wales, and her more recent memoirs which regularly proclaim the virtues of kindness. We were privileged to have seen her live on stage at Pontio Bangor in 2019 at the age of 93, being interviewed by Twm and Gwyneth and were sad to hear of her death only a year later.

Did I mention that this will be a ramble? You'll have to get used to me as I'll be doing this a lot throughout the book!

Love for the Language

I first became aware of the Welsh language at about the age of five. I remember seeing my parents' guide books when they were planning holidays to Colwyn Bay and Rhos-on-Sea and recall standing on tiptoes to retrieve one from the huge metal dustbin in our backyard. I cut out the pictures of the chubby cheeked little girl in traditional Welsh costume, which appeared throughout the brochure. The pictures were accompanied by the message **Croeso** and an explanation that this meant welcome. But I don't recall hearing Welsh spoken during any of my childhood holidays in the 1960s.

Our Edern honeymoon cottage was owned by a lovely Welsh couple. The husband, Sam, was a retired farmer, quite a few years older than his wife, Ella, and to our surprise spoke only Welsh! That was when we came to realise that, although the majority of the natives of Llŷn could speak perfect English, their first language, their mother tongue, was Welsh. I wasn't the only one charmed by Sam's musical words, as four years later, our three-month-old baby Tom giggled and cooed while sitting on his knee intent on his every syllable. I became intrigued with the language and wanted to learn more about it. I bought a Welsh – English dictionary and this accompanied me on all further trips to Llŷn. I would look up translations of words I saw on street signs, shops and houses, but unfortunately, these were forgotten again between each visit.

For several years, when the boys were small, we wanted to be within walking distance of Nefyn beach so they could enjoy the sand and the sea at what had become our favourite spot. We stayed in the chalet belonging to John and Olwen, both retired teachers and very fond of children. They were generous and charming and were keen to teach us a few words of **Cymraeg** and some interesting snippets of Welsh history and we were all willing pupils. We eventually learnt and remembered how to say 'thank you' **diolch**, 'hello' **S'mae** and a rather formal 'goodbye' **da bo chi**. We also learnt that Nefyn sounded like Nevin with a 'v' not an English 'f' sound, and that a 'ff' is needed to make the equivalent of the English 'f' sound. We also discovered that the name of the famous pub on the beach at Porth Dinllaen Tŷ Coch isn't said 'Tie Cock' as you usually hear it said by non-locals, but something more like

'Tea Coke' with a guttural sound that makes the lovely Welsh 'ch.' The same applies to the soch in Abersoch, which rhymes with coch and doesn't sound like sock at all! And Betws-y-coed sounds nothing like Betsy Co-ed as it's so often heard from the mouths of non-Welsh speaking folk, including mine until not that long ago. We were saddened to hear from John and Olwen of the gradual decline of the Welsh language during the twentieth century and horrified to hear tales of the Welsh Not. This was a piece of wood, inscribed with the letters 'W.N.' and was used in the 1800s to discourage children from speaking their mother tongue in school. The teacher would hang the sign around a child's neck if they were heard speaking Welsh, then that child would transfer it to another child who dared to do the same. This continued until the end of the school day, when the child who was unfortunate to be left wearing the sign was caned. Thankfully this barbaric behaviour was stopped in the early 1900s, but surviving Welsh Nots can be seen in museums around Wales. This imperialist system of downgrading the mother-tongue in the minds of young children did leave a long-term inferiority complex for many generations, however.

My half-hearted attempts to learn Welsh continued on and off for many years, using teach yourself books and C.D.s but I retained very little, other than the few basics instilled in us by John and Olwen. Jim and I usually share the driving on our journeys and I have the amazing skill of falling asleep very easily when it's his turn, be it night or day. Jim would regularly pull up at the same services on our trips to Llŷn; services that for a long time I thought were in the town of **Gwasanaethau**, as the sign said **Gwasanaethau** Services. Eventually an occasion arose, when I stayed awake for the whole journey and I realised that there were several **Gwasanaethau** Services. I felt very silly when I looked in my Welsh dictionary to find out that of course **gwasanaethau** means services! In 2009, and the boys now 13 and nine, we were looking for a new regular place to stay in Llŷn, as sadly John and Olwen had both passed away. We were lucky to find a lovely Llŷn family who welcomed us to their static caravan on their farm in Llannor. Brian and Amanda went out of their way to make us feel at home, providing us with freshly laid eggs and home-made **bara brith** (traditional Welsh fruit loaf). Their children Elain and Owain were similar age to Tom and Simon and the four of them got on well together, playing hide and seek around the farm and the nearby lanes. Tom and Simon began to pick up some Welsh words from their new friends and Brian and Amanda always had time to answer our many questions about the language and the area. A long-lasting friendship had begun. Wherever I go in the U.K. or abroad, I like to learn about the culture of the place and of the people past and present. I usually do this through reading novels or folk tales set in the area, listening to songs of local musicians (ideally at a local gig or festival) and visiting art galleries and museums. Amanda was a mine of information and gave suggestions of local authors, musicians and artists I might like. I began to read the books of Kate Roberts, a Welsh language author who was born in Rhosgadfan in 1891, on the east of Llŷn. Her stories were mostly set in that area and told of the everyday lives of the slate quarrying families in the early 1900s and especially referring to the poverty they suffered. Her birthplace Cae'r Gors is now owned by Cadw, the Welsh Government's historic environment service. It is a shrine to the author, and is occasionally open to visitors. I enjoyed translated versions of her books Tea in the Heather *Te yn y Grug* and Feet in Chains *Traed Mewn Cyffion* but wondered if I was missing anything in translation. I began dipping into various books and online courses that were emerging, determined to make more of an effort in learning Welsh, but nothing seemed to work for me. I wondered if maybe I just wasn't cut out for learning languages, after all I didn't do very well with French in school.

In 2011, I'd just recovered from a nasty health scare, when Jim received a diagnosis of bowel cancer. Thankfully Jim responded well to the surgery and his prognosis was good, but it felt like a wake-up call to us both. At the end of 2011, I decided my New Year's resolution for the following year was to learn Welsh properly one way or another. I finally followed advice given earlier in the year and enrolled on an online audio course called 'Say Something in Welsh' (SSIW), which later became renamed as 'SaySomethingin' as they began to offer courses in other languages. I completed my first lesson on New Year's Day 2012, pacing around the house with my MP3 player, listening to and repeating Welsh phrases as instructed by Aran Jones, and reinforced by his wife Catrin, who both then repeated them back to me and gave me lots of praise and thanks for my efforts! I had been sceptical of this course a few months previously when I'd listened to the introduction. Aran, the co-founder, had instructed me to put down my pencil as I wouldn't need it. I felt this couldn't be the right course for me, as I thought I always needed a pencil to help me to think and to scribble down vital notes, and in fact I was holding one as he said it! But on completion of this first lesson, I was totally hooked and loving all the positive feedback; I was a praise junkie! I soon discovered that SSIW wasn't any ordinary course. It was virtually being given away at this time, with the first course free and a voluntary monthly contribution after this. The Jones's mission was about increasing the Welsh speaking population, and making money seemed low on their priority list. Aran and Catrin provided the material for the northern course and Iestyn ap Dafydd and his wife Cat produced the southern course. The difference between Welsh spoken in the north and the south isn't huge and first language speakers from both regions can understand one another but I chose the northern course for obvious reasons. I later discovered that Aran and Catrin lived in Llŷn and in my early months of learning, I was lucky to have occasional Welsh speaking practices in a local pub with Aran and some other learners. I could sense the passion and the urgency from the SSIW organisers around the need to keep this beautiful language alive. At the start of the nineteenth century at least 80% of the population of Wales spoke Welsh. Most were monoglots. At the 1891 census, only 50% were speaking the language and shockingly the 2011 census showed that only 19% of the population spoke Welsh. It also showed that only in Gwynedd and Ynys Môn were more than 50% of the people able to speak the language. There are various reasons behind this decline, including changes in education and the migration of non-Welsh-speaking people to Wales. As a result of the 2007 Welsh-medium education strategy published by the Welsh government, all children attending schools in Wales now learn Welsh from the age of about eight through to GCSE level. The Welsh Government's aim of Cymraeg 2050 is that by 2050 there will be a million Welsh speakers in Wales. With the ever-increasing availability of resources for people of all ages to learn the language, including SSIW of course, I'm optimistic that this can be achieved. Alongside the downloadable lessons, SSIW also offered an online forum for learners to interact and discuss difficulties and share triumphs. I had always shied away from forums, but soon got drawn in by the warmth of the course organisers and the other learners who were supporting one another from all over the world. I began to realise that this wasn't just a place to learn to speak Welsh, it was also somewhere to discover about every aspect of the Welsh culture. Topics on the forum included music, history, art and literature. I discovered there were Welsh novels aimed at learners and learnt about some very talented Welsh singers and musicians. I was totally immersed in Welshness! I began attending a monthly group of SSIW learners in a café in Manchester and within a few months I inherited the job of organising this group as the original organiser left due to ill health. SSIW became part of my daily routine. I devoured every lesson available to me and I was surprised and proud of how quickly I was able to manage decent conversations with people in Welsh. Initially it was scary conversing with people 'in the wild' but my enthusiasm and excitement overtook my anxiety. One of these scary but exciting moments happened in June 2012, when I

was at the Urdd Eisteddfod (Welsh Language Youth Cultural Festival) at Parc Glynllifon, near Caernarfon, with Jim and the boys. Our Welsh peninsula friend Amanda was with us and she spotted Nia Parry, who at the time, was presenting a T.V. series for Welsh language learners on S4C called *Cariad@Iaith* (Love at Language). Amanda knew that I watched the show regularly so she approached her, telling her that I was a fan and wanted to speak to her in Welsh. I had only been learning Welsh for a few months at this time, so felt terrified at the idea of

At the Urdd Esiteddfod declaring my love to Nia Parry!

having a go at a conversation with a Welsh language tutor and TV celebrity. Nia immediately put me at my ease, with her huge warm smile and friendly manner, and I felt very pleased with the chat I managed to have with her. As we said goodbye, Nia praised my Welsh and gave me a hug and I tried to tell her how pleased I was to have met her, as I loved her programme, but somehow instead of this, I nervously blurted out **Dw i'n dy garu di!** which means 'I love you!'

In August 2012, to raise money for the cancer unit who had treated Jim, and to push myself to use the Welsh I was learning, I organised a Welsh Chat Challenge for myself. This involved friends sponsoring me to have as many Welsh conversations as possible during our fortnight's holiday in Llŷn. I survived it and had some lovely responses from the people I dared to chat to. One of my most exciting sponsored chats was at a gig in Bethesda Village Hall – Pesda Roc – where having arrived early, I was introduced to the person I had mostly gone to see, Lleuwen Steffan, who is a jazz/folk singer songwriter with a unique voice. She was performing with her father Steve Eaves, who has been recording blues, jazz and rock music since the 1980s and whose music I also admire. I had chatted in Welsh to the lady selling tickets on the door and she had signed my sponsor sheet to prove I'd had a conversation, then quickly went over to Lleuwen to tell her what I was doing. To my delight, Lleuwen came over to me, with her flaming red hair and friendly smile, and after a Welsh chat, not only signed my form but insisted on sponsoring me and giving me money towards the cancer unit. She explained that it was a cause close to her heart, as she had lost her mother to cancer some years earlier. This was one example of the enthusiastic and encouraging responses I received from first language Welsh speakers when I had a go at their language. Neither before nor after learning the language have I experienced anything like the urban myth I've heard some non-Welsh speakers mutter; that of Welsh speakers suddenly switching from speaking English to Welsh to friends or colleagues when they detect a non-Welsh speaker close by in a café, shop or pub. This would not make any sense, as if there is more than one first language Welsh speaker in close proximity to another, they will most certainly already be conversing in their own language. Some English words may be heard as part of their conversation, as they are sometimes used, but what usually happens is a Welsh speaking person will cleverly and quickly switch over to English once they realise they're faced with a non-Welsh speaker, then back to Welsh again to chat to a colleague or Welsh speaking customer. I once had an interesting conversation with a lady working at a National Trust property in Llŷn who explained how, for the first few weeks of the new tourist season, as visitors were welcomed back to the property, she felt exhausted at the end of each day from speaking English. She said that her 'English language muscles' had been relaxed for too long as she'd had no need to use them over the winter when communicating with friends and family.

I continue to try and keep my Welsh language muscles in shape each day by meeting up with Welsh speaking friends, listening to Radio Cymru and the talks provided in the Advanced Content on SSIW, watching dramas and shows on S4C and by reading; I can now very slowly get through non-learner Welsh books. I still struggle to read Kate Roberts' books in Welsh, as the language of her time was quite complex. My favourite Welsh novelist currently is Manon Steffan Ros, sister of Lleuwen Steffan, who writes for learners and first language readers. Welsh is now, and will continue to be, a part of my daily life. Learning to speak this beautiful language didn't just give me access to a set of words, but opened new doors to a whole new history and culture. Try it and see!

Hiraeth

2016 brought us celebration and sadness. At the beginning of the year, Jim received his five years 'all clear' from bowel cancer, but the year ended with grief when my mum passed away only three days before Christmas and shortly after her 90th birthday. We all felt the loss greatly. My two brothers and I had to sell what had been the family home since 1973, Dad having already passed away in 2005. The early months of 2017 were very painful, involving clearing out of Mum's belongings and then as it was finally sold, saying goodbye to the place which was full of memories from my teens and early twenties.

Jim and I decided to do some much needed house improvements with our share of the proceeds of Mum's house, but kept enough at one side to fulfil our dream of having a caravan in

Llŷn. I know how much Mum and Dad would have approved of this, as they knew how much the area meant to us. In September 2017, we bought a static caravan and found the perfect, peaceful spot to have it sited, with views of Cardigan Bay and the Cambrian Mountains from the living area, and Yr Eifl and another favourite hill Moel Carnguwch from the bedroom. The boys were also very pleased with the strong internet signal! The river Erch runs through the private estate where our caravan is sited and we often walk along the lane that crosses the river via the bridge Pont Rhyd Farchog. The name of the bridge means the horse rider's ford bridge or for the more romantic the knight's ford bridge. I mentioned this bridge to Twm Morys when he sent the poem to me that referred to the river Erch being the boundary between Llŷn and Eifionydd. He was amused and suggested that Jim and I sat on each end of the bridge and recite the poem to one another across the river. We've yet to do this!

The caravan felt an acceptable way to have a place we could go to whenever we wanted to be in Llŷn, but without contributing to the current local housing problems that we were very aware of. Many local, affordable houses were being bought by estate agents and advertised as 'the ideal second home' or 'suitable for weekend retreats', when local young people were struggling to be able to find somewhere to live in their home villages. Living in Llŷn has been a dream of ours for years, but circumstances have not made this possible. But if we ever did buy a house there, it would be our permanent home and we would want to contribute to the culture and economy of the area as much as possible.

Not long after we'd bought the caravan, one of my favourite Welsh singer song-writers, Lowri Evans, who I'd first heard singing on the T.V. programme Cariad@Iaith, was offering fans a chance to commission her to write a song for them. I jumped at the opportunity and asked could we have a song for the family that told of our love for Llŷn. At her request, I gave her some examples of our experiences there and mentioned about our recent delight at having our caravan and how we had thought of naming it **Hiraeth**. She created a beautiful bilingual song and recorded this onto a C.D. for us. She named the song *Fan o Hiraeth* which means 'Van of Longing'. **Fan** (said 'van') in some situations can also mean 'place' so it had a double meaning – a van or a place of longing. I loved this play on words and we decided the caravan would have *Fan o Hiraeth* as its full name. We visited Hefin, the local monumental mason in Pwllheli, and he created for us a very attractive slate name sign, with carved Celtic lettering, which is now fixed to the side of the caravan.

Christmas 2017 was celebrated in the caravan, with a tiny, locally grown fir tree from nearby Glasfryn Forest, adorned with Welsh decorations, and **Nadolig Llawen** (Merry Christmas) bunting across the fireplace. We all managed to squeeze around the tiny caravan dining table for our traditional meal on Christmas Eve. On Christmas morning, I sneaked off alone in the early hours, while the younger ones were still asleep to attend a plygain service several miles away at St Rhedyw's church in Llanllyfni, which started at 7am.These services have been a Welsh tradition for centuries and I had been intending experiencing one for many years. Plygain carols were long religious poems, sometimes described as 'sermons in song' and often told the whole story of Christ, but the accompanying music often originated from folk songs. As I arrived at Llanllyfni, dawn was almost beginning to break and the air was chilly. Groups of smiling, excited people were scurrying into the church, including some very small children. I found a space at the back of the church and became totally absorbed as I watched the scene unfold in front of me. The minister played a very small part in the service and his role appeared to be to introduce each individual or group, who took their turn to make their way to the front of the church to sing their piece, always unaccompanied. I heard a lot of familiar carols as well as some less familiar, all sung in Welsh, and I felt privileged to be part of this light hearted, yet moving service. The highlight for me and probably the rest of the congregation was a tiny boy, dressed in a donkey costume, singing 'Little Donkey' in Welsh.

By the time I got back to the caravan, the others were waking and I shared my experience with them over breakfast. After lunch, we all got wrapped up and had a beach walk at Porth Dinllaen, followed by hot chocolate and mulled wine outside the Tŷ Coch Inn, whilst watching the tide coming in.

The caravan site closes each year on the 2nd January and reopens on the 1st March, which happens to be St David's Day, Wales's patron saint day. It was now time for us to winterise the caravan before returning home and saying goodbye to Llŷn for two months.

Valentine's Day 2018 brought me more than flowers and a card; unfortunately, I also received a diagnosis of breast cancer. I'd had no indication of anything being wrong, but thankfully the lumps were detected on my routine mammogram. In March, I had a right-side mastectomy and was told that my prognosis was very good if I took tablets for the following five years. On our first visit back to the caravan, only a few days following my surgery, I looked out from our bedroom window and as usual saw Moel Carnguwch looking back at me. We have always referred to this hill as Booby Hill due to its breast like appearance, complete with a 'nipple' formed by a bronze age cairn on its summit. I have heard that locals call it similar names, including Titty Mountain in its Welsh form. I have always had a fondness for this hill and we have all climbed it on several occasions, but on this particular day, I felt amused but mostly comforted by its strong but solitary presence.

In 2018, we paid for a wooden decking to be erected around the caravan by the site manager. We asked that the gate be left for us to arrange as we had plans. We wanted to commission local carpenter and craftsman, Dafydd Davies Hughes, to make a special gate for us. As you wander around Llŷn and beyond, you may come across beautiful carved oak gates and benches created by Dafydd at his workshop at Felin Uchaf. Felin Uchaf is Dafydd's enterprise in the wilds of Rhosirwaun and is a unique place with an other-worldly feel about it. Intricately carved wooden signs lead you along grassy paths to quaint thatched roundhouses, which you could imagine being inhabited by hobbits. Another path leads you to the observatory, with stained glass windows showing the phases of the moon, and carved beams illustrating the seasons and the flora of the area. Volunteers visit from around the world to learn

traditional skills such as thatching, carpentry and boat building. We had originally come to know Dafydd through another of his talents. As a family, we have been mesmerised many times over the years, whilst sitting around the large open fire in the largest of the thatched roundhouses, listening to Dafydd telling stories. These story evenings are very popular and Dafydd grips his audience with folk tales from different parts of Wales and around the world or with stories from the medieval Welsh Mabinogion. Quite often volunteers have been present at these storytelling and musical evenings and we have felt the sense of community and friendship at Felin Uchaf, which Dafydd and his family extend to them and indeed to anyone who visits this special place. Our beautiful oak gate, with hares, birds and the word Hiraeth carved into the wood is now our treasured piece of art work, that puts a smile on our faces each time we arrive at the caravan.

The Coastal Path Walk

Throughout the years of visiting Llŷn, we have visited many of its beaches and trodden on many parts of the coastal path. We spoke often of the idea of walking the whole of the Peninsula path or at least from Cricieth to Trefor ('our Peninsula'), but had never got around to it. The breast cancer was another reminder that we shouldn't put things off for too long, and that we'd better get on with doing this walk while all of our required body parts were in reasonable working order! We knew that we wouldn't be able to manage the walk in a week as some guide books suggest. We both have restrictions as a result of our cancer treatments, including joint stiffness, fatigue, and the frequent need for a loo, so we had to be realistic. We also didn't want to rush the experience, but rather wanted this to be something to enjoy and then reflect on in our old age. Our plan was to break up the journey into manageable walks of about two to three hours, and to walk only when the weather was reasonable and we felt fit enough. Each walk would be a return trip and our choice of start and finish points would depend on a suitable parking spot and availability of loos! I've described the routes we took in detail so that it may be helpful to anyone, who like us prefer the idea of walking the coastal path in a more leisurely way than the guide books suggest. We decided to complete the path between Porthmadog and Caernarfon, which tends to be the guide book definition of the Llŷn Peninsula Coastal Path. Porthmadog was our agreed starting point, as we thought that the path looked less challenging at that end and we could gently wean ourselves into the more strenuous parts. What we didn't realise until we started was that all the guide books describe the walk beginning at Caernarfon; this made for very confusing reading whenever we referred to them. Much to the amusement of family and friends, I have a poor sense of direction and have been lost many times when alone on foot, on car journeys and especially when trying to navigate my way around Ikea! Luckily, Jim is excellent at finding his way around, especially with the help of his trusty navigational gadget that I can never remember the name of. I will refer to some of the walks as 'back to front' walks, and these are the ones where we were unable to continue our walk where we had left off on the previous walk, due to lack of access or nearby parking. Instead, we would either start the journey at what was really the end of that day's stretch and walk back, or we would start midway along the stretch and walk one way then the other. Whichever way we did it, each walk was a return journey so we in fact walked the Llŷn coastal path twice over! To help avoid confusion, the title of each walk is written in the correct order, even if it was done 'back to front,' for example Walk 16 is named Cilan to Porth Neigwl, when we in fact started at Porth Neigwl due to lack of access to the path at Cilan.

The QR codes are added to help locate the starting point of each walk on your map. If you don't already know, a QR code is a type of barcode that contains information. Some walks have more than one QR code and this is when we broke up a longer walk into sections or when we had to turn back to avoid livestock or landslides. To use the QR codes, simply point your smartphone camera close to the code for the walk you want to do and you should be invited to click onto 'maps' which will then take you to the location shown on that particular QR code on whatever map app you have on your phone. You may need to install a QR Reader App to your phone if it doesn't already have a built in one. The Ordnance Survey maps for Llŷn are OS Explorer Maps 253 and 254.

Throughout the book, I've taken the liberty of spelling Cricieth with a single 'c' in the middle. A double 'c' is never used in the Welsh language and so this is the correct Welsh spelling of the word. In books and newspapers, and on signs throughout the town, you see it spelt both ways. But as you drive into the town from either direction, an indication of how some of the locals feel about this is seen on the official town signs, where someone has blackened out one of the 'c' s.

I considered using the words **Cymru** and **Cymraeg** instead of 'Wales' and 'Welsh' throughout the book, but kept with the English words for ease of reading. I believe that the word 'Wales' is derived from the old Saxon/Germanic language and means outsider or foreigner, whereas the meaning behind **Cymru** is the much friendlier and appropriate: 'compatriot'. As I'm writing this, there is a campaign calling to put a halt to place and house names in Wales being changed into English, to avoid further decline of the Welsh language. Some examples of place names that are disappearing have been highlighted by comedian Tudor Owen, who is backing the campaign. Llyn Bochlwyd, Conwy, is now often being referred to as Lake Australia because some say its shape resembles the outline of the map of Australia. The lake acquired its name from an ancient story of a grey stag escaping a hunter by leaping into the lake and holding its cheeks above the surface as it swam. Bochlwyd means grey cheeks. How sad it would be if these wonderful tales were lost to less imaginative and anglicised naming of places and buildings.

I refer to 'we' quite often along our walk and this of course means myself and Jim. This was very much a joint walk and we shared lots of memories and admired the amazing views together along the way. I think we complement each other on our walks, as we have different interests and notice different things, for example as I'm trying to identify a bird or wild flower, Jim will be examining old metal remains from a quarry or watching the jets fly over from RAF Valley. Jim speaks a few words of Welsh, mostly greetings and thanking people and he also tries to use it with the locals. He has also mastered the most important sentence which allows him to offer me a cuppa in bed every morning in Welsh **Ti eisiau panad?** But Jim's a very private person, so most of the ramblings you'll be hearing will be mine.

We started the walk in May 2018, feeling enthusiastic and optimistic, with no mental approximation of when we would complete it. We took lots of photographs and I made scribbly notes of my observations, thoughts and our experiences, not quite sure what I was going to do with them. I gradually had the idea of putting them together to make a book for ourselves and the boys, as I had included a lot of memories of our times together in Llŷn from 1990 onwards. But during the course of the journey, I also began to reflect on what I'd discovered and was continuing to discover about the culture and people of this beautiful land – people past and present, real and of legends. I realised that many of these discoveries had come about as a result of my having learnt to speak Welsh, my eyes having been opened wider to my surroundings. This realisation led to the idea of sharing these reflections especially with non-Welsh speaking visitors to Llŷn in the hope that it may help them to appreciate some of the less obvious wonders of the place and its people and to perhaps even learn a little Welsh along the way. Apologies in advance to the locals of Llŷn for any errors or omissions I may have made with regards your rich and wonderful language, history and culture; I still have a lot to learn.

If you want to know how to pronounce the Welsh words used in this book, there are lots of videos on YouTube to help with this. A good place to start would be to learn how to pronounce the Welsh alphabet which is much easier to use than the English one, as the letter sounds are consistent, with very little deviation.

In the Appendix there is a list of some of the words I'll be using frequently, especially when describing the landscape.

Anyway (or **beth bynnag** as they say in Welsh), less rambling and let's get on with the walk.

Porthmadog

Trains, Boats and a Drunken Harpist

Porthmadog to Borth-y-gest – 6th May 2018

What better way to start our walk than with a hearty breakfast **brecwast**. The entrance to Y Gegin Gefn café is tucked away in a side street, off Porthmadog's bustling Stryd Fawr. The friendly owner responded with surprise and patience as I ordered our food in Welsh, kindly hiding any amusement he may have felt at my attempts to name each breakfast item correctly. I've noticed that many food items, despite being on the menu in Welsh are commonly asked for in English by Welsh speakers, including two of my favourite foods and Welsh food words – **sbigoglys** (spinach) and **madarch** (mushrooms).

Feeling very satisfied and ready to walk off our tasty meal, we said **diolch** to the owner who gave us a wave and a smile, quickly returning his gaze to the rugby on the T.V. I was feeling very excited about finally starting out on our adventure as we stepped back onto Stryd Fawr. It was hot and the town was noisy with traffic, despite it being a Sunday. There was no time for window shopping today as we hurried past the various craft and souvenir shops but my attention was caught by the Portmeirion Pottery shop and my thoughts drifted. Portmeirion is the nearby Italian style village, now a huge tourist attraction and wedding venue. It was designed and built by Sir Clough Williams-Ellis from the 1920s onwards. His eldest daughter Susan was the founder and designer of Portmeirion Pottery and her pretty Botanic Garden design tableware is a familiar sight in many people's homes throughout the world. My first visit to Portmeirion was with my parents in 1973, as a rather reluctant, sulky twelve-year-old, with my even sulkier older brothers, who were feeling much too old to be seen on a day trip with their parents, let alone their pesky little sister. But I admire the place and the pottery now and we have a couple of pieces of the Botanic Garden range in the caravan. Interestingly, the pottery has never actually been made in Wales, but initially in Stoke-on-Trent and currently worldwide, including China.

Puffing and hissing sounds drifted towards us from the Harbour

Station of the Ffestiniog and Welsh Highland Railway, as we made our way towards the harbour, relieved to be away from the hustle and bustle of the town centre. Fond memories of steam train journeys with Tom and Simon were shared as we looked across to The Cob, the mile long, raised strip of land which carries the railway and the road across the estuary of the Afon Glaslyn. I was also reminded of my discovery of Welsh language music in 1990 in Cob Records, situated at the beginning of The Cob; a shop renowned for tracking down rare records. I can still remember the very serious young male sales assistant handing me a cassette by the band Mabsant, when I asked him for suggestions of Welsh language music. I found it difficult to explain what I was looking for, but stated that I wanted something modern but also traditional and asked if there was a Welsh equivalent to the Irish band Clannad. I'm not sure if the term contemporary folk was used then, but that was what I was looking for. I was happy with his recommendation which was a great start for my journey into the world of modern Welsh language music. I'm pleased to be able to say that this tiny shop, which features in one of pop singer Duffy's music videos, is still thriving and continues to also provide a worldwide mail order service. Anyway, I must get on or we'll never get to Borth-y-gest!

What a beautiful day we were blessed with. Afon Glaslyn shimmered in the sunshine, beneath a vivid blue sky and boats of various types and sizes gently bobbed about on the water. We followed the path which took us past the boatyards, quiet and gated today. Dense hedgerows lined the uphill path and we were met at the top by a group of 1930s houses and their immaculately kept gardens. We continued down the steps, finally emerging into Borth-y-gest cove and simultaneously remarked on an attractive old sea-front house, Borth dairy, where we had stayed with my brother and sister-in-law, Stephen and Eileen, in 1994 BC (Before Children). In those days this old converted dairy was let out in its entirety to holiday makers, but more recently its grey stone walls have been rendered and painted white like most of the other houses overlooking the bay, and is now a very attractive looking B & B.

A thick mist had settled on the river, hiding Portmeirion across the estuary, but the mountains of Meirionydd were just peeping above it. We had reached the end of our first short stretch of Llŷn coastal path but I was eager to divert from the path to find a local landmark I had recently heard about. This landmark had a legend attached to it, with music being central to the tale, which made it irresistible to me.

David or Dafydd Owen was a composer and harpist in the early 1700s. He was said to have lived in a farmhouse close to Porthmadog, called y Garreg Wen. The story goes that he regularly entertained the locals with his harp, playing in the local hall in Borth-y-gest. One evening on his way home, possibly a little worse for wear with drink, he rested a while near a large rock and fell asleep. On wakening, he heard a lark singing and he composed the now well-known tune *Codiad yr Ehedydd* (The Rising of the Lark). I'd recently watched an interesting series on S4C, in which the Welsh singer Cerys Matthews (founding member of the band Catatonia) told the history of various Welsh folk songs. She'd shown the location of a large rock, just a little way inland from Borth-y-gest harbour, which was thought to be the very same rock where Dafydd had slept. Using Cerys's directions, we continued along Rhes Gwelfor, turning right up Mersey Street and right again just before Borth-y-gest school. Following the path which gradually wound its way through woodlands, carpeted with sweet smelling bluebells, we came across a caravan site aptly called Garreg Wen which means white rock. In the middle of a clearing close by, was the huge grey and white speckled rock, with an engraved slate plaque bearing the words **Cwyd, Cwyd, Ehedydd Cwyd** (Rise, Rise, Skylark Rise). This is a line from the lyrics added to Dafydd Owen's tune in the 1800s by the famous poet John Ceiriog Hughes (often simply referred to as Ceiriog). Whether or not the story is true, I could see how this

Jim perched on Y Carreg Wen.

Borth-y-gest

spot could be the inspiration for a musical composition. We both clambered onto the rock to witness the stunning view of the sea and the mountains, made even more dramatic by the lingering mist, but not a single skylark was to be seen or heard. The most famous tune attributed by some, but not by others, to Dafydd Owen is the sad air *Dafydd y Garreg Wen* (David of the White Rock), which has another famous tale attached to it. Dafydd died at the young age of 29 and it is said that shortly before his death he had a dream that he was in heaven listening to the most beautiful music. On waking, he asked his mother to fetch his harp and he composed the tune which shortly after, at his request, was hummed by his family and friends at his funeral procession between his home and his burial place at Ynys Cynhaearn church. Ceiriog's lyrics which were added much later, tell the tale of Dafydd on his death bed. Various versions of this song have been sung and played by many different famous Welsh musicians over the years, including the world-famous opera singer Sir Bryn Terfel and harpist Catrin Finch. My favourite is a livelier, modernised version, sung by Cerys Matthews.

We climbed down from the rock and made our way back to Rhes Gwelfor, where we enjoyed a panad and a slice of bara brith at Sea View Café, whilst discussing our plans for the next stage of our walk, before returning to Porthmadog. Despite this first walk being quite short, I still felt a sense of achievement that we'd taken our first steps along our coastal path journey.

Walk 2

Gunpowder and Graves

Borth-y-gest to Black Rock Sands – 19th May 2018

The view across the estuary was bright and clear today, with not even a hint of mist to hide the mountains and Harlech castle. Boats were bobbing on the river, which was glinting and dazzling in the hot sun. As we followed the now familiar blue and yellow 'dragon-shell' coastal path signs, we passed the rather regal looking Bron Afon. Built in the 1840s and possibly the oldest house in the village, holiday makers accommodated there have one of the most enviable views in Borth-y-gest. Shortly after St Cyngor's church, the path narrowed between sweet smelling hedgerows of gorse, entangled with brambles and fern.

The narrow branch of the river, now named Dwyryd as it divides before reaching Cardigan Bay, came into view as the path widened. We were thankful of a tunnel of oak and beech trees which shaded us for a while, as neither of us tolerate the full heat of the sun for lengthy periods of time. Continuing uphill and downhill along the path, we finally emerged at the very pretty National Trust owned Morfa Bychan beach. We stood and admired the view across the beach to the grassy and rocky headland known

Morfa Bychan

as Ynys Cyngar. Ynys means island and this was once exactly that before the build-up of dunes joined it to the mainland. Perched on top of Ynys Cyngar, we could see an interesting looking house with turrets on the roof top. We later discovered this was Y Cwt Pwdr, which in the 1700s was used as a store for gun powder after being unloaded from ships. The gunpowder was used in the local slate mines, to blast away the rubble. After picnicking on the beach, we continued along the sandy path above, which wound around the back of Y Cwt Pwdr and eventually brought us down to the edge of Black Rock Sands. The Welsh for Black Rock Sands is Traeth y Graig Ddu, but unfortunately this is rarely seen or heard. A much-needed wooden bench was waiting for us at the edge of the sand with a message carved in Welsh and English:

Blasa'r heli, gwel y nen, rhyddha d'enaid fry uwchben.
'Smell the sea and feel the sky, let your soul and spirit fly.'

I rested my achy knees and we did as the bench commanded for a couple of minutes, then continued along the beach. As we walked, we reminisced about our visits here with family and friends, pre-children. We laughed about our struggles with stunt kites and my total (sometimes endangering) lack of skill with a frisbee! Black Rock Sands is a two-mile expanse of soft, white sand, lovely to look at and play on, but weary to trudge along with aching limbs. About a quarter of the way along the beach, we had made it to our much-needed stop before turning back – the loos!

On our drive back to the caravan, there was another stop I wanted to make, which will finish my tale of Dafydd y Garreg Wen. Pentrefelin is a small village along the A497, between Cricieth and Porthmadog. An ancient, horse chestnut tree-lined causeway from the village takes you to St Cynhaearn's church. This disused church is now in the caring hands of the lovingly named organisation 'The Friends of Friendless Churches.' It stands on Ynys Cynhaearn, which was once an island surrounded by Llyn Ystum, but is now surrounded by lush green fields and overlooked by Moel y Gadair. I was hoping to have had a peep inside as I love the atmosphere of old churches, but sadly it was closed. We headed to the graveyard, which was the main reason for this visit. Jim is accustomed to trailing around old graveyards with me as I have spent years looking for ancestral graves throughout the U.K. to help fathom my family tree. He has become quite an astute grave spotter and

St. Cynhaearn's Church

once again was quick to discover the one I was looking for, despite the churchyard being very overgrown with grass, brambles and nettles, with an occasional clump of bluebells. Dafydd Owen's memorial is a flat, slate grave erected almost 100 years after his death and depicts a harp and the following words translated literally from the Welsh:

David Owen's grave or Dafydd y Garreg Wen,
The Superb Harpist buried 1749, aged 29.
He enchanted the breast, made the throng happy –
and his song was the glory of Wales.
This is where he was buried.
There is no-one like him, he was Jubal.

E.O.

It has been suggested that E.O. who wrote the 4 lined Welsh verse or englyn was Ellis Owen, a poet and farmer, born in 1798 at Cefn y Meysydd Isaf, a farmhouse north of Pentrefelin. I wonder if he was a relative of Dafydd. I've come across many variations of the story of Dafydd y Garreg Wen, including some that say he was blind. The poem that Ceiriog set to the song suggests that Dafydd had been married with children, so perhaps Ellis was a descendent who wanted to ensure that his memory lived on. He certainly wanted to emphasise how talented Dafydd was and for others to appreciate this. Jubal was a man mentioned in the Hebrew Bible and he was described as the ancestor of all who played the harp and flute.

St Cynhaearn's church was built in 1622 and is a Grade II listed building. I'd recommend anyone to visit who has an interest in historical buildings or people in this area. There are several other graves in the churchyard, commemorating locals of note. These include James Spooner, builder of the Ffestiniog Railway, Daniel Morris, the first harbour master of Porthmadog, gardener John Ystumllyn, a black man brought back from Africa by a member of the Wynn family of Ystumllyn in the 1700s and Ellis Owen the poet previously mentioned.

Ynys Cyngar and the Powder House.

Walk 3

A Long Beach Walk and Raspberry Pink Clogs

Black Rock Sands to Cricieth – 3rd June 2018

Black Rock Sands is popular with tourists, and at certain times of the year, vehicles are allowed to be parked on the beach. We set off very early from the car park on Beach Road, near the public toilets, to avoid the crowds and the midday heat. We greeted other early risers, cooking breakfast on their mini stoves on the beach by their camper vans, apparently having ignored signs of 'no overnight parking.' Heavy fines were introduced, shortly after this walk, motivated by human excrement having been found on the beaches – disgusting or **ych-a-fi** as they say in Welsh!

Criss-cross patterns from the tread of car and van tyres covered the long expanse of beach, and Cricieth castle was a distant dot ahead of us. We trudged through the soft sand for over a mile until we reached the western end of the beach, where Black Rock Café appeared like a mirage through the heat of the morning. Refreshed by an ice lolly, we continued on our way along the path by the

Black Rock Sands

exclusive lodge park, crossing the cattle grid and onto the farm track. The bright white houses of Cricieth and the sea soon became visible as we followed the low stone wall edging the fields of grazing sheep. As the track wound around the craggy hillside which is Graig Ddu itself, and we passed a grey stone farmhouse converted into a holiday cottage, Cricieth castle came into view. This ruined, thirteenth century castle, built by Llywelyn the Great and Llywelyn the Last, holds lots of memories for us. As long-time members of Cadw who own the castle, we have been very frequent visitors since Tom and Simon were tiny. Their imaginations stirred by the remains of this majestic fortress, sitting high upon the rocky promontory overlooking Cardigan Bay, led to hours of role play, often with swords and shields purchased from the Cadw gift shop. We were still adjusting to visiting Llŷn without Tom and Simon, who now as young adults were leading their own busy lives. But the memories and the tales we shared about them as we walked, added to the pleasure we got from our journey. They do sometimes come to the caravan with us when they can fit it into their busy schedules and we revisit favourite spots together including the castle.

The track now led away from Graig Ddu across a field towards the railway line, as we joked about sending photos of the castle via our phones to the boys saying 'wish you were here'. We crossed the level crossing and continued along the grassy path, which ran parallel with the line. Cricieth disappeared for a while as we strode past tall grasses, brightened by pink foxgloves, still damp from the heavy rain the day before. An occasional bluebell and the last of the wild yellow primroses brightened our path. Before too long, the whole of Cricieth was visible to us as we crossed back over at the next level crossing. We followed the grassy fenced path which soon brought us to the back of a white art deco style building. This was previously the Morannedd Café, designed by Clough Williams Ellis of Portmeirion fame. It was built in 1954 and was well known for its tea dances. Since 2015, it has been the home of Dylan's Restaurant, which specialises in local seafood. Musical events are still hosted here and it was here in that opening year, where Jim and I experienced one of our earliest Welsh language music gigs, with two very talented local folk singers – Gwyneth Glyn (mentioned earlier) and Gwilym Bowen Rhys. Gwilym Bowen Rhys is a young singer and musician with a distinctive gravelly voice, who started off his musical career as a teenager in a Welsh language alternative rock band called Y Bandana, who produced songs with catchy tunes and humorous lyrics. In addition to developing a successful solo career as a folk singer, he now often collaborates with other singers, including with his two sisters to make up their band Plu and with the South Walian musician Carwyn Ellis, plus his sisters, to create the band Bendith. Both of these bands create a beautiful unique 'retro' sound that takes me back to a phase during my 1960s childhood when I became entranced by several dubbed foreign T.V. series, all with enchanting theme tunes including White Horses, Robinson Crusoe and Belle and Sebastian.

For a while, Gwilym Bowen Rhys also worked as an apprentice clog maker in Cricieth with Trefor Owens, who was the last remaining hand maker of traditional Welsh clogs. I had often thought I'd like a pair of traditional Welsh clogs and about a year after this walk, we visited Trefor's tiny workshop in the back streets of Cricieth. I felt slightly embarrassed seeing Gwilym Bowen Rhys there, as by then I was quite a fan of his music. Even though he didn't know me, I was worried I might appear like an aged groupie, especially when I mentioned I liked his music. The situation was initially made worse by Trefor, jokingly suggesting that I was a stalker, but my embarrassment was soon dissolved by silly banter that we all entered into and which I managed partly in Welsh. Gwilym has now got used to the sight of us both frequently appearing at his gigs and the occasional appearance of my bright pink clogs. A couple of years following this visit, we were saddened to see the workshop had closed and Trefor was no longer taking orders. Also, since then Gwilym's musical career seems to have gone from strength to strength so I imagine he no longer has the time to make clogs. Did I just ramble then? Off we go again.

Buying clogs

Two giant carved

Dylan's Restaurant and Dafydd's handiwork.

wooden oars form a gateway guiding people into or out of Cricieth along the coastal path behind Dylan's. We thought we recognised the distinctive style of the carving and it was later confirmed by the man himself, that it was indeed the handiwork of Dafydd, who had made our gate. The oars are carved with images and Welsh words related to the sea and the area such as **crancod a chimychiaid** – crabs and lobsters.

As we came along the promenade we were entertained by the RNLI, who were launching their lifeboat; thankfully it was going out on an exercise and not in response to an alert. We resisted the delights of Dylan's and headed straight to Cadwalader's Café, for an ice-cream. Cadwalader's is very popular with locals and tourists alike and they proudly boast that their vanilla ice-cream is made to the same secret recipe used more than 90 years ago, when it was sold from the window of the Cadwalader family grocery store. You are lucky if you manage to get a table by the window, which overlooks the sea where dolphins and porpoises are frequently spotted. We haven't been lucky enough to spot either as yet when having lunch there, but I've been rather surprised by some of the people we've spotted. I have to confess to becoming rather like a star struck school girl when I come across famous personalities. In Llŷn this can happen quite frequently, as it is the home of many of the talented Welsh people whose work I admire – singers, musicians, authors and T.V. personalities – many of them a combination of all of these. If I hadn't learnt Welsh, it is unlikely that I would have discovered any of them as it has been through hearing about them on the SSIW learners' forum, listening to Radio Cymru or watching S4C that I have come across them. The locals don't bat an eyelid when they see these people, as they are part of their community, and our peninsula friend Amanda thinks it's hilarious when she hears of my being in awe at coming face to face with a 'celebrity.' My first encounter in Cadwalader's was in 2013, when I spotted Nia Parry, the T.V. presenter to whom, only a year before, I had declared my love! I was very touched that she remembered me and my faux pas, and we both had a giggle about it...in Welsh of course and this time with a more appropriate farewell line. On a more recent visit to Cadwalader's (yes, we're fond of ice-cream), I was awestruck by the person I spotted, and my gaping mouth gave me away. I received a modest, yet knowing smile from nonagenarian, Jan Morris, who had noticed my response as she was leaving the café with her lifelong spouse Elizabeth. I had recently read in her memoirs that they liked to visit different cafés each week for lunch. For many years they had lived not far from Cricieth in Llanystumdwy, which was to be the terminus of our next coastal walk.

Our ice-cream devoured, we returned the way we came and very slowly sauntered along in the heat until we reached Black Rock Sands car park.

Level Crossing and Cricieth Castle.

43

Walk 4

A Winding River and a Prime Minister
Cricieth to Llanystumdwy – 3rd July 2018

Since our previous walk, Jim had retired from work, which was a cause for celebration. He was very skilled at his job as a time served (but underpaid) sheet metal worker, but was glad to leave behind the dirty and noisy workshop environment. He had worked hard over the last few months, making alterations to the caravan to make it just as we wanted it and was pleased to have been able to make some very useful metal parts during his lunch breaks at work. But now he was ready to relax a little and enjoy the fruits of his labours.

With our back to the castle, our journey continued along Cricieth promenade on this hot July morning. The sea glinted in the sunshine and the seagulls were loudly announcing their presence. The fields on the right of the path and the gorse along the seaward side were scorched and brown as a result of weeks of unusually hot, dry weather. Dragonflies and cabbage white butterflies flew across our path. Further along the path and hidden behind a modern stone wall, we could just make out the flat roof and uppermost part of a large house overlooking the sea. A plaque boasted that it had won a regional architectural award in 2015. We agreed that from what we could see of it, we preferred the stone wall but in fairness, we are both drawn towards the traditional.

Grey seal

A cheeky grey seal seemed to be following us as we continued along the path, which now ran parallel to the sea. It popped its head up every so often as if greeting us, before playfully disappearing again under the gently rippling water. We stepped down onto Ynysgain shingle beach, with its pretty

44

Ynysgain

pink sea bindweed and sea thrift tangled amidst the grassy dunes. An oystercatcher was picking at its finds along the shoreline, as we clambered back up onto the path now bearing right and heading to the mouth of the Dwyfor estuary. This is such a stunningly picturesque area and just to complete this perfect scene as we were passing, two swans were gliding along the river, occasionally arching their necks, and a solitary sheep was grazing on the opposite bank.

The path became rougher as it followed the river along its course and the signs directed us onto the fields belonging to Aberkin Farm, a working cattle and sheep farm. A kissing gate led us to another field and we were directed to take a sharp right and follow the stone walled fence towards the farm. The path was wide, and bone dry as were the fields around us. There were no trains in sight as we strode across the level crossing and headed through a short tunnel of trees. We spotted two green woodpeckers taking flight from the trees and landing on a fence, close to the farmhouse. We wondered whether the circle of stones in the field were ancient or had been placed there more recently. We began to feel as if we were trespassing, as the path led us through a collection of barns and other farm buildings and houses, but we were greeted warmly by an elderly male occupant and I managed a brief chat in Welsh with him, mostly about the weather; how English of me!

We reached the A497, which although not that busy, seemed noisy after our almost silent walk so far; we were feeling hot and ready to rest. We crossed over the road and found the small wooden gate which led to the last stretch of path which cut between houses and soon brought us out into Llanystumdwy village. Llanystumdwy is famous for being the home town of David Lloyd George, who was a liberal leader and became prime minister of the UK between 1916 and 1922. The Lloyd George Museum now incorporates his childhood home Highgate and was also significant in my journey into learning to speak Welsh. In late 2011, on a family visit to the museum, I made an attempt at a couple of sentences in Welsh with the curator, a serious but helpful man in a bow tie. I tried to tell him the ages of our sons, when he asked in relation to the ticket prices. He corrected my modern usage of numbers and explained I should use traditional number words when naming ages. He recommended I use an online course called Say Something in Welsh. I didn't tell him I'd previously given it a little try and wasn't so sure about it, but this prompted me to give it another go a few weeks later. A few months into the course, I dared to respond to a request on the SSIW forum, for people to share their experiences of learning Welsh and to say what led them to using the course. I described my experience in Llanystumdwy and mentioned the 'character with a bow tie' at the museum who had suggested the course to me. I was shocked, but amused, when Aran the course director, responded to my account with the message 'guilty as charged, that's my father-in-law!' So, he was the father of Catrin, the female voice of the northern SSIW course. I have since met Emrys, the 'character in the bow tie' on several occasions, usually at Llanaelhaearn church, where he sometimes preaches and his wife Rose (Catrin's mam) always offers me a warm welcome and a seat on the old pew next to her, enabling her to guide me through the service which is performed in Welsh. **Byd bach** (small world) as they say in Wales.

Not far from the museum is Lloyd George's memorial and grave on the banks of the river, which was designed by Clough Williams Ellis, who built Portmeirion. Within the ornate walled memorial is a boulder which was Lloyd George's favourite seat by the Afon Dwyfor. Further up the lane from the memorial, you come upon Tŷ Newydd – a Grade II listed building which was Lloyd George's final

The return to Cricieth.

home. It is now the National Writing Centre of Wales, where residential creative writing courses are regularly held. I've visited the house twice and can understand why it has been the retreat of many respected authors since it became a writing centre in 1990. This large, white house is set in secluded lawned grounds and has a welcoming interior, with lots of cosy nooks to sit and contemplate, and shelves spilling over with books everywhere you look.

We found some welcome shade on the edge of the bridge near the church and rested a while before starting back to Cricieth. As we guzzled from our water bottles, we reflected on a walk we had done along the Afon Dwyfor from this same bridge only four months earlier in March, when there had been a generous coating of snow. How different from that day everything looked and felt today.

Hustle, Bustle and Heat
Llanystumdwy to Porth Fechan – 6th July 2018

It was a scorcher of a day and the first two miles of the next stage of our walk had to be along the A497, due to the position of the river. We plastered ourselves with Factor 50 and donned our sunglasses and wacky sun hats, leaving the car close to the Lloyd George Museum in Llanystumdwy village. A left turn behind some stone cottages, just before the bridge, took us back onto the short path leading to the A497. Compared to the main roads back home, the A497 isn't that busy, but the noise of speeding cars felt quite alien to us in Llŷn. The grass verges were scorched and although much of the road was lined with trees and tall bushes, very little shade was available along the way. We quietly and rather grumpily marched along, keen to feel the sea breeze on our faces. Trails of hundreds of ants frequently crossed our path. The hedgerows and the gorse were the driest we'd ever seen them, but the sweet smell of the honeysuckle and white valerian encouraged me to keep going.

The road crossed Afon Dwyfach and shortly after, a plaque announced who had opened the A497 in 2006 – I think I cursed him at this stage! We passed an attractive old white house named The Old Tollgate, which we later discovered was built shortly after the passing of the Turnpike Act in 1808. Its purpose was to control access to the Porthmadog to Porthdinllaen road. The entrance to Afonwen farm appeared on our left and triggered memories of Simon, Tom and myself having a go at horse riding there. I laughed to myself, remembering how at the time I'd thought that perhaps getting on a horse would feel like second nature to me. Prior to my being born, my dad had been a farmer and a skilled horse rider,

In the heat along the A497.

but I'd never been encouraged to give it a go. I'd only ever had donkey rides on the beach as a small child and I didn't look too anxious on the photos. As I climbed onto what seemed like a mammoth of a horse offered to me at Afonwen farm, I knew immediately I had absolutely no innate horse-riding skills. I was terrified of the beast but did my best to look calm, so that I wouldn't worry Tom or Simon who both handled the experience confidently and happily.

We approached the roundabout at Afon Wen, which is very close to the start of Lôn Goed, my favourite non-coastal walk and one frequently visited by us all in the past especially on hot summer days. Easily missed, the entrance to Lôn Goed is marked by two stone posts, each topped with a horse's head. Lined with oak and beech trees, the lane was built in the early 1800s, to transport lime, coal and peat between the sea and inland farms. We discovered it after seeing a video on S4C of Gwyneth Glyn singing her song *Eifionydd* whilst seated on a bench on the lane. The lane, which is about seven miles long, has several benches, made of stone and wood, some with accompanying sculptures, and most engraved with lines of Welsh poetry – yes, the handy work of Dafydd once again! Poet R. Williams Parry was responsible for immortalising Lôn Goed in Welsh with his poem *Eifionydd*. I've been told that in the past, Welsh primary school children were expected to learn to recite this poem by heart – and possibly still do. The poem describes the beauty of the Eifionydd area and the verse which is dedicated to Lôn Goed, describes its tranquillity, something that we have certainly experienced, but not on this particular walk.

We resisted the urge to head down Lôn Goed to escape the heat and traffic, crossed the road at the roundabout and followed the tree lined lane which ran parallel to the river. We enjoyed some much-welcomed shade until we came to the railway bridge. The lane continued under the bridge then opened up allowing us a view of the waters of Afon Wen on our left. The seagulls were calling, the sea holly was almost in bloom, Pen Ychain headland was jutting outwards ahead of us and Cricieth was in the distance behind us. We were by the sea again at last!

We walked along the stony beach in the area known as Porth Fechan, that stretches across the back of Hafan y Môr holiday park.

Porth Fechan

I can remember as a child, hearing friends saying that they were going to Pwllheli and this always meant Butlin's holiday park – its original name. I grew up thinking that Pwllheli was a holiday park. It isn't somewhere I stayed as a child and neither Jim nor I were attracted to the idea of ever visiting, apart from with an occasional day pass to use the fun pool with the boys. Llŷn means tranquillity to us and being able to roam wherever we feel like, rather than being amongst crowds of people with organised entertainment. In October 2015, before the caravan was even a twinkle in our eyes, and when friend Amanda had closed her caravan for the winter, we decided to challenge our prejudice. We booked a weekend at Hafan y Môr for us all. Our peninsula friends Amanda and family came to visit us and were highly amused as we seemed like ducks out of water. We all had fun in the pool, but none of us were interested in the noisy bars and eating places. In fact, Jim and I 'escaped' the complex on one of the days there, to have a walk along Lôn Goed.

But I have to admit that on this occasion, when we spotted the line of green static caravans from the beach, it was a sight for sore eyes – and feet! We entered the park and wandered through the play area, then used the loos and ordered a coffee in one of the bars. Now all we had to do was to walk all the way back to our car at Llanystumdwy in the blazing heat.

Towards the end of our weary return journey, as we reached the short path that took us back into the village, we noticed a paper notice pinned to the gate, with a handwritten message 'cold drinks and ice lollies for sale.' As we stepped into the village from the path, there was the tiniest of shops on the corner across the road, called **Sŵn y Môr** (sound of the sea), rather ironic after a walk with mostly the sound of traffic! A pleasant lady served us ice lollies which we devoured greedily as we sat on the bridge in the shade – a cooling end to our least favourite walk so far.

The Old Tollgate along the A497.

Walk 6

A Tepee and Some Optimists
Porth Fechan to Abererch – 6th August 2018

Porth Fechan has become known to many as Hafan y Môr beach because of its proximity to the holiday park of that name, where we parked the car on this warm but overcast morning. The narrow path towards Abererch was clearly defined and we soon left behind the caravans, and large privately owned lodges set in their prime sites with sea views at the edge of the park. We were puzzled by the sight of a large triangular structure in the distance, close to the concrete trig point marking the top of the hill at Pen Ychain. As we neared the hill, we realised it was a life size wooden sculpture of a tepee. We never discovered its significance or who was responsible for it but I liked it. Not many days after this walk there were some powerful storms that caused damage across Llŷn and I wondered if the sculpture had survived.

From the top of the hill, we could see Cricieth castle and the multicoloured seafront houses to the north-east, and Pwllheli south-westerly. A flotilla of what I thought were small yachts were sailing towards the marina at Pwllheli in the far distance. We discovered later that they were 'Optimists' – small single handed sailing dinghies. What we had witnessed was the Optimist National Championship and they were all being handled by under 15-year-olds!

Resting by Pen Ychain trig point.

We wandered down onto the beautiful stony beach near Pen Ychain, with its vast array of colourful rocks. I was spoilt for choice for my pebble collection. I have a mini printer's tray fixed to the wall at home and each tiny shelf holds a pebble from one of the beaches we have visited in Llŷn. This was one of the rare beaches that we had not yet set foot on, so I 'needed' one for my collection. Yes, I'm a geek!

We followed the natural diversion back up along the grassy path behind the dunes that led us across rough grassland and eventually to the wide sandy beach of Abererch. We rested for a while whilst being entertained by a group of common sandpipers **pibydd y dorlan** scurrying along the beach, stopping occasionally to peck at their finds.

On our return walk, we excitedly discussed plans we'd made for the remainder of the week. Tom, Simon and Tom's girlfriend Rhi had come with us to the caravan and we had some trips and treats organised. A helicopter flight across Llŷn from Dinas Dinlle had been booked for Jim and Tom. This was a retirement gift for Jim and a twenty third birthday gift for Tom. Later in the week a boat trip for us all to visit Ynys Enlli had been arranged. The coastal path walks would have to wait a little while again.

The Optimists

The wooden tepee and trig point at Pen y Chain.

Ladies of the Dawn and a Harp
Abererch to Pwllheli – 14th October 2018

Family and friend commitments plus trips to places other than Llŷn meant that we had not been near the coastal path for two months. We'd had an invitation to a housewarming party in Worcestershire in September and had decided to spend a few nights in the surrounding area, including Powys. Offa's Dyke (the linear earthwork which follows the England/Wales boundary) and the ancient oak and yew trees at Discoed were the highlights for me, but I had been disappointed at the lack of Welsh spoken around that part of Wales.

A watchful buzzard

The position of the river Erch meant that our only option for this next part of our journey, was to walk along the dratted A497 again, once we'd left the car park at Abererch Holiday Park. A buzzard eyed us suspiciously from his perch in the tall bushes as we crossed the level crossing by the railway station. It was a perfect autumnal morning, with a light breeze and bright sunshine. Thankfully the main road was relatively quiet as it was a Sunday. The leaves were beginning to turn and haybales were drying out in the fields. The Welsh for October is **Mis Hydref**, which is a reminder that autumn is here, as the Welsh for autumn is **yr Hydref**. The poet R.S. Thomas, who will be mentioned again in later walks, wrote a Llŷn Peninsula diary in Welsh, which was published in a very timely way on the 1st January 1990 and translated to English at a later date. In his October entry, Thomas, a lover of the natural world, remarked on how there is little change of colour of the leaves on the trees in

Llŷn. He describes how the trees quickly become bare and appear like scarecrows after the first strong wind. A Welsh friend who knows someone, who knew someone, who knew R.S. Thomas (or something like that), told me that he, R.S., was often heard saying that there were only two seasons in Llŷn – Summer and Winter. I have to confess that even though I'm a lover of trees, I only noticed this phenomenon, which has been attributed to the cold strong sea winds, after reading Thomas's diary.

The road crossed the river Erch which was mostly hidden by overgrown bushes and was barely noticeable. An old traditional black and white fingerpost informed us we were just two miles from Pwllheli. There are several of these fingerposts to be seen around Llŷn and they are over a hundred years old. They were erected as a result of the 1903 Motor Car Act and were all restored in 2008. I think there's something very charming about them. Shortly after the sign for Pwllheli, our attention was drawn to the small terraces of houses along the main road. Although we had driven along this road many times, neither of us had noticed how close they were to the rocky, wooded hillside behind them. They almost looked as if they were built into the rocks and we wondered about how much daylight, if any, the occupants got into their back rooms.

We turned left at the sign for the marina and the road took us past the outskirts of the Glan y Don industrial estate and across the level crossing. I noticed a quirky looking green and white house, simply called 'Crossing' which I believe is where the original Pwllheli station was situated before land was reclaimed. The current station was built and opened in 1909, about half a mile further along and nearer to the

The old station house, Pwllheli.

Pwllheli Harbour

town centre. This is the terminus of the Cambrian Coast Railway which runs to Machynlleth and then onwards to Shrewsbury or Aberystwyth and today it was the terminus of our walk.

Before returning to Abererch, we paused to admire the view across the water to Plas Heli and the yachts of the sailing club. Plas Heli is a modern, space age looking building, home to the Welsh National Sailing Academy. It also has a restaurant with stunning views across the harbour, which is often used as a venue for events. One event that Pwllheli music lovers were proud to be able to hold there was the **Gŵyl Cerdd Dant** in 2016. This is an annual festival held in different parts of Wales and dedicated to a special form of music known as **cerdd dant**. My simplistic explanation of **cerdd dant** is that whilst a melody is played by a harpist, a singer or singers concurrently sing lines of poetry to a different tune. Unfortunately, we missed the festival but we did attend a fundraising event for it in April 2015, which was held at Capel y Drindod, in Pwllheli. It was called *Sioe Cân a Chomedi* (song and comedy show). The star of the show was Pwllheli's own Gwenan Gibbard, who specialises in this unique art and is one of the few people who can self-accompany on the harp. The first performance was to be a short comedy play by the local **Merched y Wawr**. **Merched y Wawr** translates to Daughters or Ladies of the Dawn and is an organisation for women which aims to promote women's issues and to support culture, education and the arts in Wales, similar to the UK Women's Institute (WI). Before the start of the performance, I managed to have a conversation in Welsh with a friendly, chatty lady, a little older than myself, called Gwen, who was sitting on the pew next to me. She was very interested in how and why I was learning to speak Welsh. She then turned to chat to friends who were sitting behind her and then to others to her other side. About ten minutes later, the chairman of the local committee for the **Gŵyl Cerdd Dant** – a comical character and ex head master of a local school – began his welcome and introduction to the evening. We got quite a shock when not long into his welcome speech, he asked everyone to give Jim and I a special welcome as visitors from Manchester and to congratulate and thank us for learning their language. This was followed by a round of applause from the audience! I was very touched but also amused and wasn't sure whether to laugh or cry. Jim said that he didn't deserve the applause as he only speaks a few words of Welsh, but I disagreed as he always tries to greet people in Welsh and is very supportive of my learning. That evening, we discovered that word spreads quickly in a Welsh chapel, but also that there is nothing warmer than a Welsh welcome! Not long after this happened, I also received an invitation to have coffee at Gwen's home.

Dewi Pws and the Trespassers (no it's not the name of a band!)

Pwllheli to Penrhos (Traeth Crugan) – 29th October 2018

Bright blue skies awaited us on this cool morning as we left Pwllheli station behind and strode out along Embankment Road, known to many as The Cob and a great place to find a free parking spot for those who don't mind a short walk to the town. We passed the war memorial dedicated to those who lost their lives in WW1 and 2, with the statue of a soldier as if standing guard with his back to the harbour. We passed the council offices Swyddfa Dwyfor on our right where a few months later we were to witness the colourful and musical St David's Day parade **Parêd Dewi Sant** begin its journey through the streets of Pwllheli. The parades were introduced to Pwllheli in 2014 and are held every year on the Saturday nearest to St David's Day, depending on the weather. They are part of a week-long celebration in Llŷn, when the shopkeepers of the town decorate their windows in a St David's Day theme, ready to be judged on parade day, and local cafés offer *Tapas Llŷn*, where they add various tapas dishes to their regular menus. In 2017, local singer, poet and actor Dewi 'Pws' Morris, who

is a bit of a comedian and usually part of the event along with other local talent, wrote and composed *Cân y Parêd* (the parade song), a short catchy song, which has been sung by school children in the parade ever since.

We passed the play park as we approached the promenade and fondly remembered Tom and Simon showing off their prowess on the skateboard ramps many years before. It's only in recent years that I came to understood what the

Pwllheli war memorial.

58

circle of stones were on the field by the park. In the past, I had wondered if they were a Neolithic stone circle or maybe a replica put there for the children to enjoy. I hadn't realised that they were Gorsedd stones which are an important part of the National Eisteddfod and were placed there when Pwllheli hosted the event in 1925. The National and the Urdd (under 25s) Eisteddfods are held annually and are week-long events, alternating their venues between the north and south of Wales. They are one of the highlights of the lives of many thousands of people in Wales and an opportunity for them to show off their creative talents, especially in the field of music and poetry, and to compete against their fellow Welsh folk for coveted awards. The most prestigious award is the chair which is awarded to the winner of the **cynghanedd** poetry competition. The winner is referred to as **Y Prifardd** (the chief/master poet) and is presented with a specially designed chair at the chairing of the bard ceremony. The other desired award is the crown, again designed by a crafts person each year and presented to the winner of the **pryddest** (free verse poetry competition). Both of these ceremonies are presided over by the Archdruid and are full of pomp and customs including the wearing of long robes. According to tradition, a proclamation of the following year's National Eisteddfod is completed a year before its official opening by the Archdruid of the Gorsedd of Bards. The Archdruid is the presiding official of the Gorsedd which is the society of Welsh language poets, writers, musicians and others who have contributed to the language and to public life in Wales. He or she stands upon the central **Maen Llog** (logan stone), surrounded by the circle of 12 standing stones while announcing the event. These circles of stones can be found throughout Wales where other National Eisteddfods have been held. I have yet to witness one of these ceremonies but it's on my to do list! An Eisteddfod is an ideal opportunity for anyone learning to speak Welsh who wants to immerse themselves in the language, as it is an all-Welsh event. You can either watch competitors performing inside the huge pavilion, listen to a variety of musicians and singers in the surrounding tents, or browse the hundreds of stalls on the Maes which offer Welsh goods of every kind. There is even a special area where Welsh learners can meet up called Maes D.

Just before the promenade, by the South Beach or Traeth

Marian y De, we passed the deserted café, that has stood empty for many years. It was built in 1959 and has had several names and owners, including Curds Café (after its owners), Caffi Melyn because of its décor – **melyn** means yellow, Caffi Glan-Môr and then Rita's, after it featured in an S4C film *Stormydd Awst* (August Storms). It had been very popular with locals and visitors alike, but was now an eyesore. We had heard rumours of it being renovated but there was no sign of this today. We walked for a while along the long stretch of sandy beach, then stepped back up through the dunes and onto the prom without dawdling, as we had read the signs warning of adders in the grass. Along the promenade, we continued past the remainder of the pastel coloured three storey houses, which are almost all converted into flats. The grassy path at the end of the promenade led us past some attractive bungalows and houses with terraces looking out to the sea, then further along we passed the popular golf course where there was already quite a lot of activity. I tend to agree with an anonymous quote, usually but apparently not correctly, associated with the nineteenth century author Mark Twain that 'Golf is a good walk spoiled' but I know many would disagree.

We shortly came upon a rambling ruin of a house, which was barely a shell of the beautiful farmhouse it had probably been in the past. An elderly lady approached us and, speaking in a firm American voice, told us that we were actually trespassing and should have been on the higher path. Feeling rather embarrassed, we gave an apology but due to my inquisitive nature (nosiness) I needed to know more. I asked her was she the owner of this house

The Ruins near Traeth Crugan.

Jim at Traeth Crugan.

and commented on its beauty but dilapidated state. She said that the house had been in her family for generations and she was going to have it renovated. We said goodbye and did as we were told, with some muttering to each other, and clambered up onto the grassy bank towards Traeth Crugan. She called after us, saying that it was a beautiful spot for bird watching.

With the headland Carreg y Defaid to our right, we sat on one of the huge orange boulders on the beach and admired the views across the rocky sands, which was deserted of birds and people. We continued our muttering about whether or not that stretch of the path, which was clearly marked as the coastal path, was really private land. A horse drawn tramway used to run between Llanbedrog and Pwllheli. It was originally constructed in 1893 to allow the carrying of stone from Carreg y Defaid quarry to Pwllheli and was extended to Llanbedrog in 1897, allowing the transportation of visitors to the recently opened art gallery at Glyn y Weddw, Llanbedrog. I will mention more about this unique place in a further walk. As we began our return walk, we pondered about where the tramline would have been and decided it could only have been along this very path, which passed the American lady's ancestral home. So, did we remain on the higher path on our return? I'll let you guess!

Three Men and an Oystercatcher

Penrhos (Traeth Crugan) to Llanbedrog –
6th November 2018

There is no easy access directly to Traeth Crugan so we had to start at Llanbedrog and work our way back. We parked the car in Llanbedrog village, where we often find a handy space, close to St Pedrog's church hall, along Pentre Llan. We walked to the junction where Lôn Nant Iago met Pentre Llan and turned right into the lane which leads down to the beach. We passed the very pretty church of St Pedrog and the gateway to Plas Glyn y Weddw Art Gallery, which will be talked about more in the next walk. As we reached the end of the lane and stepped onto the beach, despite the cold and grey of the day, many happy memories of times spent here with the boys came flooding back. One of my fondest was of Tom and Simon taking part in a summer workshop with other children, when they proudly showed off their works of art, made using driftwood, pebbles and shells under the direction of a local young artist employed by the gallery. As we trudged along the beach, we did the obligatory glance up at the familiar Iron Man (or Tin Man as he is sometimes known) who stands at the tip of the headland, Mynydd Tir y Cwmwd, and was barely visible today. I'll introduce him to you properly in the next walk. Below was the typical Llanbedrog picture postcard view with the old converted boathouse and the very photogenic white Foxholes Cottage, a Grade II listed building, both nestled amongst the autumnal woodland. The beach was empty apart from a solitary oyster catcher **pioden y môr** intent on finding itself some breakfast from amongst the seaweed and stones. In the summer, Llanbedrog beach is very busy and is usually

Approaching Llanbedrog beach.

Llanbedrog boathouse and Foxholes Cottage.

decoratcd with brightly painted National Trust owned beach huts, that are brought out of storage for the holiday season, but they hadn't made an appearance at all this year as the sand level had been too low following storm Emma in March. We reached the wooden steps that led up onto the grassy coastal path and were rewarded with a stunning view of the headland and the beach. While I was distracted by the remnants of wild flowers on the path, Jim spotted a plain, square, concrete building that we'd never seen before, sited at the end of the headland. Having forgotten our binoculars as well as our walking poles once again, we depended on our phone cameras to obtain a closer picture. Later, when studying the maps and guides, we discovered that this was the abandoned Quarry Hopper Building, used originally for the storage of stones from a nearby quarry, while they were waiting to be shipped out. The path, lined with browning ferns and gorse bushes, followed the edge of Carreg y Defaid, the small headland west of the beach and eventually took a 90-degree turn bringing Traeth Crugan into view, with the hills in the distance beyond. An opening appeared along the path to our left with a lane that leads to the A499. We continued straight ahead and the path widened out as it followed

Traeth Crugan with Pwllheli in the distance.

the curve of the bay, which was lined with large boulders acting as a sea defence. We passed through a small metal gate and the path now led us across the edge of a field along what probably used to be the tram line. As we reached a large wooden gate, we clambered up onto the grassy bank via a kissing gate and wandered down onto the beach from where we had distant views of Pwllheli promenade. We continued along the seaweed and pebble strewn beach until we reached the ruined house but there was no sign of any activity there today.

We were now close to Penrhos, but even though our walk didn't take us through the village itself, I can't continue until I mention some important events and people connected with it. My awakening to these events happened when we were enjoying a gig in the tiny Tafarn y Fic pub in the village of Llithfaen – Gwilym Bowen Rhys yet again! A drunken young man was being reprimanded by a very tipsy older lady who may have been his mother. She spoke passionately in her Llŷn tongue, but too quickly for me to follow easily and pointed towards us, or so it seemed. I was confused until I realised it was the picture behind us on the wall of three male faces (two wearing hats), that she was drawing his attention to, and I managed to grasp that she was telling him that he should be ashamed of his behaviour in front of them. The other faces on the walls of 'Y Fic' are of local singers who have performed there over the years, but I had often wondered who these three older looking men were. I contacted my font of all knowledge about things related to Llŷn, friend Amanda, who suggested it was probably the three men famous for the **Tân yn Llŷn** (fire in Llŷn). So, naturally I needed to know the whole story. The 'Three' were all members of **Plaid Cymru** (The Welsh Party) – Saunders Lewis (dramatist), Lewis Valentine (poet and preacher) and D.J. Williams (novelist). In 1936, the UK government, decided to establish RAF Penrhos bombing school and air base at the site of Penyberth, an old farmhouse in the village. This led to protests, as Penyberth was a very important part of the history and culture of Llŷn, having been the home to generations of poets and a resting place for pilgrims on their way to visit Ynys Enlli. The destruction of Penyberth and building of the bombing school went ahead despite the protests but on the 8th September 1936, the 'Three' decided to take action, setting fire to the new building and according to reports, immediately turning themselves in to the police. They were sentenced to nine months imprisonment but on release were greeted as heroes by a huge rally of 15,000 people in Caernarfon. This event is seen as very significant in the history of Welsh politics and continues to be remembered in stories and songs. In 1949, the Penrhos Polish Home was founded to provide accommodation and support to Polish ex-service men and women who remained in the UK following the Second World War. It was built on the site of the RAF base. A few weeks following this walk, we visited the grounds of the Polish Home to pay our respects to the 'Three,' who are remembered on a brick memorial close to the entry. Engraved slate plaques are built into the brick, showing their faces, the details and dates of the event and a picture of Penyberth.

On our return, the sky showed a hint of blue and we strode out, eager to get back to Llanbedrog, where Plas Glyn y Weddw art gallery had everything that we needed – a loo, café and interesting art to admire – in that order.

The Tin Man and Bear Grylls
Llanbedrog to Traeth Tan y Mynydd – 19th November 2018

Plas Glyn y Weddw art centre is my most frequented art gallery and the next stretch of our walk began at this beautiful 1857 gothic mansion, which has a fascinating history that I can't do justice to here, but which is available to discover in the Madryn Room and the Ap Tomos Room in the **Plas**. The display there especially focuses on Solomon Andrews who first established a gallery here in 1896 and Gwyneth and Dafydd ap Tomos who rescued the place from dereliction in 1979. I look forward to each new exhibition in the gallery, especially the summer exhibition which showcases and sells the work of many local talented artists. This is where I first saw the stunning art work of my favourite Welsh artist Tess Urbanksa, with her signature blue that is so recognisable in her paintings, which are often of local villages and beaches. I've been fortunate enough to meet this lovely young artist a few times and she is always incredibly modest about her work.

We drove into the gallery car park for the second time in two days. The day before we had enjoyed the annual Welcoming Christmas Event at the **Plas**, with live music, carol singing, mulled wine and a glowing open fire. By the side of the wide, sweeping drive of the **Plas** is a brightly painted red and white tramcar which is the only surviving horse drawn tram used on the tramway mentioned previously, taking visitors back and to between Pwllheli and the gallery. Following the closure of the track in 1927, it was used as a feed store on a local farm, then in 1986 it became a novelty tourist information centre in Pwllheli, before being taken to the Steamport Museum in Southport, where it was rebuilt. In 2013, it was refurbished and later given on long-term loan to the gallery by Pwllheli Town Council. Just by the entrance to the car park is the elegant Giant Sequoia tree which is thought to be the tallest tree in Llŷn.

We left the car in the gallery car park, next to the John Andrews Amphitheatre. which is built into the woodlands. The sea and headland provide an amazing backdrop for this theatre, where we have all enjoyed various performances, many by a regular travelling theatre company called Illyria. One performance that will stay in our memories forever was the concert to celebrate the opening of the theatre in 2012. I had only glanced at the programme for this event when booking the tickets and had thought it had been described as a Welsh variety concert. My taste in music is very wide, and I can enjoy most genres with the exception of rap and any rock that involves growling. Tom, our eldest son was seventeen, played electric guitar and was into heavy rock at the time and Simon was twelve, learning to play drums and liked mostly pop. Jim's preference has always been for quite gentle and tuneful music, with an aversion to jazz and opera. We had seen the forecast wasn't looking good for the night of the concert and went prepared (we thought) with raincoats and umbrellas and took our place on the back row of the packed amphitheatre. Not long after the introductory announcements, the heavens opened and the sky became aglow with lightning flashes. The classical singers and musicians – we soon realised the whole concert was classical – bravely competed with the loud thunder claps. I was enjoying the music and drama of it all, but was also feeling sorry for the organisers, singers, harpist and other musicians who, less than halfway through the concert, had to call it an evening. The expressions on the faces of Jim, Tom and Simon reinforced my thoughts that this may not have been my best idea for a family evening out together. Glad to say we're all still speaking to one another and we will always remember and laugh about the night we got soaked to the sound of Welsh opera.

Thanks to a huge amount of clearance, replanting and maintenance work which has taken place over the last few years, we were able to follow the trail along the original old paths through the woodland known as **Winllan** (translates to vineyard, but in Llŷn the word is used for a nursery of woodland). The woodlands were in

Winllan woodlands at Plas Glyn y Weddw Llanbedrog.

The Iron Man, Mynydd Tir-y-Cwmwd

existence before the mansion and have been given Ancient Woodland status. They were closed in 1939, when the Plas ceased to be an art gallery and remained in private ownership until they were purchased and reunited with Plas Glyn y Weddw and its current gallery in 2008. We crunched our way along the leaf carpeted path, then trudged up the stone steps, admiring the views of the sea and beyond through the trees. We followed the direction of the hand carved wooden fingerpost pointing **At y ddelw** (To the statue) which took us to the last stretch of uneven stone steps, lined with brown ferns. The view at the top is always worth the effort. We stood next to the iron man, who faces away from the headland, Mynydd Tir y Cwmwd, and shared his view of the sea, the mountains and the **Plas** in all their glory. We simultaneously began recounting a memory from one of our walks here with Tom and Simon who, like us had been unable to hide their amusement, at overhearing two Americans commenting on the amazing view and the 'beautiful lake!' Everything is so much bigger in America!

There have been three different statues in position here. The first one was wooden, a ship's carved figurehead, placed in 1911 by Solomon Andrews who established the first art gallery at the **Plas**. This was set on fire by vandals and in 1980 was replaced by the one that Jim and I first 'met' and was often referred to as the 'Tin Man' or 'Iron Man.' Made from steel by local artist Simon Van de Put, it represented an ancient warrior, but sadly he could not cope

68

with the exposure to the sea winds for too long and was replaced in 2002 by the present statue, the one we introduced to Tom and Simon. This one was also created by local craftsmen and continues to be known as either the 'Tin Man' or the 'Iron Man.' He is hollow and on a windy day can be heard singing but this was quite a still day so we parted in silence.

The stony path which winds its way up and down around the headland cuts through an immense carpet of heather, ferns and gorse interspersed with white boulders, which my legs found a bit of a challenge especially after the steep steps. We stopped occasionally to catch our breath, give my knees a break and admire the consistently stunning view. Finally, the two main St Tudwal's islands came into view. Both of these islands have become famous due to their owners. The eastern island was owned by the author Carla Lane, creator of the Liverpool based TV series The Liver Birds, until her death in 2016 and the western island is owned by T.V. celebrity and adventurer Bear Grylls. I've heard various interesting tales about the use of the islands by both of these characters, but I'm not one to gossip!

Due to the sheerness of the headland, we had to head inland and follow the hairpin shaped path to return back to our destination for today – the area known as The Warren. The Warren is a long sandy beach with Tan y Mynydd or Lan Môr Gwaith (quarry beach) at its eastern end and Traeth Tywyn y Fach at the western end close to Abersoch. It is backed by dunes and the busy Warren Holiday Park with its exclusive chalets. We rested at the deserted Traeth Tan y Mynydd, while we ate our sandwiches and kept an eye out for seals which are frequently seen swimming

Traeth y Mynydd

around the islands ... but not today. We had to be satisfied with the view of the islands and the sea which glowed in the rays of the sun, which were forcing their way through the low dark clouds. I selected a pebble for the collection before we hurried back, hoping to reach Llanbedrog before a downpour. We made it just in time!

There's No Sock in Abersoch!
Traeth Tan y Mynydd to Porth Mawr Abersoch
– 9th December 2018

With the sound of the dulcet tones of two local singers, Alys Williams (of The Voice fame) and Glain Rhys, still resonating in my head from a gig in 'Y Fic' the night before, we arose early to an ominous sky. There wasn't enough blue 'to make a workman's overall' as Jim's mam would have said, meaning that we were likely to have wet weather for the day. Jim's mam lived to 99, or 'ninety flippin' nine?' as she used to say in a questioning tone in her broad Bolton accent, whenever her age was mentioned. She was a straight-talking Lancashire lady with a gift of the Irish blarney inherited from her maternal grandparents and adored by all. I loved her quirky sayings, but I was always a bit puzzled about how you figured out the amount of blue sky needed to make a workman's overall! I've since discovered that in Llŷn, they tend to use a pair of sailor's trousers as a guide, equally puzzling but amusing nevertheless. The weather forecast was mixed and we decided to take a chance but the low, dark clouds looked rather menacing as we trudged across the beach from Traeth Tan y Mynydd towards Traeth Tywyn y Fach.

The sun, fighting its way through the cloud, cast a shimmering glow on the sea between the St Tudwal's islands, and the steady

Porth Mawr and beach huts.

sounds of the waves gave a rhythm to our steps in the soft sand. We were glad we had chanced it. The tightly packed row of various shaped holiday homes of The Warren holiday park, lined up higgledy-piggledy above the dunes, seemed to go on forever. The day began to brighten, but still we

River Soch, Abersoch.

were glad of our warm hats and gloves. We climbed the steps off the beach at Tywyn y Fach to the wooded walk leading to the A499, then followed the coastal path sign which pointed us in the direction of Abersoch town centre.

Jim and I had joked in the past about how, if we ever walked the peninsula coastal path, we couldn't avoid walking through Abersoch, which is our least favourite part of Llŷn in the peak season. Abersoch is a picturesque harbour town, but has become heavily populated by wealthy non-Welsh speakers, many being second home, yacht and huge off-road vehicle owners. It is often nicknamed 'Cheshire by the Sea,' as so many of the temporary residents are from wealthy areas of Cheshire. In the summer especially, its trendy bars and shops (almost all with English names) are heaving and the roads are noisy with traffic.

The poet Myrddin ap Dafydd, has written an amusing yet poignant Welsh poem, *Gwledigaeth yr English Pyb* (Vision of the English Pub), about Abersoch and how anglicised it has become, with so many of its houses, shops and pubs being renamed with English names and even its own name rarely being pronounced correctly by people staying there. Ap Dafydd is a familiar character around Llŷn with many strings to his bow. In addition to being a writer, and founder of Gwasg Carreg Gwalch publishing company, he is also director of two other companies – Cwrw Llŷn (Llŷn's very own craft brewery based in Nefyn) and one of my favourite shops in Pwllheli, art gallery Oriel y Môr Tonnau.

We followed the road as it passed the river Soch then into the town centre which was relatively quiet on this Sunday morning. Lôn Traeth took us to the end of our journey for today onto the northern end of the beach at Porth Mawr, often just referred to as Abersoch main beach and dominated by the old concrete beach huts which despite renovation still look rather unattractive and remind me of coastal lookout bunkers from the Second World War. Porth Mawr is the home of South Caernarfonshire Yacht Club and is also where only a year earlier a very small and simple wooden beach hut had sold for a staggering £160,000! We decided we could wait until the continuation of our walk the following day to try and guess which one it was. We needed to get back to the caravan to try and look half decent before joining the carol concert at Plas Glyn y Weddw that afternoon. What wild lives we lead!

The sun breaking through and shining between St Tudwal's Islands

Walk 12

Luxury Sheds and a Cornish Mine

Porth Mawr Abersoch to Bwlchtocyn –
10th December 2018

The weather and the tide both contributed towards our decisions about days and times of walks, but we both preferred mornings while we had more energy and enthusiasm. The best option for us on this particular day was to walk to Bwlchtocyn via the golf course then return along the beach when the tide was lower. As we turned into Lôn Golff on the outskirts of the town centre, my attention was drawn to a rather run-down looking wooden house, not much larger than a shed, but with a chimney and traditional front door with a letter box which suggested it was inhabited. We joked about how much it would sell for if the beach hut prices were anything to go by. We made a right turn down the lane that soon brought us to Clwb Golff Abersoch, which was empty of golfers, probably as the ground was very wet after a night of heavy rain. We dodged the puddles formed in the large pot holes along the way as we trekked through the golf course which is designated as part of the coastal path and useful at high tide. Machroes beach and the sea loomed into view at Bwlchtocyn as we exited the golf course onto the tarmacked road leading to the car park, but we were saving that for the return walk as we wanted to find our starting point for the next journey and to allow the tide to lower. We took a sharp right turn along the narrow road and continued a few hundred yards before taking the wooded path to the left which soon brought us back to a view of the whole of the bay, with Port Mawr in the distance and the trendy Mickey's Boatyard and Beach Café at Machroes, which was closed for the winter. We continued towards the end of Penrhyn Du headland with the familiar white painted house on its tip, once the old lifeboat

Jim navigating his way around the puddles along Abersoch golf course.

station and now a holiday home with its own slipway. Near the gatepost signed 'The Old Lifeboat House', the rough stony path heads inland again and widens out to a very uneven, wide bumpy track where we had

Machroes

planned to park our car for the start of our next journey. We noticed a tall ruined stone building almost hidden by trees at the end of a private lane. The sign at the end of the lane informed us that the cottages were called 'Cornish Row.' We later learnt that the ruined building was known as the Cornish engine house and had been built in the 1860s to house a steam engine which pumped water from a lead mine at Penrhyn Du. The cottages get their name from their past occupiers who were mostly families who had moved north from Cornwall and Devon to provide work in the mines. It is thought that the engine house may well have been built by Cornish workers.

The Cornish engine house at Bwlchtocyn.

We retrod our steps to the beach and walked back along the sands to Porth Mawr, dodging the wooden breakers. The sky had remained grey with clouds but we could still make out the beautiful Cambrian mountains in the far distance. We ended our journey none the wiser about which beach hut had raised such a large sum of money. However pretty any of them were, as Jim said, his Bolton accent emphasising it well, 'at the end of the day they are all just sheds'.

Walk 13

Islands and Love
Bwlchtocyn to Porth Ceiriad – 22nd April 2019

It was great to get back to our caravan and coastal walk once the site reopened following its usual winter closure in January and February. We miss the caravan in these months but we are allowed to visit to check its safety and often incorporate a short stay somewhere close by. We had visited in March, which had been quite a wet month, but our time had been taken up with catching up with friends, watching the St David's Day parade and taking a long-intended trip on the train from Pwllheli to Machynlleth, another very interesting place, steeped in Welsh history.

We left the car on the rough track at Bwlchtocyn which we reached this time via the road near Porth Tocyn Hotel. The kissing gate greeted us with a familiar blue and yellow coastal path way marker sticker, with its distinctive dragon shell logo and the wording **Llwybr Arfordir Cymru** – Wales Coast Path. It was a beautiful bright, sunny morning and T-shirts were the dress code for the day. A gentle incline took us past fields with grazing sheep on one side and hedgerows on the other. We stopped to look at the view from another gate at the end of this straight path and were able to see the top of the Cornish engine house and a hint of

Approaching Porth Ceiriad.

St. Tudwal's Islands

Porth Mawr. The path continued upwards and opened out onto common land, with improving views with every step. By doing a return journey on every walk we reap the rewards of seeing the views from all angles, but we still can't resist looking behind us to get a sneak preview of the return views, especially if we're heading uphill. Our reward today was St Tudwal's Islands again. They looked close enough to swim out to and we had a clear view of the lighthouse on the western island. We continued along the grassy path, which was lined with fern and yellow flowering gorse. On and on the path continued; a motorboat sped past the islands and the sun was warm to our skin. Clumps of pink sea thrift were clinging to the edge of the headland and blew gently in the breeze. This was our favourite kind of coastal path with sea views all the way. The path headed downwards and a short wooden bridge took us across a stretch of land that was dry today, but deep hard ridges and footprints in the soil suggested that it was normally very boggy. The land was now quite bare and the islands dipped in and out of view. Finally, we got our first glimpse of the white sands at Porth Ceiriad and this spurred us on to continue trudging our way around and along the cliffs to the car park at the western end of the beach, which was our stopping point. We propped on the wooden stumps by the fence and tucked into what we agreed was our well-deserved lunch, whilst admiring the stunning view across Cardigan Bay, with the silhouette of the Cambrian Mountain range beyond. Porth Ceiriad is very popular with surfers but the sea was too calm for any sport today and the beach was deserted. Ceiriad is very like the Welsh word for love which is **cariad** and some say that it has derived its name from this, so after lunch, Jim took on the challenge of finding a heart shaped pebble for our collection and succeeded. I tried to ignore my stiff, aching joints as we managed the return journey at a much slower pace, once again wondering how we had forgotten the walking poles which were in their usual obvious place in the boot of the car. As we trudged along, we discussed our plans for our visit to Ynys Enlli the following day.

The path from Bwlchtocyn.

Lion's Teeth and Dolphins
Porth Ceiriad to Cilan Uchaf – 22nd June 2019

Porth Ceiriad

The kissing gate near the car park at Porth Ceiriad beach was our starting point on this beautiful summer's day. We were feeling ready to continue our journey after a break for a couple of months due to other events taking over, including a weekend long celebration for the tenth birthday of SSIW, held at Galeri in Caernarfon, and our eldest son Tom's twenty fourth birthday. It was a Saturday but not quite holiday season, so the beaches were still quiet, just how we like them. A group of people were daring the chilly waters below us as we followed the grassy path between the double row of wooden and wire fences leading westwards. Bright purple foxgloves stood tall between the gorse and several of the fields we passed along our way were carpeted with dandelions shining in the sunshine. How different they seemed to the dandelions that I uproot from our tiny lawn back home. I love wildflowers and do allow many to grow amongst our perennials in the garden, but our lawn is so tiny, that they would takeover completely if allowed. I enjoy finding out the Welsh words for wildflowers, which are often much more interesting than the English names. Foxglove in Welsh is **bysedd y cŵn** which translates as dog paws and dandelion is **dant y llew** which means lions' tooth as does dandelion if translated into French. One of my favourites is **llygad y dydd** (daisy) which translates as eye of the day.

As we strode along the steep path and through a couple more kissing gates, we could now look down on Trwyn Llech y Doll point, flanked by lush green fields. We were thankful for the wooden steps built into the path that helped us manage the steepest part and were rewarded at the top by a wonderful view. The distant range of Cambrian mountains appeared blue and merged with the expanse of Cardigan Bay, which was glinting an even brighter blue in the sunshine. A fellow walker was also appreciating the view and we chatted a while and shared our admiration of the area. He told us that he had seen dolphins from a little further along the path, so after we said goodbye, we kept our eyes on the sea as we continued on our way. We didn't have to wait long until a pair of beautiful bottle nosed dolphins appeared and delighted us with a display that made our day. We are both still adjusting to going away from home without our sons and it's at times like this when we see something extra special that we feel it the most and wish we could share the moment with them. We comfort ourselves knowing that we have shared many special holiday moments with them over the years and occasionally still do if they join us on our travels. We reminisced about a previous dolphin sighting when in 2010, we took a family boat trip one afternoon from Pwllheli. Jason, a friendly young local who ran a fishing charter agreed to make an exception and took us out on a pleasure trip to the Tudwal's islands on his boat Haf-Aled III. He knew where to go to almost guarantee we would sec dolphins. We weren't disappointed and had an amazing afternoon watching them play around in the waters near the western island. I digress as usual – onwards!

Stopping to take a pic at Cilan Uchaf.

We continued a little further along the path which now zig zagged around the farmer's fields, where grazing cows ignored us as we passed... on the other side of the fence of course. We were now in the area known as Cilan Uchaf. We stopped to make a mental note of a fence post (marked with a familiar blue and yellow coastal path walk sticker), where we had decided to stop and return to Porth Ceiriad. We both laughed at the idea that we would remember and agreed that we needed to take a photograph! This is where we would need to stop on our next walk as we would be starting the next stage a little inland so that we could park the car. As we made our way back to Porth Ceiriad car park, I was still grinning from ear to ear about our dolphin sighting and greedily hoped to see more but it wasn't to be.

View from Cilan Uchaf.

Choughs and Islands

Cilan Uchaf to Cilan – 14th July 2019

This was one of our 'back to front' walks, and we began near Castell Bach holiday cottage at Cilan. The car park was on the edge of a wide expanse of dry scrubland dotted with clumps of purple heather and with various defined grassy paths leading to the coastal path. We headed diagonally towards fields and followed the line of the fences to help guide us to the section of path we were aiming for. Two large black birds were perched on the top of fence posts and we were just able to make out their red bills and legs, which to my delight identified them as choughs, one of my favourite birds. We then spotted several more pecking at the ground in the fields beyond the fence and as we approached, they all flew up high and gave us a spectacular aerial display, diving and swooping and floating on the gentle breeze. My day was complete already and we hadn't even reached the coastal path. The chough is the rarest member of the crow family and currently three-

Cilan

81

Quietly approaching choughs on the fence at Cilan.

quarters of the UK's population live in Wales. Its Welsh name is **brân goesgoch** (red legged crow) and it features on the logo for the Llŷn Peninsula **AHNE – Ardal o Harddwch Naturiol Eithriadol** (AONB – Area of Outstanding Natural Beauty). From the nineteenth century onwards there had been a decline of choughs throughout the U.K., partly due to their being trapped and shot as agricultural pests (which they are not) and partly by trophy hunters and egg collectors. Jim and I are wary of cows along the coastal path, as you will read about later, but another reason for the decline is said to be the reduction of animals grazing along coastal paths, resulting in a decline of the local habitat where choughs like to feed. Thankfully, the ten yearly surveys of choughs are showing that there are gradually increasing numbers in the U.K.

As we approached the coastal path near Mynydd Cilan trig point, we stopped to admire and take photographs of the amazing panoramic view around us. The whole stretch of Porth Neigwl beach was now in view, with the hill Mynydd Rhiw, Ynys Enlli and the smaller islands Ynys Gwylan Bach and Ynys Gwylan Fawr to the west. To the north were the glorious Eifl hills and to the east Abersoch and Llanbedrog headland. The poet R.S. Thomas was very fond of Cilan and its hilly landscape which he described as bare and untidy and he talked of it being the part of Wales most like western Ireland.

The clearly marked grassy path led us through the continuing scrubland, curving its way around Mynydd Cilan headland and its tip, Trwyn Cilan. We eventually reached a kissing gate and on passing through, beyond the ferns, we were able to see the dramatic stratified cliffs below, which I believe are popular with climbers and breeding sea birds. There was no fence between us and the cliff edge and I felt safer once the path opened out to rough grassland again, with patches of prickly flowering gorse and heather. We passed through a very pretty spot where a wooden bridge took us safely across a spring, which had caused the rocks below to be covered in bright green moss. This was reflected in the turquoise waters, close to the opening of a cave carved into the low cliffs. Wooden steps took us up to another gate and Porth Ceiriad loomed into view. The view motivated us to keep going as we had begun to feel weary and overheated. We pushed ourselves onwards up the steep dry stony path beyond and finally spotted the familiar fence post, where we had stopped on our walk three weeks earlier. It was time for a well-earned rest and a picnic before we started the return journey.

View of Porth Neigwl and the stratified cliffs from Trwyn Cilan.

Sunshine and Surf

Cilan to Porth Neigwl – 5th August 2019

We timed our next stay at the caravan around the National Eisteddfod which was being held in Llanrwst this year. There had been flood warnings and the site of the event had been altered to reduce the risk of it having to be cancelled. We decided to get tickets for the first day of the festival – Saturday the 3rd August. This is the quietest day of the Eisteddfod as everyone is arriving and preparing for the main events which start on the Sunday, but I was keen to see the musical show that evening *Y Tylwyth* (the folk). This was an amazing production that incorporated folk tales from the area of Llanrwst and had been produced by Gwyneth Glyn, Twm Morys (who also starred in it) and Myrddin ap Dafydd who only the previous year had aptly been elected Archdruid for 2019 to 2022 (he was born in Llanrwst). It was performed by members of Pontio Bangor Theatre and an Irish Contemporary Circus Troupe called Fidget Feet who created some amazing effects from high wires! Some of my favourite Welsh musicians were also involved so it was a 'must see' for me and it will be something I will remember for a

Surfers at Porth Neigwl.

Heather in full bloom on the summit of Mynydd Cilan.

long time. We planned to return home on the 9th August, allowing us to spend a full day on the Eisteddfod Maes on the way. This gave us almost a week at the caravan and plenty of time to make some progress with our coastal walk.

We were blessed with a beautiful sunny day for this next 'back to front' walk. Porth Neigwl beach car park was our starting point, as there was nowhere to park near the spot at Cilan where we'd left off last time. We felt a bit out of place with our rucksacks and walking boots, amongst all the enthusiastic surfers, pulling on their wet suits in the backs of their vans and probably looked quite comical trudging along the sandy path in line behind them as they carried their boards to the beach. Porth Neigwl beach is about four miles long and the bay is the broadest in Llŷn. Its English name is Hell's Mouth due to its potential danger to sailors from its huge waves and lack of shelter, but this is also what makes it so popular with surfers. We left the surfers to enjoy themselves and headed east along the beach which soon became quite rocky. We reminisced about bringing our youngest son Simon here for surfing lessons years before. He had picked it up very quickly, probably due to already having excellent skateboarding skills. I looked ahead to our path up the cliffside, which from a distance looked quite precarious. We scrambled up off the beach and onto the grassy path leading to the headland – Mynydd Cilan. Near a kissing gate, we passed a tiny ruined house which overlooked the bay. I wondered who had lived there and what views they must have seen from their front windows, most likely including shipwrecks, of which there had been many in this area. In the distance inland we could see a tall old chimney, which we later discovered was the remains of Llanengan lead mine, which closed in 1892. As we approached the beginning of the incline to the headland, we greeted campers in the fields, relaxing and reading in the sunshine. It was all uphill now to the summit of Mynydd Cilan. Thankfully it wasn't quite as precarious as it had looked from a distance and although steep, there was a fence between us and the fern covered cliff edge – something that is always very welcome! The path proceeded immediately beneath the uppermost rocky part of the headland and the fence came to an end! We headed slightly inland and our legs gave a sigh of relief as the path began to level out for the last stretch to our chosen stopping point from our previous walk. We found a smooth patch of ground and sat down, avoiding the patches of prickly gorse, and the heather which was now a beautiful bright pink. Time for refreshments before our return journey.

Llanengan lead mine chimney.

An Ancient Forest and an Old Boiler
Along Porth Neigwl Beach – 7th August 2019

After a day of rest at the caravan, we were ready to continue. Today's walk was nice and level, an approximately four-mile return trip along Porth Neigwl sands, so no chance of getting lost and a bit of a rest for our old knees. The car park was quieter than our last visit, with no sign of surfers today and only a young couple with a small child and bags of seaside toys, accompanied us along the path to the beach. There was a cool sea breeze and we were surprised to need jackets for the first time this week.

In the early spring of 2014, at low tide, after heavy storms, roots from an ancient submerged forest were exposed on Porth Neigwl beach and on other beaches in Wales. Unfortunately, we didn't get to see it but we heard about it from Dafydd the story teller at Felin Uchaf, when he wove it into one of his stories and shared hazelnuts with the audience that he said were over 5000 years old and had been found on the eroding surface of the forest. There was no sign today of the forest even though it was quite low tide; the sand now having blown back and buried it again. The further west we went along the beach, the more atmospheric it became. We kept a distance from the cliffs but were fascinated by their interesting shapes created by severe erosion over the years, especially one part that looked like a pirate's face complete with long beard! Quite apt as this beach has seen many shipwrecks during the last 200 years.

Having fun with shadows on Porth Neigwl sands.

We stopped to look at a dead jellyfish on the sand. The Welsh name for jellyfish is **slefren fôr** (saliva fish) but they are sometimes jokingly referred to as **pysgod wibli wobli** (wibbly wobbly fish). Further ahead

Pirate's head on the cliffs at Porth Neigwl.

on the beach we could see a large rock and decided this would be our turning back point. About level with the rock on the cliff top was a square concrete building which looked like the remains of a war time lookout. The tide was quite a way out and a large colony of herring gulls pecked at the wet sand along the shoreline. As we approached the moss-covered rock, on closer inspection we realised it wasn't a rock at all but a large metal container of some kind, half buried in the sand. Jim suggested it looked like a boiler and with the help of Google later that day, we discovered it was exactly that. It has been identified as the remains of the ship the Aggravator, a wooden steamship built in 1860 which was stranded on the beach in 1898. It had been delivering a cargo of coal when it was caught by a force ten gale. We did an about turn at the boiler and trudged back along the soft sand, which hadn't been as easy to walk on as I'd anticipated.

Porth Neigwl and the old boiler from the shipwrecked Aggravator.

A Still Heron and a Stern Poet

Porth Neigwl to Plas yn Rhiw – 8th August 2019

We had a short stretch of Porth Neigwl beach to complete before continuing on to Plas yn Rhiw. There was a conveniently situated parking area close to Treheli farm near the western end of the beach. The surrounding farmer's fields were filled with cheerful campers with their tents and vans, some cooking a late breakfast on their camping stoves in the sunshine, while their children played close by. We found a spot where we could scramble down to the beach from the site overlooking the bay. Natural steps had been formed in the cliff from frequent use but I was thankful that someone had secured a rope to a nearby tree which helped us to get down without injuring ourselves!

A welcome piece of rope to help us climb off Porth Neigwl Beach.

The tide was quite a way out and the silhouette of a heron perched on one leg on a distant rock immediately caught our attention. As we slowly walked towards it, we noticed a second heron pecking at the seaweed close by. We were struck by how perfectly still the heron on the rock remained, even as we approached close enough to take a photo – quite a feat on one leg!

Sand ripples shone in the sunshine and several gulls flew low across the sea. A solitary

A very still heron on Porth Neigwl beach.

oystercatcher was looking for a snack in the wet sand. We could see our turning back point – the boiler on the beach – not too far ahead. Again, we steered clear of the tall bone-dry cliffs. One large section had a huge vertical crack and looked ready to collapse onto the beach at any minute. Jim inspected the old boiler again. Anything metal or mechanical grabs his interest due to his engineering background.

We returned back along the beach and pulled ourselves up the steps with the rope, leaving the heron still standing tall and very regal looking on the rock. He looked as if he hadn't moved a feather all this time, still gazing in the direction of the headland and the old stone house on the rocks below.

We left the car where it was and walked back along the road, passing more campers and Treheli farmhouse. We were glad of some shade as the road narrowed into a leafy country lane. I was quite excited as I knew from previous visits that along this lane was a very special little house that I was eager to see again.

Five stone steps led up to the inviting open iron gate which was almost hidden by tall shrubs. Feeling a little like intruders but unable to resist a look, we justified our nosiness by there not being any 'keep out' signs. Sarn y Plas is a very pretty eighteenth century, whitewashed, single storey stone cottage with a slate roof and is part of the Plas yn Rhiw estate. The tiny garden at the side of the cottage was very overgrown with wild geraniums and other rampant perennials. Brambles were creeping across the one small four paned window, through which we took a peek, only to see bare walls and floors. We had heard that there were plans to make it into a museum dedicated to the poet R.S. Thomas who had made it his retirement home between 1978 and 1996. Thomas was one of the leading poets of twentieth century Wales. He was passionate about the Welsh language, but having only learnt it from the age of 30, he felt he was too late to use it for his poetry, which primarily contained themes of the Welsh landscape and its people. He did write some prose in Welsh and wrote one of my favourite Welsh language books about Llŷn – *Blwyddyn yn Llŷn* (A Year in Llŷn). This short book gives a month-by-month account of the landscape that surrounded him, as well as his observations of the local wildlife, especially the birds as Thomas was a keen birdwatcher. I keep the book in the caravan and often return to it to read the

Sarn y Plas, once the home of poet RS Thomas.

chapter related to the current month and if I'm feeling lazy, I refer to my translated version. I have spoken to friends who live or have lived in Llŷn who were lucky enough to have met Thomas and describe him as having been quite a formidable character, who would not stand for any nonsense and this comes through in his writing. He was also the vicar of St Hywyn's church in Aberdaron, where our walk would soon be taking us. As we returned to the lane, I wondered what Thomas would have made of our uninvited visit. I like to think that if we had greeted him in Welsh, he would have welcomed us and invited us in for a panad.

The lane soon joined the main road which we followed in the direction of Rhiw. Not so far along the road, we reached Plas yn Rhiw, a place very familiar to us, having visited frequently in the past with Tom and Simon. The **Plas** is a manor house built in the early seventeenth century. Its most recent occupants were the three spinster Keating sisters who acquired and renovated it in 1939. They were passionate supporters of conservation and finally donated the hall and surrounding land to its current owners, the National Trust. The inside of the house remains as the sisters left it and is a treasure trove of their fascinating collection of furniture, household items, art, books and clothing. Outside is a beautiful organic garden, from where there is one of the most incredible views of Porth Neigwl and Cardigan Bay beyond. The **Plas** is

Eroding cliffs at Porth Neigwl.

surrounded by woodland, which look especially stunning in early spring when the ground is carpeted with snowdrops and visitors are invited to come and view on 'Snowdrop Weekends.' Several years previously I had one of my first 'proper' conversations in Welsh with Ann, a very friendly and patient lady who greeted visitors (always using Welsh and English) into the **Plas**. Today we weren't going to look around the house itself but we were keen to use the loo and the café, before completing our walk and heading back to Treheli farm.

I'll ramble a little away from the coastal path, if I may, and share our Eisteddfod experiences from the following day. Unfortunately, Llanrwst had seen a lot of rain since our visit a week earlier, but it was worth trudging through the mud to see some of our favourite artists in the **Tŷ Gwerin** (the folk tent). It was yet another very wet day in Llanrwst and we spent the morning dodging the heavy showers and people spotting as we browsed the various stalls, absorbing the Welsh language from every direction. We saw a few familiar faces from the Welsh T.V. Channel S4C and I was amused and surprised when a very familiar voice asked me in Welsh where the toilets were! It was T.V. presenter Aled Samuel who provided the comedic voiceover for the S4C programme Cariad@Iaith, which I've mentioned previously. I managed to recover from my shock and pointed and stuttered in Welsh that they were **rownd y**

gornel (round the corner). I hope he found them! After lunch we decided to take root in the crowded **Tŷ Gwerin**, to shelter from the rain and to ensure we had seats to see our favourite singers, scheduled to appear on and off throughout the afternoon. We began by watching band Plu from a bench at the back of the tent, with our view rather restricted by the huge tent poles. I spotted a couple of other Welsh learners who I was in touch with mostly via social media and we chatted in Welsh. Jim and I were glad of our inflatable camping cushions, as the wooden benches weren't the most comfortable, and we took turns to stretch our legs and to bring refreshments back from the outdoor stalls. In between each act, as people moved in and out of the tent, we edged forwards, until by the time Gwyneth Glyn and Twm Morys were performing we were on the front row. I was thoroughly enjoying the performance – Gwyneth with her sweet voice accompanied by Twm on the harmonica or the **pibgorn** (a very old and loud traditional Welsh musical horn) – when Gwyneth looked towards us and gave a knowing smile. We have seen her perform several times not just in Llŷn but also at gigs closer to home. My immediate thought was that she would be thinking 'Oh no, not those two again!' and I felt a little embarrassed as we were sitting so close to the stage. Following their performance, Twm and Gwyneth were mobbed by a small group of Welsh celebrities, who wanted to pose with them for a photograph including ITV's ex-weather forecaster Siân Lloyd. Immediately after the photo shoot, we were taken by surprise and felt quite touched when Gwyneth made her way to us, hugged me and thanked us for coming to see her yet again. Incidentally Twm Morys has written a moving poem about R.S. Thomas. The poem is called *R.S.* (which is how he was referred to by many) and disputes his reputation of being cold and unapproachable, describing his warmth and devotion to friends, family and wildlife.

Walk 19 — Wild Horses and an Even Wilder Pheasant

Plas yn Rhiw to Penarfynydd –
20th September 2019

Since our last walk we'd had quite a few interesting events, my favourite being a get together at the caravan over the August Bank Holiday weekend with Tom, Simon and Tom's partner Rhi. We squeezed this in before Simon moved out again, to a flat in Manchester, to continue his university studies. Instead of continuing along the coastal path, we took them to see Cilan, one of our favourite sections of the walk so far and somewhere we had never taken them as children. We also managed to fit in a storytelling session with Dafydd at Felin Uchaf. Then in early September Jim and I flew to Iceland and stayed in Reykjavik for a few days, something I had wanted to do since childhood. We were amazingly lucky to see the Northern Lights from the rooftop of our flat, fulfilling another dream. Another of the attractions of Llŷn is the ability to see the night sky so much more clearly than back home due to there being a lot less light pollution. On clear nights, we love gazing at the milky way and spotting shooting stars from the decking. Tom is a keen stargazer and we've spent many chilly nights enjoying him pointing out planets and galaxies to us with his giant telescope. I digress...

The sky was a brilliant bright blue with not a cloud in sight so we donned our sun hats for our walk to Penarfynydd. We parked at Plas yn Rhiw car park and headed along the main road in the direction of Rhiw, soon coming upon a kissing gate at the side of the road with a coastal path sign directing us across the field beyond. At the end of the field a wooden gate led us into a small deciduous woodland, which was very welcome

Approaching Penarfynydd.

on this hot late summer's day. Our view as we emerged at the other side was spectacular, with the whole of Porth Neigwl bay, and Mynydd Cilan headland. The grassy path led upwards and around the edge of Mynydd y Graig, cutting through the scrubland of fern, heather and gorse which were all now beginning to lose their colour. A dry-stone wall appeared and lined the path for a while in an area that looked as if it had been inhabited in the past, with remains of stone buildings and some small intact buildings that looked as if they may still be used for storage of some kind. The path took a 90 degree turn and headed uphill following the side of the wall for a short distance before turning to run parallel with the cliff edge again. We continued for some time along the path, and the hill Mynydd Penarfynydd finally came into view as we crossed an open grassy stretch with a wooden gate not far ahead. Through the gate, we continued left towards Penarfynydd, soon following the line of another long dry-stone wall and passing a small sewage farm, which looked quite out of place in such a beautiful spot. A National Trust sign marked the start of Penarfynydd and three stone steps led us through a kissing gate onto the hill. Our legs were beginning to feel the pull but we were eager to see the view from the summit. A fellow walker was on his way down the hill and greeted us in Welsh. I greeted him back in Welsh and then had my first (albeit brief) Welsh conversation so far on the coastal path! I was very chuffed. We soon switched back to English so that Jim could understand and he said that he was from Ynys Môn and had completed the coastal path there several months ago. He'd come to the conclusion that there could be no finer views in Wales than those seen along the Ynys Môn coastal path, but then added that now he had to confess that the views along the Llŷn coastal walk had 'knocked spots' off them. We agreed that they were stunning, but also mentioned that we had not done enough of the coastal paths of Ynys Môn to be able to compare. We said our goodbyes and after a good guzzle of water, we forced ourselves onwards and upwards towards the trig point, now visible at the summit.

The view was spectacular of course. To the west was Ynys Enlli and the smaller isles of Gwylan Fawr and Gwylan Bach and the two headlands flanking Aberdaron which was hidden from view. To the north was Mynydd Rhiw, easily identified with its radio mast.

Jim and the pheasant seconds before the attack!.

Something very unexpected suddenly caught our attention and delighted me. A short distance away on the lower part of Penarfynydd was a small herd of horses grazing peacefully on the rough grass! We hadn't realised there were any wild horses in Llŷn. We later discovered that they were Carneddau mountain ponies and that ten of them had been introduced to the area by the National Trust to help maintain the landscape by grazing there. The name Carneddau comes from the group of mountains in Eryri, where these ponies had originated and where there are about 300 of them helping to conserve the landscapes of the National Park. We could only see five of these beautiful animals today, three brown and two white. We kept our distance from them as we made our way downhill, but I continued to glance back at them, still rather amazed at having seen them there.

On our return walk, some other walkers with small dogs passed us along the way. One of the dogs especially was quite lively and rather yappy. A little further along we were surprised to see a male pheasant strutting along through the heather, making his way towards us until he was walking parallel to us along the widened path. Pheasants are plentiful on the site where our caravan is situated and we often have to slow down in the car along the drive to allow them to nonchalantly walk across. They regularly make us jump on our walks along the wooded lanes near the caravan, when they nervously take flight out of the hedgerows at the last minute as we pass by only about a metre or less away from them, making their strange loud mechanical sound with their wings. A year previous to this, I grew quite fond of one pheasant who I named Phil. We used to watch him each evening as he flew up to roost on a large bare branch on the ash tree close to our caravan. We hadn't seen him this year and had presumed the poor thing had been shot. We joked that maybe this was Phil and on recognizing us he'd come to greet us on our journey! I was thinking how lovely that he was so friendly towards us and started to take pictures of him, and Jim began to film him with his phone camera. He seemed especially interested in Jim, cocking his head to one side and looking at him. Then suddenly without any warning he lunged at Jim and tried to peck at his legs! Jim jumped back but he kept on trying to attack him. I quickly remembered some advice a friend had given me about how to scare geese away by making loud squawking noises and waving your arms as if you're a huge bird. I gave this a go with the pheasant but it didn't deter him one bit. He seemed determined to get a chunk of Jim's leg. In the end Jim resorted to launching the pheasant into the air with his foot and we hurried along the path away from him. As we looked back, we could see he was stunned but unharmed as were we! We wondered if the little yapping dog had unnerved him and he'd decided to take his revenge on us instead. When we got back to the caravan, Jim found the video clip he'd taken on his phone and realised filming had continued during the attack! We laughed as the whole thing seemed like something from a comedy sketch, but I was horrified at the inhuman sound coming from me as I squawked at the pheasant – a sound I'd not heard coming from me since I gave birth! I hoped that no one had heard or seen us at the time! I'm not sure if it's my imagination or not, but since then Jim's foot doesn't seem to touch the brake pedal quite as quickly as it used to as we approach pheasants on the drive leading to the caravan.

View from Penarfynydd including Ynys Enlli

King Arthur and a Poetry Recital

Penarfynydd to Llanfaelrhys/Porth Ysgo – 23rd September 2019

There was no way of beginning our walk at Penarfynydd without trespassing, which we would never do, so we began at Llanfaelrhys and did a triangular journey. We parked the car by old St Maelrhys church in Llanfaelrhys, a simple building with many medieval parts

St Maelrhys's Church

and a bell cote that was added in the nineteenth century. **Llan** means a parish or church dedicated to a saint so Llanfaelrhys means the parish of St Maelrhys but the M has changed to an F due to a rule used in the Welsh language called a soft mutation **treiglad meddal**. St Maelrhys was thought to have been Breton and is honoured as a saint on Ynys Enlli. He is commemorated on the first of January by the Church of Wales. R.S. Thomas, who preached here as well as at nearby Aberdaron and Rhiw, was said to have been especially fond of this church due to its peaceful location. I wanted to explore inside, but I decided to save that treat for the end of the journey.

We started off along the main road towards Rhiw, and continued until we came to a sharp bend in the road with an adjoining road to the right. We took the right turn and immediately on our right again, we could see a kissing gate and a grassy path beyond a clump of trees, leading downwards into a valley – Nant y Gadwen. Kissing gate in Welsh is **giât fochyn**, which means pig's gate but for once I think I prefer the English name, as the Welsh name conjures up unpleasant images from the uncorroborated anecdote known as 'Piggate' involving former Tory Prime Minister

David Cameron! A stream ran parallel to the path for a while, then disappeared into the hillside. Very soon we could see Ynys Enlli and the Gwylan isles again and a large rock Maen Gwenonwy, which faces the tiny beach of Porth Ysgo, which was still out of our view. It was cloudy and much cooler

Remains of Manganese mine near Porth Ysgo.

than our walk three days ago, but the sun peeped out every so often, making it a perfect day for walking.

We ignored the gate on the right leading down to the beach and instead followed the cleared grassy path that wound around the hill and led towards Penarfynydd. On top of the hill, which we discovered was a disused manganese mine, we could see the remains of a building and rusting winding gear. We continued until we got as close as we could to the base of Penarfynydd. I wanted to go and see the ponies again, but Penarfynydd summit wasn't as accessible from this side so we followed our tracks back to the rusty metal kissing gate. Shortly after the gate, the path divided and we took the left fork and were soon able to see Porth Ysgo. Steep steps zigzagged their way to this tiny secluded beach and we merrily trotted down them without a thought of having to make our way back up again later! We sat on a large rock to get our breath back and devour snacks from our rucksacks, taking in the view with Maen Gwenonwy in the foreground. This rock, which is attached to the mainland by shingle, takes its name from King Arthur's sister as many believe that the nearby island, Ynys Enlli, was the real Avalon where King Arthur was buried. I was spoilt for choice on this rocky beach when looking for a small pebble for our collection.

Quite a lot of moaning and groaning was to be heard, thankfully only to our ears, as we trudged back up the steps to re-join the coastal path. Instead of continuing further along the coastal path, we took the path heading northwest towards the village of Ysgo. We passed further remnants of the manganese mine and

Steps down to Porth Ysgo and Maen Gwenonwy jutting into the sea.

eventually emerged onto the main road near several farm buildings. We walked back along the road to the church, feeling satisfied with our walk but also ready for a rest. The church was unlocked and a sign welcomed visitors to enter. I couldn't resist of course. I was met with that lovely familiar musty smell that all old churches have, and are part of their appeal to me. The box pews looked well cared for and polished. A handmade cardboard sign invited me upstairs to visit the R.S. Thomas loft, so it would have been rude not to. The loft or **lloft**, is a tiny room with a shelf of books, by and about Thomas, a kettle with tea and coffee to help yourself and a CD player with CDs of Thomas reciting his poetry. What a lovely welcome. I resisted the cuppa, but sat for five minutes on the small wooden chair provided and listened to Thomas, whilst admiring the view from the small window, with shells and pebbles on its deep whitewashed sill. I could see why this was one of his favourite retreats as I looked out across the lush green fields with Ynys Enlli and the sea beyond.

View from the RS Thomas loft in St. Maelrhys's Church.

Pilgrims and a Polyglot

Llanfaelrhys/Porth Ysgo to Aberdaron –
6th October 2019

On our previous walk, we had noticed herds of cows further along this stretch of coastal path, with no fence for protection for the walker. So, we made the decision to walk into Aberdaron from Llanfaelrhys along the main road to avoid any conflict. I had always thought that cows were docile creatures, but we'd had a close-up encounter with a herd of them quite recently, which had changed my view. Our caravan is situated on a country estate, where a farmer keeps cows and sheep, which graze in the different fields in rotation. As we approach the caravan site at the beginning of each stay, we play a game of 'cows or sheep?' as we guess which of them will be grazing in the fields that line the mile long drive from the main road. More often than not, some of them are walking or sitting on the drive itself and we patiently wait for them to move and let us go on our way. One day when we thought this area was empty of cattle or sheep, we had a leisurely stroll along the drive

Aberdaron, looking across St. Hywen's Churchyard.

towards the lodge by the gateway. Suddenly, as if out of nowhere, a herd of about ten cows stampeded towards us. We ran onto the field and towards a tree to avoid them, our hearts pounding, but thankfully they carried on along the path and ignored us. We've been wary of the beasts ever since.

It was a day for coats and hats, with only a peep of blue sky between the heavy clouds. The road was narrow and winding, flanked by fields of grazing sheep, many of which raised their heads to stare as we passed. The hawthorns were laden with berries and the last of the blackberries were still juicy and inviting. I felt rather cheated of my sea views, but I knew that we would not have long to wait as the sea is never far away on the Peninsula. We came through Ysgo village, with its hotchpotch of farm buildings and a stream-fed pond close to the roadside. Gradually the sea came into view behind us as the road inclined and we passed more farm buildings and houses. At the cross roads, the sign announced that Aberdaron was only a mile away to the west and Pwllheli 17 miles eastwards. We strode out along the road, passing a terrace row of old cottages and other occasional stone houses, and ahead of us the western headland of Aberdaron, with Pen y Cil at its tip came into view. We wandered past Morfa Mawr farm where a row of brown cows seemed to eye us up suspiciously as we passed them in their large outdoor pen. Maybe we could have walked along the coastal path after all, I thought. The farm campsite had a few late visitors with their touring caravans in the field. Just as we approached Aberdaron village, after passing several modern

Arriving at Aberdaron.

detached houses (holiday homes we guessed), we passed a very plain looking large house, which advertised itself as being home to the Aberdaron Coastguard and the Llŷn Boys' Sailing Club. Its plainness was compensated for by its stunning view of the sea, the beach and the village, which was now also our view as we neared Aberdaron.

We have been frequent visitors to Aberdaron over the years, often calling for a day with the boys when holidaying in Nefyn or stopping off for some bread from the bakery before a day trip to Ynys Enlli. We have usually approached the village from the north east via Sarn Mellteyrn, so as we reached the village sign, we paused and leant on the corner of the long stone wall of St Hywyn's church to take in the view from this less familiar angle, across the graveyard. Several couples, wrapped up for the weather, were walking on the beach and the sun was beginning to break through the clouds above Mynydd Anelog in the distance. The well-known white painted Gwesty Tŷ Newydd Hotel takes command of the seafront at Aberdaron. It has envious views and quite a few years ago was used for an S4C television family drama *Porth Penwaig*, which we watched with English subtitles not long after I began to learn Welsh.

As we walked into the village, we realised it was Sunday and that meant that our favourite bakery was closed; not very good planning there. Becws Islyn is owned by Geraint Jones, a friendly baker, who produces the most delicious bread in Llŷn. We can remember buying the bread many years earlier when the bakery was a tiny corrugated metal hut. In 2015, this was transformed into a beautiful thatch roofed building, still selling scrumptious baked goods, but now with the addition of an upstairs café with a terrace, offering hot and cold drinks and tasty home-made savouries and cakes. The café interior has been decorated by Darren Evans, a local talented decorator and artist and husband of Welsh artists Tess Urbanska, mentioned earlier. He paints incredible murals on the interior or exterior of buildings around Llŷn, many which tell a tale about the area where they are situated. The mural in the bakery provides an informative, illustrated history of Aberdaron whilst you're enjoying your lunch. It includes the tale of Dic Aberdaron, real name Richard Robert Jones, who was born in Aberdaron in 1780 and was said to have taught himself 14 or 15 different languages by the time he was 11! And I was feeling so pleased with myself at having learnt one language in my 50s! Geraint now has plans to transform the thirteenth century mill, situated across the road from the bakery as well as to extend the café further. Melin Daron was one of five mills owned by the Abbey on Ynys Enlli. Grain was grown on the island and transported to the mill for grinding. Geraint hopes that the mill can eventually be restored and once again be able to grind local grain which can then be used in the bakery. Situated between the bakery and the church is another café worth mentioning although also closed today. Y Gegin Fawr (the large kitchen) is a Grade II listed building thought to date from the seventeenth century and legends record that in medieval times it was visited by pilgrims who could claim a meal here before crossing the waters to Ynys Enlli. Tom and Simon, who are both tall, will remember this pretty whitewashed stone building as the café with the winding stair and low ceilings where you have to watch your head!

Before heading back, I tried the door of St Hywyn's church to see if I could do my usual look around, but surprisingly it was locked. This atmospheric stone church dates from the twelfth century and has been the last stop for pilgrims past and present, before they take the boat across Y Swnt, which are the notorious tidal waters between Aberdaron and Ynys Enlli. It has a small exhibition which celebrates R.S. Thomas's time there as vicar between 1967 and 1978. About three years previously, we attended a gig held there, which included a favourite band Plu. I'm not sure what Thomas would have thought about his church being used as a venue for musical events, but the acoustics sounded great. I think he would have approved, especially as it was all performed in Welsh and by a band whose members are very proactive in keeping the language alive.

When we arrived back at St Maelrhys' church, I had one last mission before we returned back to the caravan for lunch. Since our last visit, I had discovered that R.S. Thomas's wife Mildred Elsie Eldridge (known as Elsi) was buried in the graveyard and I wanted to see her gravestone. Elsi was a very talented artist who created detailed studies of flowers and birds especially. She also painted an impressive mural, called 'The Dance of Life' which we went to see in 2018 at Wrexham's Glyndŵr University where it is now exhibited. It had been commissioned by a hospital in Oswestry for the dining room of a nurses' home, where it was previously hung and is illustrated with scenes of the countryside and seashore. Elsi lived with Thomas in Sarn y Plas until her death in 1991, nine years before the death of Thomas himself. The grave was marked by a tiny memorial stone and below her name and date of death was an added inscription *ac yn ei ysbryd* R.S. Thomas – and in his spirit R.S. Thomas. Just behind the stone was a simple wooden cross with the name Andreas Gwydion Thomas, now almost faded by the sun. This was their son who died in 2016 and was also buried there. Thomas's ashes are buried close to the door of St John's Church in Porthmadog.

St. Maelrhys's Church and memorial for Mildred Eldridge,
RS Thomas and their son Gwydion.

20,000 Saints and Almost as Many Steps
Aberdaron to Craig Cwlwm –
28th October 2019

For our next walk, we were blessed with a brilliant azure sky and a dramatic display of clouds, including lots of huge feathery looking ones, which I think were cirrus and scatterings of bold cotton wool like formations of various shapes and sizes, which were probably cumulus or is that cumuli? Apologies to the Cloud Appreciation Society (yes there is one) for my appalling attempt at cloud identification! We left the car at the National Trust car park by the river Daron, and walked past Porth y Swnt, the National Trust Exhibition Centre, which is well worth a visit. It tells the story of Llŷn and especially of its relationship with the sea, and is bursting with amazing sculptures, many made with natural materials by local talented artists, with bilingual audio and video accompaniments to compliment them. We didn't stop to look today, but instead took a left turn along the road, following the sign directing us towards Rhiw up the steep hill until we reached a lay-by.

Along the wall at the back of the lay-by, someone had graffitied in white paint the words **Cofiwch Dryweryn**, which means remember Tryweryn. Signs with this message had been popping up all over Wales, this year especially, usually painted in white on a red background. They are copies of the original sign, which was painted on the wall of a ruined cottage in Ceredigion, by author and journalist Meic Stephens in the 1960s. He did this as a demonstration against the decision by Liverpool City Council to flood the Tryweryn valley in North Wales to create a reservoir. In 1965, the valley was flooded and several old communities including Capel Celyn were lost, despite many protests, including those made by the villagers themselves, who eventually lost their homes and many their livelihoods. In 2017, the words **Cofiwch Aberfan 1966**, were added to the original sign to also remember the 116 children and 28 adults killed in the Aberfan disaster, when a colliery tip collapsed into homes and a school. Early in 2019, the original sign was vandalised by someone who painted over the

Looking down at Aberdaron village with Cofiwch Dryweryn graffiti in foreground.

writing with the name Elvis. There was a huge outcry across Wales, and since then hundreds of Cofiwch Dryweryn murals have been appearing across the country, including a tiny one on a pebble in our caravan garden. A couple of years after this walk, a short documentary film was produced called The Welshman, which told the story of Owain Williams, one of the founders of the Movement for the Defence of Wales. He was imprisoned for planting an explosive device at an electricity transformer powering the reservoir project near Bala in 1963. The film includes recent interviews with Owain who was previously chairman of Gwynedd Council. Now where were we?

We looked back at the rooftops of Aberdaron, before heading through the gate marked 'Porth Simdde' which is the local name for the western end of Aberdaron beach, and meandered along the fenced path towards the headland. Not too far along the path, we came across a simple wooden bench offering views across the bay, with sayings carved on the seat in a familiar, swirly, script. This looked like the handiwork of Dafydd from Felin Uchaf once again. 'Time and Tide Wait for no Man' it said in English and **Fel yr Afon i'r Môr yw Bywyd Dyn** which literally means 'As the River to the Sea is Man's Life.' The path wound to the right and then a long flight of stone steps, surrounded by browning ferns, led us to a wooden

Bench with a view at Porth Simdde.

bridge which crossed a stream feeding into the sea at Porth Simdde. We stepped down onto the stony beach and watched hundreds of gulls breakfasting on pickings brought in by the tide, while we snacked on our apples. We examined the remains of some old stone quarry buildings and a wooden pier which we later read about. The pier had been built in the early 1900s to allow shipping of the quarry's output, but was barely used as the quarry closed soon after. A rusty kissing gate directed us upwards again via more steep steps and we paused to get our breath and admire the view when we reached the grassy path at the top. The open path followed the line of the coast and the Gwylan islands seemed to follow us as we trudged along it. The view of Aberdaron was picture postcard pretty with the beach, white cottages and a turquoise sea shimmering in the sunshine, with the hills providing the perfect backdrop behind. By the side of a modern looking bench, was the remains of an old stone building, possibly once a house and we were intrigued by an engraved slate plaque which had been wedged between the stones of the wall and read **Ysgol Farddol Caerfyrddin, Medi** 2015 – 'Caerfyrddin Poets' School, September 2015.' I had visions of a group of poets sitting amongst the ruins, composing verses inspired by their scenic surroundings.

Finally, we reached a wooden gate where we could see a green leafy headland ahead which we recognised as Porth Meudwy, a secluded lobster fishing cove which is also used as the embarkation point for trips to Ynys Enlli. We could see a familiar yellow boat heading towards the cove – Colin Evans the boatman was on his way back from the island. Colin has been running the Ynys Enlli boat trips for as long as we have been visiting and probably longer. It felt strange to be approaching the slipway from this direction as previously, we have only ever arrived at it from the car park at Cwrt farm ten minutes' walk inland. It felt even stranger to not be taking a trip across to the island. Since our youngest son Simon was only a few months old, we have taken a trip with Colin to the island every few years, then earlier this year Jim and I did our fifth visit but our first one without the boys. The island has lots of history and legend attached to it and for centuries it has been seen as a place of pilgrimage. Legend has it that 20,000 saints are buried there and it is said that three trips to the island are worth a pilgrimage to Rome! I'm not sure what five means but presumably we've qualified! It's still on my bucket list to spend at least one night on the island, to experience one of the darkest skies in the U.K. Jim may need a little more persuasion, as he is slightly put off by the lack of electricity and flushing toilets. The island is a very important place for wildlife and birds and has been listed as a Special area of Conservation for its habitats and species and a Special Protection Area because of the breeding birds, particularly the Manx shearwater of which there is a breeding colony of 20,000 pairs. We have been lucky enough to see puffins near the island and every trip guarantees close up sightings of Atlantic grey seals. Colin was born on the island and I believe he and his family still live there at least for part of

Steps down to Porth Meudwy.

each year. When he gives visitors his introductory talk as they land at Enlli, you sense the passion that he has for the island and his determination to help to protect it for the future. His mother Christine Evans is a poet and her collection of poems about Llŷn is on my 'still to be read' book shelf.

As we got to the bottom of the steps and onto the rocky beach at the port, we could see the red tractor in position ready to pull the boat onto dry land. The sea looked calm and still today as Colin approached, but often trips to Enlli have to be cancelled due to the powerful tides in Swnt Enlli. This year there have been discussions about an Ynys Enlli tidal energy project, which could involve placing turbines in the Swnt, to create energy for the local communities. Maybe electricity and flushing toilets will arrive on Enlli in time for our future overnight stay after all!

We left Porth Meudwy, the fishing boats and lobster pots and our memories behind, as we slowly trudged across another wooden bridge and up another large flight of steep stone steps, before continuing along the fern lined narrow path towards the area known as Craig Cwlwm, our turning back point for today. We reached the bottom of another hill and more steps and decided this was the perfect place to stop, as we had plenty steps to negotiate on our walk back and we could save these for tomorrow when we hoped to continue our journey.

Colin the boatman arriving at Porth Meudwy with the Gwylan Islands in the distance.

Volcanic Rocks and a Violet Lagoon

Craig Cwlwm to Porth Felen –
29th October 2019

We parked the car at the National Trust car park named Braich y Pwll, above Porth Felen, and prepared ourselves for another back to front walk. The view from here is one of the best to be had of Ynys Enlli. We trotted downhill alongside the farmer's fencing, with Mynydd Gwyddel, on our right, until we could see Porth Felen ahead and the gate and stone steps to our left, leading to the grassy coastal path. Tufts of fading pink sea thrift were clinging to the cliff edge and the turquoise sea glinted in the sunshine. **Gwyddel** in modern Welsh means Irishman but has derived from the Old Welsh word **Guoidel** which means pirate or raider. I could imagine pirates of old, landing in this beautiful hidden cove. As we strode out along the path, a few sheep quickly scattered as we approached. Ynys Enlli came into view again, with Trwyn Gwyddel in the foreground.

As we reached a kissing gate, we could see Bychestyn headland and the rocky islet Carreg Ddu ahead. We greeted another walker with his Welsh border collie dog which was off its lead. He seemed to be just out for a stroll but we wondered if he was a farmer looking for his straying sheep. The path narrowed into what looked more like a sheep trail and was a little too near the cliff edge for my liking, but thankfully it soon veered upwards and a welcomed fence followed the curve of the next bay, Parwyd, where the cliffs are said to be the steepest in Llŷn. Through another kissing gate we stopped to catch our breath at a conveniently positioned large white rock, perfect for perching on. The path was almost a straight line for a while but continued to climb and just as

Negotiating a narrow path on the way to Craig Cwlwm.

Ynys Enlli and a lagoon.

my legs were beginning to say 'no more' an amazing panorama opened out before us. Aberdaron bay and the Gwylan islands gleaming in the sunshine to the east, with the hills Garn Fadryn and Yr Eifl in the far distance and Carreg Ddu to the west, and there was Ynys Enlli sitting neatly on the horizon. We paused for a while, to rest and to take in the sight before us.

As the path continued downhill along the eastern side of Parwyd, we came upon a flooded area that had created a pond. The sun was shining on it and gave the illusion of a deep violet coloured lagoon. Had the weather been warmer it would have been very inviting for a wild swim. I left those dreams behind as the path headed northwards across Pen y Cil headland, passing through more gates. We reached the official National Trust sign for Pen y Cil and on a nearby rock, an engraved slate plaque, yellowed with lichen, informed us that the North Wales Centre of the National Trust had raised the funds to buy this headland in 1970. The narrow, open path now wound around the bays, Hen Borth and Porth y Pistyll, close to the cliff edge again and before long we reached the steps near Craig Cwlwm where we had ended our walk the day before. Craig Cwlwm, which means 'knot rock' is an outcrop of magmatic rocks, which was quarried on and off during the early nineteenth century and shipped abroad via Porth y Pistyll. Our return walk was brisker and motivated by the call of our packed lunch which we'd left in the car. We were care free and pleased at realising that we had now reached the approximate halfway point of our journey, with no idea that this was to be our last coastal walk for quite some time.

Ynys Enlli from Porth Felen.

Strange Times and Uncertainty

Between October 2019 and January 2020, we had several short breaks at the caravan, but for various reasons, including meeting up with friends and a trip to Aberystwyth, we didn't get back onto the coastal path again. The caravan site closed as usual on the 2nd January 2020, but we looked ahead to two months later, when it would be reopening on St David's Day.

In early February, we booked tickets to see a newly formed musical duo at Galeri in Caernarfon. They were called Tapestri and consisted of Lowri Evans, who had written our Fan o Hiraeth song and another female singer whose music we admired called Sera. We arranged to stay for two nights in the Travelodge in the town, which is almost next door to Galeri, and used this as an opportunity to also check on the caravan. On the day of the gig, the UK, especially North West England and North Wales, was hit by Storm Ciara, a powerful cyclone, with accompanying heavy rain. It swept across the whole of the UK and caused a lot of damage and some fatalities. We cancelled plans to visit Ynys Môn in the day time and decided it would be safer to stay in our room and read, especially after a member of staff at the Travelodge informed us that he'd just seen a lady and her full supermarket trolley being blown over. We waited hoping it would calm down and checked on social media for plans for the gig and news of the restaurant, as we had also booked to have an evening meal at the same venue. We eventually heard that there was damage to the roof of Galeri and the gig and meal were cancelled. The gig took place instead in Sera's living room on Ynys Môn, where Lowri had been on standby with her and they managed to broadcast it live on Facebook. We were able to watch it on our mobile phones, from the comfort of our Travelodge bed, dining on sandwiches that we bought on a very cautious but hasty trip on foot to the local supermarket across the road. The gig was rescheduled for July 2020, but little did we know what lay ahead.

On the 5th March 2020, four days after the reopening of the

site, and following a short break in Bruges, we returned for a long weekend at the caravan. Our usual excitement at returning to the caravan after the long break was dampened as March 2020 saw the beginning of the rapid spread of Coronavirus (soon to be known by all as COVID-19) to the U.K. The first case reported in the U.K. was at the end of January in York and Wales's first reported case was a person returning to Swansea from Italy on the 28th February. By the beginning of March news of COVID-19 spreading across the U.K. filled the newspapers and social media sites. We were uncertain about visiting, not wanting to add any unnecessary pressure on the services or the people of Llŷn. We didn't feel our usual elation at being back at our special place. We took our own food and avoided the towns, but enjoyed quiet walks within a few miles' radius of the caravan. We had originally planned to return for a further weekend towards the middle of March, but decided against this as we had seen on the news and social media that the people of Gwynedd were rightfully becoming scared about the transmission of the virus by the thousands of visitors who were beginning to arrive.

We received an email from the caravan site owner on the 23rd March, explaining that the park was closing with immediate effect in line with government guidelines, who that day had announced a national Lockdown, which was to be reviewed every three weeks and which restricted travel. It had been announced that the death toll at this time was 335 people in the UK, with 16 of these being in Wales. All of the UK were being told to 'Stay at Home' and to continue to wash their hands with soap and water for at least 20 seconds, as advised by Health Secretary Matt Hancock, who also suggested that singing the Happy Birthday song whilst washing hands could help children to gauge the time. We were treated to a live handwashing demonstration on T.V. by Prime Minister Boris Johnson, whose popularity was quickly waning, due to his slow reaction to the pandemic. We had been expecting this communication, as we had seen the announcements and were making plans to bring Simon home from his student accommodation in Manchester. Like everyone, we felt very worried about family, friends and the future; everything was so uncertain.

Over the next few months, we kept in touch via technology with our friends in Llŷn and compared how we'd had to change our work and leisure routines. I had already been working at home for one of my three days each week, to help me to manage the side effects of my cancer meds. I used this day to write up reports and complete admin duties, with the other two days used for face-to-face work with clients who attended the Adult Autism Diagnostic Service Clinic, where I was working as an Occupational Therapist/diagnostician. I now had to work all three days at home and quickly had to adapt to assessing people over the phone or using video consultation. The NHS Trust Information Technology staff worked amazingly hard to make all this technology available to thousands of employees within days of people being told they were to work from home wherever possible. Within a couple of weeks, myself and my colleagues became experts at using various video conferencing platforms to meet with clients and each other.

I began to do our weekly shopping at 6am, in the hour allocated for NHS staff, at our local supermarket, to reduce my contact with other people. Supermarkets were unable to keep up with the stock and many shelves were bare as a result of panic buying. For some reason many people felt the need to stock up on pasta and toilet rolls especially and these soon became scarce. As I write this months later, I imagine there are still households around the U.K. where bags of pasta fall out of crammed cupboards when opened and where loo rolls are being used in various imaginative ways around the home! Despite virtually self-isolating, including having been working from home for several weeks, I contracted the virus in May 2020. Luckily it was a mild form with atypical symptoms, but scary nonetheless and it seemed to exacerbate the side effects of my medication leaving me feeling even more fatigued than usual for many weeks. I remained in contact, via Messenger or WhatsApp, with our peninsula friends and we chatted about our goings on and our concerns for our families. A couple of days after I'd shared my news of having contracted the virus, a large package arrived in the post, with peninsula friend Amanda's familiar neat, bold handwriting (she teaches young children), containing home-made **bara brith** and Welsh cakes to help speed my recovery. It certainly helped.

We missed Llŷn desperately, but never at any point felt it was acceptable to visit during these months. We heard tales of visitors breaking the rules and being caught travelling to their second homes and trying to trick the police by sending their luggage separately by courier to make it look as if they were permanent residents. We began to realise that coastal walks were off the agenda, possibly for the whole of 2020. I gained comfort and help with my **hiraeth** throughout these times by reflecting on our coastal walks so far and looking over the photos and my jottings. That's when I decided to start writing this book – I had more free time on my days off as I wasn't able to socialise with friends and family and we were now having shopping delivered to reduce contacts with others.

I experienced this first lockdown, in a similar way to many, in that once over the initial shock, I began to enjoy the slower pace of life imposed upon us and to appreciate the peacefulness brought, especially by the huge reduction in traffic on the roads. We were all allowed one walk a day from our own doorsteps and Jim and I began to appreciate our surroundings more than ever before, with walks along a nearby meadow or the canal. We joined in with the weekly Thursday evening clapping, where we stood outside on our front drive and at 8 o'clock precisely we clapped to show appreciation for NHS frontline workers and carers, who were putting their lives at risk on a daily basis, helping people with this deadly disease. This would always be followed by waving to neighbours in the street and applauding one who brought his accordion out with him each time and played a tune for us all. We chatted to neighbours we had barely seen before, despite living only a few doors away and there was an increased sense of camaraderie in our village as there was in many others around the country.

I, like many others, began to discover the pleasures of using video conferencing platforms to pursue my interests, including meeting up with Welsh speaking friends. Until now, the Manchester Welsh Learners' Group had been continuing to meet up on the third Saturday of every month since 2012. Our venue had changed over the years but since early 2018, a few months after its opening, we discovered a little café in the trendy Northern Quarter 'Siop Shop' – **siop** means shop and sounds the same. When we realised it was run by a Welshman, we all agreed this was the perfect meeting place and moved on from the city art gallery café. Iwan, who originated from Dolgellau, gave us a very warm welcome and was happy to chat and take our orders in Welsh. From March onwards, non-essential shops and eating places were closed during the Lockdown, so our meetings in Siop Shop had to stop. Luckily our group already kept in touch via a Facebook page, and in April, I suggested we meet via video conference platform Zoom on our usual third Saturday. I was pleasantly surprised by the enthusiasm and by June, I was arranging the group twice a month. One of the benefits of this socially distanced way of meeting was that we had the pleasure of Welsh learner 'visitors' joining us from various places outside of Manchester, including Australia and Wales! It was agreed that when 'normality' returned, we would aim to continue twice a month, with one meeting in the café and the other via Zoom, which would enable people who may otherwise find it difficult due to health or travel reasons to continue to meet up. Prior to COVID-19, I had also been attending a similar monthly group, but this was in the evening and for fluent and first language Welsh speakers. The organiser of this, my fluent learner friend Simon, moved these to a virtual platform, which meant these were also able to continue.

I've always been ambivalent about using Facebook, being quite a private person, and would never dream of sharing my day-to-day events with the world across social media, but I love being able to access information about events related to my interests, especially music and the arts. During Lockdown, some of my favourite Welsh singers, musicians and writers began to offer free live-stream gigs on Facebook and YouTube and some of them recorded the musical contributions they gave in their own streets on 'Clap for the NHS' Thursday. Some of these were singers Al Lewis and Glain Rhys, who happened to be in the same street but across the road to one another. They duetted from a distance and performed some songs, that would have been sung in Al's tour that had been cancelled much to the disappointment of ourselves and many others. I was so grateful to these musicians for helping to keep me sane as I was really missing the experience of seeing live bands. Lowri Evans and her partner Lee Mason gave wonderful performances with excellent sound quality from their garden or house (depending on the weather) in Newport and another favourite, Lleuwen Steffan (then living in Brittany), offered an intimate gig from her attic, occasionally whispering to avoid waking her children below! Dafydd, the storyteller, wrote inspiring poetry and posted these on Facebook and YouTube, accompanied by uplifting music and films showing scenes around Llŷn and local wildlife. A favourite lively Welsh folk band, Calan were trying to keep busy during Lockdown in the absence of gigs and to help raise some income they offered various deals to their fans including commissioned music by one of the band members. I bought a tune to play on my low D whistle, composed by Beth, the singer and accordionist from the group. She titled it *Jig i Jean* (Jig for Jean) and it will always be a reminder of these strange times. Beth also clog dances and often incorporates this into the songs, with her clogging providing a great percussion sound. She put some free clog dancing lessons on Facebook and yes, I had to give them a go, but wearing my trainers not my clogs to reduce the risk of breaking my neck! They were a great way to keep fit and have fun but apart from Jim and Simon occasionally catching sight of me in the kitchen, thankfully no one else had to tolerate my clumsy attempts at following the steps!

The 2020 Welsh National Eisteddfod **Eisteddfod Genedlaethol Cymru** was due to be held in Tregaron, Ceredigion during the first week of August. Due to COVID-19, it had to be postponed, which was a huge disappointment to many. As you can imagine, a huge amount of preparation is required and this begins a couple of years before the actual week of the event. The people of Llŷn and Eifionydd had been excitedly making their own Eisteddfod preparations as they had been chosen to host the event the year after Tregaron had their turn, but they now knew that they had a long time to wait. But it wasn't all despair; during August, a host of innovative people got their heads together and created the **Eisteddfod Amgen** (Alternative Eisteddfod) which highlighted the many talents of Welsh musicians and poets and was broadcast live on Facebook or YouTube. Some of my favourite performances were those by **Pedair** (meaning four), a newly formed group made up of four well-known female Welsh singers/musicians – Gwyneth Glyn, Meinir Gwilym, Siân James and Gwenan Gibbard, three of whom live in Llŷn. Together they created three songs, which they performed simultaneously from their own homes. These were recorded and could be watched live or at a later time on the

Eisteddfod Amgen YouTube channel. One of the songs was dedicated to Rhodri Dafydd, a well-known Natural Resources Wales warden who had done a lot for local conservation and had died recently of cancer. Another touching song was *Cân y Clo* (Lockdown Song) which was about the longing everyone was feeling for the people and places they loved.

During our separation from Llŷn, I began to miss some of the local produce that we usually bought and enjoyed there. We also felt concern for the small businesses and wanted to support them, as we had been trying to do with those near to home. So, throughout May and June, interesting parcels regularly arrived through the post as treats for ourselves or as gifts for friends and family. This included our favourite curds and chutneys from Welsh Lady Preserves (a small company within walking distance of our caravan) and Welsh cheeses wrapped in sheep's wool to keep them insulated! Beautiful wooden and rainbow coloured cord tealight holders made by the talented young woodturner Miriam Jones who lives near Porth Neigwl were perfect as gifts, especially as part of the proceeds was given to charities supporting people during these difficult times. A beautiful framed print of a painting of Porth Nefyn was ordered from Tess Urbanska – my favourite Welsh artist and my favourite beach – to be added to our 'Tess' wall in our extension.

Various interesting new Welsh language Facebook pages began to appear during the Lockdown to try and lift people's spirits and motivate people to keep going. These were entertaining and great for my ongoing efforts to continue developing my Welsh vocabulary. One of these was **Curo'r Corona'n Coginio** (Beat Corona by Cooking). This was created by **Merched y Wawr** and people were encouraged to share their culinary talents with pictures and recipes. I had thought of submitting one of my baking creations, but when I saw the amazingly high standard of the cakes and savoury dishes presented by other members, including friend Amanda, I thought better of it! Another Facebook page that inspired and encouraged me was **Garddio Corona** (Corona Gardening) where people shared their gardening successes...or disasters later in the year following the storms. Like many people's gardens ours had been having a lot more attention than usual during Lockdown, but I was concerned about our little caravan garden especially after the very dry, hot spell we'd had throughout May. **Côr-ona** was the cleverly named Facebook page for singers to show off their talents and to raise people's spirits; **Côr** means choir. One man from Llŷn, Dylan Morris, won the admiration of tens of thousands of followers who watched videos of him singing popular songs in Welsh and English, sometimes with his young daughter duetting with him. The culmination of this was the release of an E.P. called *Haul ar Fryn* (sun on the hill), which was also the title of one of the tracks and part of a saying that was beginning to be used frequently throughout Wales to encourage optimism about the future.

At the end of June, the Welsh government announced that holiday parks in Wales could reopen on the 13th of July. Wales residents had only just had their travel restrictions lifted which had prevented them from travelling more than five miles from their homes. Wales had taken a stricter line with restrictions than the rest of the U.K. and we knew that many feared the reimportation of the virus. Scenes of crowds of people on English beaches, not respecting social distancing guidelines and leaving tons of waste including human excrement, appeared on the T.V. and in newspapers which fuelled the fear. We waited and allowed time to see how the reopening went and asked our friends about the feeling of locals. We eventually made a cautious visit at the end of July, taking our own food and avoiding busy areas again. We had strolls on an empty Nefyn beach in the early hours of the

July 2020 Happy to be on Peninsula sand again despite the rain.

July 2020 Cricieth and social distancing reminder on the pavement.

August 2020 Visit to
Plas Glyn y Weddw Art Gallery
wearing masks.

August 2020 Cafe at Nant Gwrtheyrn
with socially distanced tables.

morning and walks through peaceful Lôn Goed. We were a little nervous to be there and very careful to follow guidelines at all times but so happy to finally be back in this special place. Everywhere looked more beautiful than ever in Llŷn apart from our caravan garden, which as expected was a mess. All the potted plants had died from the heat and our small raised garden was a tangle of weeds and perennials, fighting for space. But this was little to worry about and was soon sorted.

On the 7th August, the day after helping to move Simon into his new flat in Manchester to begin his third year of university, we returned to the caravan for another weekend, again avoiding supermarkets and busy areas at peak times. We visited Plas Glyn y Weddw art gallery and I soaked up the beautiful art work at the Summer Exhibition, where staff and visitors wore masks, which by now were mandatory in public places, and people gave their contact details for 'Track and Trace' if necessary. We even managed to visit some cafés at quieter times, where the tables were distanced from one another and temperatures were taken on entry. We visited Pwllheli and had a walk along the beach, admiring the long snake of painted pebbles along the nearby wall, which the local children had made to raise community spirit. We adhered to warning signs about being aware of real snakes (adders) in the dunes as more than usual had been sighted this year. Everywhere seemed alien, with signs reminding of restrictions of numbers of people in the shops. We had grown accustomed to this at home but it seemed more shocking somehow to see it here. Pwllheli is a treasure trove of some great

August 2020 Pebble snake at Pwllheli

independent shops and cafés, which we regularly frequent. We were saddened to see that some hadn't survived during Lockdown. We were shocked to see Taro Deg Café for sale. To me, this modern yet cosy café, had always felt the most traditionally Welsh place to eat in Llŷn, with Welsh language music playing in the background and **bara brith** and Welsh cakes always on the menu. We were happy to see that *Llen Llŷn* was still surviving. This is the place to go for all Welsh language books, magazines, music and much more. I popped in to buy a copy of both of the Welsh language local monthly papers. They are a great way of keeping in touch with what's going on in the area and good reading practice for me. They are a work of love, produced by the communities of the peninsula, and as well as giving up to date news from the various towns and villages, often include short stories, poetry and articles about the art work created by the talents

August 2020
Felin Uchaf Craft shop..

August 2020 Encouraging Rainbow sign near Y Ffor.

August 2020 Carys Bryn sign in Llanaelhearn.

of the area. Prior to COVID-19, each month a different village or town took responsibility for the folding and distributing of the papers, with volunteers meeting in their local community halls to organise this. During Lockdown, both papers were digitalised and made available free online. Not surprisingly my favourite page was missing from both papers – Y Dyddiadur – The Diary – which lists dates and venues of local events of interest such as gigs and art exhibitions. Everything was cancelled until further notice. We were pleased to see that the shop Glasu, where they sell ice-cream made in Edern, was still going strong and on the way back to the caravan we called in to buy a tub to enjoy later from our freezer.

On our travels to and from Llanbedrog and Pwllheli, we noticed several new and colourful signs outside of houses and schools, many adorned with rainbows similar to the signs that children near to home had been putting in their windows, to offer a ray of hope during Lockdown. Many had the words **Daw Eto Haul ar Fryn,** a Welsh saying which translates as 'The Sun will Shine on a Hill again' and means that all will eventually be well again. This saying had been adopted throughout many parts of Wales and used to offer hope to the communities. I began to notice it appearing on cards, T-Shirts, mugs and even Covid masks. The saying is a line from a **Hen Bennill** (old verse) – a form of folk poetry. There are many collections of these anonymous verses, often with themes of love and nature. They were usually four lines in length and thought to have often been written by women. They were composed to be spoken or sung to a harp accompaniment and have been performed for centuries at Welsh social gatherings. Two of the signs that we saw on our travels were immediately recognised as the brightly coloured work of local artist

August 2020 Tecwyn Tractor, Carys Bryn picture and raised garden at Ysbyty Bryn Beryl Pwllheli.

Carys Bryn, but without her usual signature paint splats across the completed image. One of these was in the village of Y Ffôr and had the message **Cadwch yn Saff!** (Keep Safe), with a caricatured house surrounded by her frequently painted bright hearts. The other was positioned outside the local hospital which had been converted to a COVID-19 Unit – Ysbyty Bryn Beryl – and featured a red tractor with a smiley face and a speech bubble announcing **Bib-bib Daliwch i Wenu!!** (Pip Pip Keep Smiling!!). This face will have been recognisable to many local people – young and old – as Tecwyn the Tractor, the character who featured in a series of 1990s Welsh children's books illustrated by Carys and later transferred to a T.V. series. At the front of the hospital was also a large flower bed filled with colourful plants, forming a rainbow pattern to cheer patients, staff and the passing community. Gardeners, Sioned Edwards and Meinir Gwilym (also a singer as previously mentioned) were responsible for creating this and we later watched them doing so on their regular S4C television programme *Garddio a Mwy* (Gardening and More). The

August 2020 NHS sign at Nefyn

August 2020 Sign supporting the NHS at Llanaelhaearn.

August 2020 The Pizza van at Llanaelhaearn.

plants were all kindly donated by our favourite Welsh garden centre, Tyddyn Sachau, which is situated just down the road from the hospital and as it is close to our caravan, its café is a regular lunching venue for us.

In the middle of August, we decided to have a fortnight at the caravan. I was feeling rather low after the sudden death of a young work colleague, and the tranquillity of Llŷn was just what I needed. We took some basic supplies with us and decided to continue avoiding large supermarkets as we'd heard they'd become extremely busy with the influx of visitors. We discovered that a pizza van, owned by a young local couple, now visited our closest village of Llanaelhaearn every Friday evening. This took care of one of our meals during our stay and we were happy to support a small business as well as enjoy their tasty fresh pizzas. We ordered boxes of fresh fruit, vegetables, eggs, cordials and preserves to be delivered from a local organic farm in nearby Llithfaen and the remainder of our needed supplies we bought from Pwllheli Spar (who stock a lot of locally produced goods) at

August 2020 Rhoshirwaun

quieter times of the day. We sported our Welsh dragon face-masks, an anniversary present from a friend, when entering any shops. We avoided busier parts of Llŷn and enjoyed exploring areas closer to 'home' that we sometimes take for granted, including strolls around Llanaelhaearn village. During walks along the lanes by the caravan, I gathered blackberries which I added to the locally grown apples, given to us by friends from their orchard, to make jelly.

At this time, COVID-19 regulations restricted the numbers of people attending funerals and weddings to 30. On the day and time of my colleague's funeral, I made a solitary visit to St Beuno's church, Pistyll, which sits in a most beautiful and peaceful spot overlooking the sea. The church is usually open to visitors but due to the virus, the doors were locked so I sat outside on the wall for an hour and wrote a short tribute to her which I later added to the remembrance book that was to be presented to her family from myself and my colleagues.

On another day, I made my first ever appointment to visit the workshop of artist Carys Bryn which is only about a mile from the caravan and housed in a large shed next to her house. I entered the shed cautiously, wearing my mask and Carys, wearing paint

August 2020 Carys Bryn in her studio at Rhosfawr.

splattered black jumper and trousers, gave me a warm welcome, offered me a **panad** and allowed me to browse. I was like a child in a sweet shop. The walls were full of her colourful creations – large canvases with stormy scenes, portraits of dogs and lots of her familiar hearts and flowers on smaller square canvases. I trod the floor, carefully avoiding a myriad of pots and jars of paint and partly completed works of art. Then I spotted a little red tractor, presumably the model for Tecwyn with his bright yellow chimney. I managed some Welsh chat with Carys who proudly also showed me her son Cian's detailed pencil caricatures of local villages. I chose a Cian print of Nefyn and a small Carys canvas with a cartoon style house and the word **Cartref** (Home), for the caravan. The colourful canvas was similar in style to Carys's Lockdown signs and I thought it would be a reminder of these strange times.

We were keen to continue our coastal walk but only if it didn't put ourselves or others at risk. We began with some shorter walks along parts of the coastal path that we had already walked to weigh up the situation. It was strange to see temporary signs by the coastal path, reminding us all to maintain two metres social distancing and some remaining red and white plastic tape strips,

where paths had obviously been closed until recently. We saw few other walkers, so we decided to keep an eye on the weather and re-join our coastal walk on the next suitable day, which was on one of the few calm days between the departure of Storm Ellen and the arrival of Storm Francis!

August 2020 *Coast path at Cricieth with social distancing sign*

The Edge of the World and an Embarrassing Accident

Porth Felen to Mynydd Mawr – 24th August 2020

It had been ten months since our last coastal path walk and it felt strange but wonderful to be back. It was the day before our 29th wedding anniversary and a perfect way to celebrate. We have always worn appropriate footwear on our walks and kept to designated paths to minimise our risk of falls. Several years ago, we had also invested in some walking poles, but on almost every walk these have been left behind in the car, forgotten about until our knees started to complain. On this occasion, we prepared extra carefully, even though this was going to be quite a short walk. We were determined to be safe and not need rescuing along this rather remote section of the coastal path, conscious of the pressure the NHS had been under recently. So, with walking poles at the ready, sun hats on, sun cream applied and rucksacks stuffed with water bottles, first aid kit and snacks, we set off. Now is perhaps the appropriate time to reveal a little secret I have about something I do, or rather don't do, when walking along the coastal path. I've never been able to answer the call of nature by squatting behind a bush in the way that many of my friends are able to. But with advancing years, I have had to devise a system as my bladder isn't what it used to be! I have an old denim dress that I'm very fond of and I discovered that it was perfect for going commando as it allows me to stride out but doesn't fly up in a breeze, so I remain decent at all times and it allows a quick pee behind a bush when needed. I've named it my 'wee in the wild dress.' Until now I've only shared this secret with close family and friends and in fact my friend Letizia (whose first language is Italian) had to correct me when I told her that I was now going 'combat' on my longer walks! I've inherited my occasional use of malapropisms from my dear mum.

We decided to start from the upper car park on Mynydd Mawr, and to do a reversed trip, walking back to Porth Felen where we had finished last time. Absence certainly makes the heart grow fonder and I felt blissfully happy to be continuing on our journey.

Arriving back at Mynydd Mawr

The Coastguard's Hut on Mynydd Mawr and Ynys Enlli.

All of my senses seemed on high alert after our long break as I took in our surroundings. The sun was shining, the birds were singing and the colours of nature looked more vivid than usual. This area is known to many as **Pendraw'r Byd** (The Edge of the World) and each year Aberdaron hosts the Music and Arts Festival – **Gŵyl Pendraw'r Byd**, but not this year of course. We tend to refer to this beautiful most westerly part of Llŷn as Uwchmynydd, which is really the name of the main village in the area. Some people call it the 'Land's End of Wales' and there is certainly a wild and dramatic feel to the stretch of the coastal path around this area, especially between Aberdaron and Porth Colmon.

The coastguard's hut and shed are the only remaining buildings on the summit of Mynydd Mawr. The hut is now sometimes used by National Trust volunteers to provide information to visitors, especially about the local wildlife to be seen in the area, including porpoises, choughs, hares and grey seals. In the past it had been a lookout point for the coastguards until 1990 and had been part of a chain of signal stations guarding against invasion during WW2. We have driven to this spot many times over the years with Tom, Simon and their friends to take in the view and depending on the weather to experience the force of the wind at the summit. As we looked towards Mynydd Gwyddel, we were saddened and shocked by a sight we had never seen here before. Two men had driven off the large car park area and headed across the grass to the edge of the headland, finally stopping to sit

Watching choughs near Mynydd Mawr.

and look at the view from behind the steering wheels of their huge Land Rovers. There were more people around than we were used to in this usually very quiet spot, but as with us, the sunshine had brought people out who had not been able to go very far for months. We saw the look of horror on the faces of other walkers, who like us, felt this was unacceptable behaviour, totally lacking any consideration for the wildlife and landscape. We'd heard a few locals saying that Llŷn had been attracting a lot of non-regular visitors this year, who as a result of COVID-19 hadn't been able to visit their usual resorts abroad and that not all, but some of these, didn't seem to have the same respect for the environment and the local people that regular visitors showed.

We followed the concrete steps and path, then strode across the foundations of some WW2 buildings, demolished many years ago. As we approached the coastal path, we noticed large patches of burnt fern, a reminder of the heatwave fires of 2018. Ynys Enlli was in full view and we could even make out the red and white lighthouse as we turned left to follow the rough grassy path towards Mynydd Gwyddel. We giggled at a man repeatedly attempting to make his serious looking bulldog keep still while he took its photograph on a grassy mound with Ynys Enlli in the background. As we wandered downwards following the narrow sheep trail path, we were overtaken by two cheerful runners. One was a bit less enthusiastic and joked with us about needing to get back for a pint. As we stopped to let them pass more easily, we were rewarded with the sight of a seal close to the rocks below. Further out we spotted the familiar yellow boat of Colin, the Ynys Enlli boatman on his way back to Porth Meudwy after dropping off passengers to enjoy a day trip on the island. What a lovely day for it. The path took us down and around Mynydd Gwyddel with its patches of low growing pink bell heather and yellow common rock roses and several sheep were grazing peacefully on the grass close by. We eventually reached the gate on the path above Porth Felen, where we had ended our walk last time.

We turned back and were glad of our walking poles as we trudged back uphill along the narrow path. We were amused by, and took photos of, our long shadows ahead of us and grazing sheep gave us puzzled looks. Yes really, sheep do have all kinds of facial expressions – most often puzzled! As the steps to Mynydd Mawr appeared ahead of us, we were treated to a wonderful display by a flock of choughs, playing in the sea breeze, with their familiar chee-ow sound. A grey seal, choughs and one of my favourite views in Llŷn – I thought that my day was complete! Little did I know what still lay ahead of us.

As we approached the car park, a family of four were on their way down the steps and I recognised the mother. It was Nia from the farmhouse café, Caffi Ni, just outside of Nefyn, which I tend to refer to as Café Nia. I was surprised that Nia recognised us with our sunglasses and hats and we stopped to chat, while her husband and children continued on to admire the view. She commented on us wearing all the right walking gear and I joked about how I didn't want an injury like the one I'd had a few years ago. About four years previously on Jim's birthday, during a much-anticipated family quad bike trek at a local activity park, I had badly sprained my ankle and lost consciousness after coming off my quad. Once I'd revived, we'd stuck to our plan of lunch at Nia's and I'd hobbled into the café still in quite a lot of pain. Nia remembered this event and we laughed about it. I asked her how business had been during the COVID-19 restrictions and we were pleased to hear that even though the café was still closed, she had been inundated with takeaway orders for her delicious afternoon teas, which have always been popular in Llŷn. It was good to hear of a small business thriving in these times and as we said goodbye, we asked if we could place an order in a few days.

Today, we had planned to visit yet another favourite café, Caffi Tŷ Newydd, situated on a campsite in Uwchmynydd on the way back to Aberdaron. We were greeted like old friends at the back door by Marian and family, who asked were we on our way back from Enlli again as this is when we have

The ambulance setting off home from Ty Newydd Cafe.

sometimes visited in the past. We explained what we had been doing and ordered our lattes and scones and sat on one of the outdoor picnic benches. Marian's husband saw us admiring the view and pointed out Fishguard in the far distance beyond Enlli. We chatted with an elderly south Walian couple and joked about the north/south rivalry and how the southerners are often referred to as **Hwntw** by the northerners, who in turn are referred to as **Gogs**. **Hwntw** is derived from the phrase **tu hwnt** meaning 'over there' and **gog** is short for **gogledd** which means north. The gentleman was also a learner so we exchanged a few sentences in Welsh before they went on their way as our food and drink arrived. As I turned to say goodbye, my serviette flew off the tray in the breeze and I leapt off the bench to grab it. The next thing I knew, I was lying on the ground, regaining consciousness with a very painful foot. I had sprained my left ankle yet again! I had passed out cold and three very worried faces were looking down at me – Jim, Marian and one of her adult daughters. I tried to sit up but passed out again and after my failed third attempt of sitting and remaining conscious, Marian took charge and insisted that I stay lying down and she phoned the ambulance service. I argued against the ambulance being called for and felt sure it was just a sprain but Marian was more concerned about my passing out and explained that they had first responders not far away. The whole experience felt quite surreal. Various faces appeared above me as I lay on the ground. The south Walian couple had returned to see how I was and various children came to have a look at me – most of them Marian's grandchildren. I started to feel more alert and suddenly remembered about my lack of pants and muttered something to Jim about it. Jim being Jim, had already dealt with it and had straightened my dress as soon as I had fallen, to ensure I maintained my modesty. I just hoped no one got a flash of my bum as I went down! Marian made me comfortable with blankets and she and her daughter stayed by me checking on my colour and updating the ambulance staff when they rang back. Understandably and much to my relief, I wasn't being treated as an immediate emergency. We laughed together as I shared my pant free situation and the conversation turned to alternative methods of having a pee in the wild.

The cheerful and friendly Emlyn and Wyn finally arrived in the ambulance, immediately put me at my ease and dismissed my feelings of guilt at needing their services for a twisted ankle, especially in the current times. They'd travelled from Blaenau Ffestiniog almost 50 miles away! I had a little chat in Welsh with them and they were surprised and intrigued as to why I had learnt to speak the language. They checked my foot and my vitals and seemed confident it was just a sprain and that all was well. I offered to buy them a coffee and scone but Marian appeared with a tray for them on the house. We finally enjoyed our jam and cream scones and a fresh hot coffee, then thanked Marian and family before heading back to the caravan.

A couple of days later, Jim chauffeured me back to Caffi Tŷ Newydd so that I could take a bouquet of flowers for Marian and her daughters to say thank you. Shortly after, I made a donation to the Wales Air Ambulance and thanked God that I hadn't needed their services. My leg was black and blue between my toes and my knee, and I had orders to rest it for several days. I felt gutted. We had only just resumed our coastal walk after so long and now we would be unable to go any further during our last few days at the caravan. The future was also beginning to sound uncertain again with regards the COVID-19 situation.

Another Lockdown

During September 2020, we made a couple of cautious weekend visits to the caravan, following our local and Wales's COVID-19 guidelines. My foot wasn't up to any strenuous walking yet and we were avoiding contact with other people as much as possible. We managed some slow, quiet early morning walks and ate the food we had taken with us, avoiding the need for supermarkets. One shop we did visit was the tiny craft shop at Felin Uchaf. We saw no one and left payment in the honesty box for the beautiful woven willow bees and dragonflies made by the wife and daughter of Dafydd the carpenter and storyteller. These were to be birthday and Christmas gifts for friends and family but somehow one of each also ended up in our own garden when we returned home! I felt sad at how deserted Felin Uchaf seemed as we wandered back to the car with our treasures. From previous visits we were used to seeing the fresh young faces of volunteers, full of passion and enthusiasm for whatever they were engaged in, whether it be thatching, building, wood working or gardening. These volunteers would often also be around for Dafydd's storytelling sessions and would sometimes offer their musical talents to the evening. COVID-19 meant no volunteers and no storytelling. Jim was about to start up the engine for us to leave, and I heard 'Jean!' Dafydd had spotted us as he was heading away from his boatbuilding shed. He gave a huge welcoming smile as we jumped out of the car to greet him. Arms were reached out from a distance but our hugs had to remain virtual. Dafydd updated us about the situation at Felin Uchaf and dispelled the rumours I'd heard that there was little hope for the enterprise as a result of the losses made during Lockdown. Volunteers hadn't been allowed to work there but he was hopeful that things would pick up and told us that his carpentry business remained busy. Dafydd was very encouraging when I told him about my coastal walk writings and helped me with some pieces of information I'd been unsure about. He understood when I explained that the writing would help with my **hiraeth** for Llŷn as we were pretty sure this would be our last visit for a long while. I told him that the beautiful poems he had put onto YouTube recently would do the same and thanked him. In true modest Dafydd style, he swept away the compliment and wished us well as we set off back to the caravan.

On the 15th October 2020, we visited the caravan for one night to winterise it, as the Welsh government had announced a 'Circuit Breaker Lockdown' from 6pm the day after. This meant that there should be no visitors in Wales and all residents of Wales should return to their homes by this deadline. The following morning, we quietly watched the sunrise from the coastal path above Nefyn beach, said our goodbyes and after a quick lunch and packing up, we headed for home, crossing the border in plenty of time before Lockdown began. We were both in our own thoughts for much of the journey home, wondering when we would be able to return to the caravan and enjoy our walks again. But our thoughts were mostly with friends and family in Llŷn and at home, wishing to see an end to this terrible virus and the suffering it was causing to so many.

Our family had two special birthdays in November 2020; my 60th and Simon's 21st. All that was allowed at this time was outdoor distanced visits with one other household. My birthday was celebrated by a local walk with Jim, some doorstep visits from friends and family and a video chat with Tom, Simon and Rhi using FaceTime. This was followed throughout the week, by some slightly restricted walks around the grounds and parks of some local National Trust properties. Snacks and drinks were on sale but had to be eaten on the move and one-way systems were in place to reduce contact with others. On Simon's birthday, Jim and I hand delivered his gifts, birthday cake and balloon. We weren't allowed to meet indoors, so we got together in the park close to his Manchester flat and had a takeaway seated at a picnic bench! This was followed by a full family video chat session using FaceTime in the evening, when his brother Tom had finished work. Tom had been lucky to not have to be furloughed throughout the pandemic. None of us are wild party animals but this wasn't quite what we'd had in mind to celebrate our birthdays!

Shortly before Christmas, Simon was allowed to return home for a couple of weeks, after testing negative with a lateral flow covid test. These were being made available for university students to help detect and reduce the spread of the virus. The highlight of December was Christmas Day as this was the only day that the COVID – 19 regulations allowed all of our close family to get together indoors over the holiday period. An email arrived in December from the caravan site owner, informing us that the site would not be closed during January and February 2021, as it had been forced to close for so long already. He explained that if COVID-19 guidelines for Wales and England allowed we could return for visits. We both felt that this was very unlikely to happen and continued to get on with life and enjoy more local distractions including a very heavy snowfall on New Year's Eve.

As I worked for the NHS, I received my first Pfizer covid vaccination in January 2021 and gradually began to do small amounts of work in the clinic, but mostly continued to work from home. For much of the time between January and March, when I wasn't working, I was joining Jim in doing some much-needed repainting of bedrooms, hall, stairs and landing. At the Easter weekend, with the gradual lifting of restrictions again, we were allowed a garden meet up with Tom, Simon and Rhi. Two days later, Simon decided to complete the last few weeks of his degree from home and moved back. It was lovely to be able to see family again. In March, it was announced by the Welsh Minister that from the 12th April 2021, the Welsh border could be opened up and people could travel into and out of Wales again, including those wishing to stay in self-contained accommodation. Four days later, and exactly six months since we had said goodbye to Llŷn, we made a cautious but emotional return to the caravan for a week's stay. We were able to have some socially distanced meet ups on the decking and local walks with friends, which felt like a real treat. On our drives, I noticed that many of the bright rainbow signs had now been replaced with boards promoting local councillors who were preparing for the forthcoming elections. Many of the hedgerows and verges looked stunning with the white blossom of blackthorn. There was an atmosphere of hopefulness and looking ahead to the future and we were looking forward to getting back onto the coastal path.

Choughs to the Rescue
Mynydd Mawr to Braich Anelog –
19th April 2021

April had been unusually dry and warm and we were blessed with sunshine for the whole of our week's stay. As Jim drove towards Uwchmynydd, I soaked up my favourite sea views along the quiet north coast road. Along the narrow winding roads between Aberdaron and Uwchmynydd, we followed a school bus for a couple of miles. As in the rest of the UK, the education of children in Wales had been disrupted greatly due to the pandemic and they'd had long periods of time being home schooled by their families and by school staff via video. Secondary schools had also been providing lateral flow tests to detect any asymptomatic children with the virus. Only a week before this walk, the Welsh government had announced that all children could now be back in school. As we followed the bus, I thought about how I might have felt if this had happened when our boys were of school age. I empathised with the mixed feelings the parents must be experiencing about their children being back with their friends, and with the huge responsibly the teaching staff had been given with their duty to keep the children as safe as possible.

We passed Tŷ Newydd café and campsite, where I'd injured my foot after our last walk. We'd seen on Facebook that the café extension was well on the way to completion and I was hoping we could stop by for lunch after our walk. We spotted a couple of camper vans on the clearings by the roadside on Mynydd Mawr and guessed the occupiers had slept there overnight to take in the amazing views of Ynys Enlli under the stars. There were no other cars on Mynydd Mawr car park as we reached the top, beneath the coastguard buildings. We had been surprised at how quiet Llŷn had seemed so far on our return.

We set off across the level grassy path with large confident strides, eager to get going again. It felt unusual to be heading north from the summit of Mynydd Mawr and not southerly to view Ynys Enlli. Our surroundings looked quite mystical as a result of the bright yet hazy sunshine. Eastwards towards Aberdaron bay, a silvery glow encircled the islands, Gwylan Fawr and Gwylan Bach, and the headlands and mountains were covered by a misty veil. Clumps of dry heather were beginning to show signs of regrowth. As we saw Mynydd Anelog ahead of us we realised that this was new territory for us, which felt exciting.

Heading for Braich Anelog.

Our large strides were soon replaced by tentative steps along the steep stony path which led downwards to the base of Mynydd Mawr. Since our last coastal walk, to my disappointment, a bone scan had revealed I had osteoporosis, a common side effect of my cancer tablets. So, I was feeling a bit cautious about any uneven walking, despite being well equipped with walking poles and new

Interesting terrain on the way to Braich Anelog.

extra sturdy walking boots. For the first time on our walks, I felt anxious about falling and wondered if I should carry on – I didn't want to break any bones and certainly didn't want to put myself at risk of needing emergency services again! Jim was his usual calm self, reaching out his hand to help me at all the right moments as always. We joked about how the previous day we had been bursting with enthusiasm and we began to modify our ambitious plan of doing a walk on each of our seven days' stay at the caravan. My knees were already feeling the strain and as the path levelled off again, we could see that the remainder of our walk would involve further steep inclines and declines and of course we then had to turn around and come back. I was feeling rather despondent and for the first time ever, I wondered about quitting, when a familiar loud 'chee-ow' from a nearby fence post interrupted my thoughts. The chough flew past, close enough to prove its identity to us, with its now visible red bill and legs. This wonderful sight somehow gave me a burst of renewed enthusiasm and energy to keep going. The power of nature!

We admired the views of the bay, Porth Llanllawen ahead of us with Mynydd Anelog beyond. There had been very little rain for weeks and the surrounding area and clay path was bone dry. In contrast, the walled fields of Uwchmynydd were green and lush in the distance. As we progressed, our surroundings gradually came to life, as the path took us through farmland, where free roaming sheep munched on the grass as they watched us pass. Bright yellow lesser celandine flowers were plentiful in the fields and along the edge of the path, with an occasional tiny violet adding variety. Jim was amused by my sniffing at each violet that we came across. I was checking if they were sweet violets but they were all dog violets, which are as pretty but lacking in scent. Golden gorse bushes shone in the sunshine distracting our attention from the large patches of dry bracken.

We came to a wooden kissing gate and followed the narrow clay path onto the ridged grassy hillside which was covered in large tufts, which from a distance gave the illusion of waves. Jim joked and said the hill was having a bad hair day, something we had all been extra familiar with until recently. Hairdressers had only just reopened after months of closure due to the most recent lockdown. As we neared the inlets of Llanllawen and Ogof Goch, we could hear the loud and eerie calls of the gulls and other sea birds that I was unable to identify, echoing between the cliff sides and we were soon able to see them perched on the rocks and flying in and out of the caves, presumably building their nests or feeding their young. Another steep path downwards took us across a wooden bridge spanning the stream which fed into the sea at Porth Llanllawen. The banks of the stream were decorated with sturdy clumps of yellow primroses, one of my favourite spring wildflowers. We passed the National Trust sign for Porth Llanllawen and followed the zigzagging path which led to a makeshift bridge – a slab of concrete – which crossed a small gully. As we began a gentle incline, we were surprised to see another walker heading towards us. By leaning into the spaces between the gorse bushes, we managed to negotiate a socially distanced cross over and exchanged greetings before continuing.

We passed through a wooden gate and followed the path upwards, close to the turf covered stone walls. These walls are a very familiar site around Llŷn and I had recently discovered that they were known as **clawdd** in Welsh and that they do a good job of sheltering the fields from the harsh winds from the Irish Sea. As we looked back, we could see two dots on the summit of Mynydd Mawr that we realised were people, and the coastguard buildings looked tiny. As we looked again, Ynys Enlli was beginning to appear, peeping from behind the hill. We worked our way around the foot of Mynydd Anelog and kept to the left of a solitary cottage, called Mount Pleasant, where more sheep grazed peacefully. I felt quite relieved and a sense of achievement, to see the coastal path signpost not far ahead of us at Braich Anelog, which we had chosen as our turning back point. The path opened out and we enjoyed stunning views across the village and fields of Anelog, with Porthor to the west, Llanbedrog headland to the east and Garn Fadryn and Yr Eifl almost hidden in the distant mist. The silence was broken by an occasional industrial sound which we guessed came from Tŷ Newydd farm in Uwchmynydd, where they were working on their new café extension. That reminded me to give them a call to see if they were serving food today. Sadly, they weren't but the lady who took the call was the daughter of the owner who had so kindly helped to take care of me after my injury last year. I was quite touched that she remembered me and I said that we looked forward to seeing them again soon when the COVID-19 restrictions were further relaxed and they were allowed to serve food to people in their outdoor seating area. All we had to do now was to walk back!

Becws Islyn, Aberdaron Bakery.

As we arrived back at the car park at Mynydd Mawr, the sun was getting much warmer and a lizard scuttled into the short dry grass near the car. It was still only April, yet felt like a warm summer's day. Jim drove down into Aberdaron and I called at Becws Islyn, our favourite bakery, where I bought delicious cheese and onion pasties, cakes and coffees for lunch and a full bag of bread and Welsh cakes to take back to the caravan. I had a muffled conversation behind my mask (still compulsory at this time) with owner Gillian. We had been excited to hear that they were renovating the old café on Nefyn beach and would shortly be opening up another Becws Yslyn there. What a wonderful combination – our favourite bread on our favourite beach! Gillian said they hoped to be open by the summer and until then they were continuing with deliveries across Llŷn and I was thrilled to discover that they would happily deliver to our caravan! As we greedily devoured our goodies in the car, scattering flaky pastry everywhere, I updated Jim and we considered calling into Nefyn on our way back to the caravan to have a look at the progress of the café. As Jim was about to drive out of the car park, I was just in time to jump out of the car and capture on camera a man in a small cart, being pulled by a heavy horse. It was one of those magical moments and the scene could quite easily have been from the early 1900s with the thatched roof of Becws Islyn in the background.

We postponed our visit to Nefyn as we were both feeling in need of a shower and siesta. Later that evening we were shocked to see on the news that there had been a mud slide on the north side of the beach there. Some homes had lost part of their gardens which had fallen onto the sand along with a large area of the cliff face and the whole of the beach was currently closed. A few weeks earlier, we had heard of smaller mud slides behind the white cottages on the southern end of the beach. Luckily there had been no one hurt in any of these recent incidents but we remembered how 20 years previously, a mudslide at Nefyn had swept a car off the car park and onto the beach, causing the death of a lady and serious injury to her husband. We wondered about the future of our coastal path walk and hoped the cliffs would be safe enough for us to be able to complete it this year.

View from Braich Anelog.

Welsh Cakes and Squeaky Sand
Braich Anelog to Porthor – 21st April 2021

The forecast said it was going to be hot and sunny, so we set off extra early to avoid the full sun. We parked the car at Porthor National Trust car park and followed the signs directing us to the short gorse lined path which would lead us to the coastal path. We could see the path which led to the beach in the other direction and the embankment at the side which was covered in blackthorn blossom, that from a distance gave the impression of a snow-covered hill.

We were relieved with the start of the walk which was grassy, wide and level and felt comfortable under foot. We had allowed ourselves a day to rest after our previous walk. This 'rest' had involved cleaning the caravan and a walk along Lôn Goed; neither of us are good at keeping still. We were heading south towards our turning back point from two days ago at Braich Anelog. There had been no way of re-joining the path where we had ended last time. As we looked back, the headlands of Porthor and Porth y Wrach had come into view. It was another hazy day and distant views were hidden from us. The grassy cliff sides sloped steadily down to the sea and were carpeted with primroses. This walk felt so much easier than our last one that I heard myself saying confidently, 'Maybe after

Arriving at Porthor.

Dinas Mawr and Dinas Bach islets.

lunch, we could do the next stretch from Porthor northwards.' Jim wasn't so sure. To the east we could see Mynydd Carreg with its circular stone wind shelter on the summit, an easy climb we had done with the boys a few years ago, or at least it felt easy then! An information board at Porthor had explained that in 1904 a jasper quarry had been developed there and there had been an intention to build a jetty at Porthor to export the large red stone blocks. This however did not happen and the jasper was transported by road.

We passed two islets Dinas Bach then Dinas Mawr, which translates as small and large city or stronghold, although there looked very little difference in their sizes. Dinas Bach looked especially inviting, with its tiny beach where gulls and oystercatchers were enjoying their isolation. I vowed to return soon, to have a picnic there when the tide was even further out, if my legs would allow the downhill scramble needed to get there. We could see Braich Anelog in the distance now. There was a cool breeze but the sun and the walking were warming us nicely. We noticed that some of the path was eroding and sunken and we had to be a bit creative to work our way around safely. I heard the fleeting buzzing of bees as they flew past, a sound which always makes me think of childhood summers. We were close enough to the sea to hear the gentle ebb and flow of the waves today, unlike on our previous walk where the cliffs were much higher. The path zigzagged downwards to a wooden railed footbridge, which we crossed. I was intrigued by another bridge and a stile to our left and wondered where this led to, but I had to continue wondering as we had to focus on the steep upward path ahead of us. I began to think Jim was right in saying that this would be enough of a walk for us today. We passed grazing sheep and stopped to rest on our walking pole seats and feasted on Becws Islyn Welsh cakes which gave us some energy to manage the incline. As we reached the top of the hill, the path curved to the left and we could see the spot where we had finished two days ago. We enjoyed the same view again, looking out across Llŷn, but with even more haze than last time.

On our return walk, we could hear the beautiful sound of the skylarks singing high above us but they were nowhere to be seen. We shared our childhood memories of lying on a lawn or a field, trying to spot this elusive bird and enjoying listening to its song. About half a dozen choughs flew past playfully. Porthor is known as Whistling Sands to many and gets this name from the squeaking noise made by the sand underfoot as you walk along the beach. This sound is apparently caused by the unusual shape of the sand particles. We couldn't resist pressing our feet hard into the sand to make it whistle as we headed along the beach to the café which was open for take-out only. In the early twentieth century this same building was known as the 'Coal Hole Café'. It had previously been used as a coal yard where imported coal was stored for local use. When Porthor became popular with tourists, a roof was added and it was converted into a café. I enjoyed a behind mask Welsh chat with the young lady in the café who said things had been quiet so far this year, but she was looking forward to when the COVID-19 guidelines would allow tables to be placed outside again for people to sit and eat their food. We sat on the wall outside to eat our picnic and did some people watching. The beach was empty apart from one family with two children, who were just setting out their buckets and spades. We reminisced about coming here with Tom and Simon not many years before on a very windy day. I could still picture them both laughing as they leant into the strong wind on the cliff tops. This was where we would be heading on our next walk, which we were hoping to manage the following day, stiff legs allowing!

Mynydd Carreg in the distance.

Walk 27

A 'Lovely' Boat and a Newborn Calf
Porthor to Penrhyn Mawr – 22nd April 2021

We returned to the National Trust Car Park at Porthor, but this time followed the signs for the beach and soon spotted the coastal path sign which guided us across the beach road and onto the path which was lined with sweet smelling blackthorn laden with blossom. We could soon see the whole of Porthor beach and the sea which glistened an emerald green in the sunshine. The narrow path remained close to the cliff edge for most of the way. A wooden bench dedicated to all who loved the area had been placed in an ideal spot for viewing. 'For all who love the Llŷn Peninsula' and its Welsh translation **I bawb sy'n caru Pen Llŷn** was carved on the seat. The swirly script looked familiar but it was many months later that I checked with Dafydd the storyteller and he confirmed it was another one of his benches. Despite the sunshine and clear sky, the cool breeze deterred the celandines and daisies along the path from opening. We spotted the tiny islet of Maen Mellt off the headlands between Porthor and Penrhyn Mawr. This side of Llŷn

Bench on the path above Porthor beach.

Blackthorn in bloom at Porthor.

Heading back to the cafe at Porthor.

is especially notorious for its shipwrecks and I later discovered that a schooner called *Lovely* was wrecked on Maen Mellt in 1802. It had been mostly carrying food produce from Chester and many items of interest have been discovered by divers around the islet since then, including elephant tusks and copper hoops from casks of butter.

The path widened out and I became over confident in my striding out and fell onto the soft grass which cushioned me nicely. Jim was walking ahead of me and I tried to get up quickly before he noticed but he misses nothing! The path headed down, but not too steeply across a stream and back up again. Jim now walked behind me keeping an even closer eye on me. It was still quite chilly and even the sea thrift flowers were too cold to open up yet. The path continued close to the cliff edge as we worked our way around Porth y Wrach, then widened out again allowing us to pick up a bit of speed. Not far ahead of us was a huge rook on the post of the gate we were heading for. It looked as if it was guarding its territory and we could see that this was its regular viewing spot as the gate post was caked in its droppings. It flew off into the breeze as we approached. Beyond the gate were fields of cows, and a tiny black calf lay in the corner of the field closest to the path. As we approached, it was soon clear which was mother cow, as she kept a close eye on us as we passed and stood guard by her baby. I was concerned that the calf may have been unwell as it was perfectly still, apart from an occasional very slow blink.

We were almost at Porth Iago and could see camper vans on the headland above it. The sun was getting warmer and the

Porth Iago.

celandines and sea thrift were beginning to open up now. Herring gulls were having fun and mating on the rocks below. As we followed the path along the southern edge of Porth Iago, I could see a steep winding path leading down onto the beach at the northern side. The beach was empty and with its golden sand and turquoise water, looked the perfect place for a rest and I hoped to myself that the path would be manageable for us to get down. We greeted a couple of campers who were getting their breakfasts as we neared the start of the path down to the beach. Jim smiled as he looked at me and said 'You have to go down there, don't you?' I laughed – he knows me so well. We managed to get down to the beach unscathed and sat on a rock and ate homemade chocolate chip muffins as we watched the tide slowly creeping inwards – bliss. I collected a pebble for our collection before we made our way back up to the coast path. This was our first time on Porth Iago beach, but it was definitely a spot to remember and return to.

The path now headed across a large empty field and we went to look at the trig point at what must have been the highest point as we neared Penrhyn Mawr. It was encouraging to see the familiar silhouette of Yr Eifl in the distance. The next stretch of coastal path became very narrow and steep and I tried to avoid looking at the rocks below us. We reached a wooden gate with a few steep steps beyond, which Jim noticed were made from recycled plastic. We looked at the map and decided that the top of the steps could be our turning back point for today as it looked like a manageable distance from Porth Colmon for our next walk.

On our return walk, it was a joy to see the calf, obviously damp and new-born, now on its feet and suckling on its mother, who again followed us with her large brown eyes until we were far enough away to not be a threat. We had a quick chat with a couple of walkers from South Wales who didn't speak Welsh but who spoke with a wonderful strong Swansea accent. We came down from the path and onto the north side of beach where there used to be a lime kiln. As we squeaked our way across the sand to the café for an outdoor lunch, there were only two other people on the beach. To our horror they were sitting on their camping chairs facing the cliffs, very close to a rather obvious old landslide. We wondered if they were oblivious or just thrill seekers!

Tales of Shipwrecks, Whiskey and a Piano
Penrhyn Mawr to Porth Colmon –
30th April 2021

On the 29th April we returned to the caravan for a long weekend and before setting off, the morning post brought my mammogram results which gave me the all clear from breast cancer again for the 3rd year running – a wonderful start to our break.

For parking reasons, we began this walk from Porth Colmon and planned to continue to the top of the steps where we stopped last time at Penrhyn Mawr. The small car park was used mostly by fishermen for their vans and tractors, so unsurprisingly there was a strong smell of fish as we set off. There was low cloud but blue skies and we soon began to feel quite warm. This walk afforded us sea views all the way – my idea of a perfect coastal walk. A wooden gateway at the side of the information board led us out onto the grassy path which led around Carreg y Defaid. Several concrete steps took us up to a wide and even grassy path. We passed fields of sheep and cows and as we continued, we came upon a young lamb that had somehow managed to get through the fence and onto the coast path, and mother and baby were crying out to each other from either side of the fence. We wanted to help, but knew that intervening could cause more distress, so we took a wide berth to avoid frightening the lamb further and hoped it would find its own way back to its mother soon. A little further along, a ewe with her three lambs, all of them loose on the path, scurried away as we approached.

The clay path that ran along the sloping grassy cliff top was crumbly and became narrower and tricky to walk along at times. Jim commented dryly that this wasn't a coastal path but a sheep trail! I noticed an additional plaque on the coast path signpost, showing that we were now also following the Taith Pererin Gogledd Cymru – 'The North Wales Pilgrim's Way'. This is a route which links ancient churches dedicated to the saints of the seventh century. It begins at Basingwerk Abbey which was used as a hospital for pilgrims going to nearby Holywell in medieval times and ends at Ynys Enlli. Ahead of us we could see a brightly painted, white wooden bench overlooking the tiny coves of Porth Wen Bach and Porth Tŷ Llwyd, which looked very prominent and a little out of place.

We passed through more gates and negotiated steps leading upwards then down again and the path became more winding, very narrow and sunken at times. We stopped to gather ourselves and listened to the skylarks high above us. We had brought our monocular to help us to get a closer look at some of the small birds which frequently flitted about at speed ahead of us along this stretch of the walk. We managed to identify stonechats by spotting their pink breasts and confirmed this using my new favourite phone app 'Chirpomatic' which helps to identify birds from their call. My dad taught me the names of many birds but I'm no expert and can only identify a handful of birds from their call.

As we looked out to sea, we spotted a fishing boat heading back towards Porth Colmon. The wind had picked up and the sky began to darken in the distance behind us and we could see the heavy rain over Yr Eifl. We checked our weather apps and it was forecasting the same for us shortly. We hadn't planned for this as the earlier forecast had said it was going to be fine all day. I began to form a plan B in my head in case it became stormy – we could continue to Porth Iago and get a taxi back to Porth Colmon. Part of me would have been disappointed to have not managed the return walk, but another part of me quite liked the idea of not having to repeat some of the tricky narrow paths. I suddenly heard a loud, deep rumbling sound that filled me with dread. I've had a fear of thunder and lightning since childhood. This has lessened over the years, but I'm not keen when I'm exposed to it in the great outdoors. My fear was brought on by one misinformed, hysterical, primary school teacher who, one day in a storm, told all of her pupils, including me, to drop our scissors immediately. She explained that if we were touching anything metal, we were at a greater risk of being struck by lightning! I can remember throughout my childhood, being scared of wearing shoes with buckles on if it was ever stormy. The rumbling got louder and changed its tone and to my relief, I realised it wasn't thunder I was hearing, but the sound of jets flying over from Valley R.A.F. on Ynys Môn. This kept Jim entertained for several minutes as I recovered from my catastrophising, but the idea of the taxi journey back remained with me as the sky darkened further.

We crossed an open grassy area, which was punctuated with what looked like huge grass covered mole hills that we later discovered were ants' nests. I recognised the dainty pale pink cuckoo flowers that always reminded me of walks with my dad and of him helping me to learn the names of wildflowers. A simple wooden bridge took us across a narrow ravine, where clumps of marshmallows grew on its bank. We could now see Porth Tŷ Mawr, where at low tide it is said you can see the remains of the ship *The Stuart*, which was shipwrecked there in 1901. She had left Liverpool and had been bound for New Zealand, carrying porcelain, whisky and pianos amongst other things. There are lots of stories about how locals raided the wreck and even buried barrels of whisky to collect later. I find it difficult to believe the tale that someone even managed to rescue a piano and carry it up to the top of the cliffs! But many people are said to have intact pieces of the porcelain on their Welsh dressers and various items can be seen in the fascinating maritime museum in Nefyn. A few years ago, we visited this spot at low tide after learning about *The Stuart* and Simon scrambled down onto the beach where he found some tiny fragments of blue decorated pottery which we have kept and would like to think are from *The Stuart*.

Soon after Porth Tŷ Mawr, we came upon a wooden plank bridge which crossed a very uneven section of path where white spoonwort flowers were growing profusely amongst the thick clumps of hard rush grass. A herd of very serious looking cows stared at us as we passed. I was glad they were behind the fence. We could see the campsite at Iago, and Penrhyn Mawr headland, as we followed the winding path between Porth Tŷ Mawr and Porth Widlan. As we approached a tiny port, there was a large collection of farm buildings

Not more cows!

Interesting graffiti!

to our left and a small grass covered stone bridge crossed a stream. We followed the steep path upwards after the bridge and were bemused by some graffiti on a large white rock, which read 'Walk fast I hear banjos we-e-e-e-e.' When I later tried to find the meaning of this, I read that it had probably been taken from a phrase used in a 1972 film, Deliverance, 'Paddle faster, I hear banjos.' The film apparently involves a canoe trip and an encounter featuring a banjo which results in some unpleasant events. At least we couldn't hear any banjos and thankfully neither had we heard any thunder! The port had some small sheds built into the rocks that we presumed were for fishermen to keep their gear. We stopped to allow a fellow walker and his dog to pass us, still very conscious of the need to social distance. He said he was camping at Porth Iago in a campervan and that he had been travelling around England and now Wales for a while whilst waiting to buy a house. He was also concerned about the weather and said he had timed his walk to be back at his van by the time the heavy rain was meant to reach us, which was in about half an hour. It still looked very dark over Yr Eifl but didn't seem to be heading our way after all. We checked our weather app after he carried on his way and were pleased to see it now said it was going to be fine for us for the rest of the day. Maybe a taxi journey wouldn't be needed after all. We followed the path around Porth Ferin, which also had a small wooden shed built into the grassy slope leading down to a stony beach. We arrived at the top of the steps where we had turned back just over a week ago and found a sheltered spot to prop on our walking poles and eat part of our lunch. We watched about six grey curlews take off together from the rocks below and fly above our heads, their long downward curved beaks helping me to identify them.

On our return walk, the wind had dropped and the skies looked clearer. We saw the travelling man again and he told us that he had just seen a fox creeping down to the rocks probably to steal eggs from the gulls. We looked out for it as we walked on, but there was no sign. A young lady with a huge back pack passed us in the opposite direction. She told us that she was wild camping as she walked the Llŷn coast path and was hoping to complete it in the few weeks she had allowed herself. We said that we wished we had done it at her age and explained how we were doing it in very small parts and had started it over two years ago! The white bench that had looked out of place as we set off, now looked very inviting and we were pleased to rest there for a while as we finished our lunch, whilst watching a large black cormorant on the rocks below, drying its wings in the sunshine.

Porth Colman.

More Cows, Mudslides and a Potato Shed
Porth Colmon to Porth Towyn –
2nd May 2021

Two days later we arrived back at Porth Colmon, to continue northwards this time. We hoped to reach Porth Towyn but it depended on the ease or difficulty of the walk. The rain was just easing off and the forecast looked promising. We were early enough to see the fishermen preparing to launch their boats and towing them into the sea. There was a cool breeze as we headed towards the steps to the coastal path and we were shocked to see that the sign towards Towyn had been covered with a sheet of white plastic, but there was no message to say the path was closed. We felt uncertain about proceeding and I decided to ask a young fisherman who was about to join his colleagues. He said there had been some landslides there about three weeks ago, but that people had still been using it by keeping further away from the edge. As always, when I heard his local accent, I took the opportunity to have a short chat in Welsh with him and he praised me for my efforts. The local people really do appreciate even a 'Good

Mudslides at Porth Colmon.

Morning' **Bore Da** in their own language. We thanked him, with **Diolch** and climbed the steps to take a look. We stayed well back in the field backing onto the cliff, but were able to see several mud slides below on Penllech beach. We decided it was too risky and headed back onto the lane. We knew of a path, a few minutes' drive away that also had a nearby car park, that led to the centre of Penllech beach. This would take us beyond the landslide area and we could then climb back onto the coast path at the northern end to continue the walk towards Towyn. Before doing this, there was somewhere I wanted to visit.

The previous day we had met with Dave and Chris, our apple providing friends from Mynydd Nefyn. During our walk with them, they had told us about a protest they were going to join, starting off in Nefyn and ending at Porth Colmon. The protest was about the increase in affordable housing being sold as second homes, which was making it difficult for local young people to buy their first home in the area. The reason for them choosing Porth Colmon as the finish of the march was because they wanted to highlight the situation of two eighteenth century cottages, which were being advertised for sale. These Grade II listed cottages, built by an old traditional method using **clom** (a mixture of clay and fibre) were purchased in 1788 for £40, with money left in the will of a local man called Richard Griffith. Since then, they have been rented out to local people by a charity and have been under the care of the vicar and churchwardens of Llangwnnadl church. The protestors were supporting the community, who were shocked to discover that the cottages had now been put up for sale on the open market. A petition was started to try and remove them and transfer them to the care of the community, to be renovated and rented out to local people again. I wanted to take a closer look at the cottages, which were only a short walk from the car park. One of them was quite hidden by overgrown hedging but there was no sign advertising their sale. These pink single storey cottages, named Llain Fatw 1 and 2, had corrugated roofs, and despite looking in need of a lot of care were full of character and charm, but also looked perfect as first homes for local young people. I hoped that the petition would be successful.

I admired the bluebells and sniffed the leaves of the three-cornered garlic growing along the edges of the lane as we returned

Llain Fatw Cottage at Porth Colman.

Walk 29b

to the car. We soon arrived at the car park at **Pont yr Afon Fawr** and followed the signs to the beach. I remembered what a pretty walk this had been from a previous visit, with the path following the river with its gentle waterfalls along its course. The beach was empty and we were glad to see that the mud slides were some distance away. We walked along the wide stretch of sandy beach, enjoying being so close to the sea again. The northern end of Penllech beach is a mass of huge rocks inhabited by barnacles, limpets and sea anemones. We noticed that the tide was coming in quite quickly now and realised that we may not be able to get back across the beach later on. We could also see that there were cows along the cliff tops, so once we'd walked the length of the beach, we decided the best plan was to return to the car, head to Porth Towyn and walk back as far as we could along these cliff tops, cows allowing.

As we arrived at the car park at **Towyn Farm**, fond memories returned to us both from our visits to this area. When honeymooning in Edern, we had made a few trips here to watch the sun setting into the sea. We both remembered the car park being carpeted with chamomile and giving off a heady sweet smell when we drove onto it. I tried to find remnants of chamomile as we

Walk 29c

got out of the car, but there was none to be seen or smelt. In 1996 we stayed in Morawel, the white cottage along the lane from the farm. This had belonged to the mother of the owner of Towyn Farm, and possibly still does. We had spent a lot of time on the beach making sandcastles and flying kites with Tom, who was only a year old, and walking to the farm to see the animals, especially a large black pig that I seem to remember was called Ellis. Daloni Metcalfe, who continues to run the farm with her husband, is now a very familiar face to viewers of S4C as she is also a TV personality, having presented news shows and the farming programme Ffermio. A few years ago, she also established a shop close to the farm, selling luxury household goods and designer clothing with a café next door, which she has called Cwt Tatws and Caffi Tatws, named after the building that houses them, which used to be the potato shed. Cwt means shed and tatws means potatoes. At this point, I would like to ramble off the path again to tell a short story about a **tatws** experience I had in my earlier years of learning the Welsh language. It involved the use and understanding of something called a **to bach** accent. It looks like a Chinese hat and is equivalent to the French circumflex, causing a longer pronunciation of the vowel. The word **tatws** doesn't have this accent but the word **tatŵs**, which means tattoos does. I was reading a book, called *Inc* (Ink), which had been recommended to me and was written for Welsh learners by Manon Steffan Ros. Having not read the blurb I knew little of the topic of the book. I read the first few pages about a person using different coloured ink with the **tatŵs** and was convinced that the main character of the story was creating potato prints (something I'd done in primary school myself) and not tattoos! My mistake slowly dawned on me when I read further and there was a description of needles being used with the ink to create the **tatŵs**. I now keep my eyes open for those important little roofs!

Porth Towyn bay was as picturesque as ever, but a lot busier than when we had stayed here. We remembered there being just a couple of static caravans in the field overlooking the bay and now there were many more as well as tourers at the back of the farm. Cwt Tatws was also attracting a lot of business and the outdoor seating areas at the café were beginning to fill up as we walked past to get to the coast path. The beach was empty and looked very tempting, but the path down was long and winding and we didn't want to add too many more steps to what was already quite a long walk for us. We stayed on the coastal path that skirted the fields and gazed at the long golden sandy beach from above as we strode out, adding it to our mental list of places to come back to soon. We crossed a bridge by a waterfall just before the campsite at the next bay, Porth Ysglaig. Wooden steps then took us down to a board walk and up again before we crossed the campsite, which was busy with large touring caravans. We passed through a farmer's gate and followed the path around Porth Llydan. Llydan means wide but the path was very narrow, dry and crumbling in parts with large holes that we had to stride across. We reached a trig point in a field just before Porth Ysgaden. I believe there are people that 'bag' these concrete triangulation pillars, that were installed by the mapping agency Ordnance Survey from 1936 onwards, often taking selfies whilst standing posing on the top of them. Jim and I prefer to lean on them while we get our breath back and admire the scenery around us.

The walk became easier for a while as the cliff top widened out into a field. Ahead we could see an old fisherman's hut, painted green, on the headland above Porth Cychod, which is a pretty horseshoe shaped bay, with a pebbly beach. I imagine there are lots of seafaring tales to be told around this area, which has been home to the boats of many local sailors for years. We had been to this part of the coast path before and knew what to expect as we crossed the grassy headland towards Porth Ysgaden, but people new to this area will be taken by surprise by a rather unexpected sight towards the end of the promontory. A tall gable end of a stone house, complete with chimney, stands tall with a recent addition of a wooden bench sheltering by its side. It is said that in the 1700s a customs officer lived in the house there and that it also served as a lighthouse. The last occupants, who were coal merchants John and Hugh Daniel, moved out in 1935, after their sister fell to her death down the nearby cliff. **Ysgaden** is an old Welsh name for herring and in the past salted herring were exported from here. The tide was out at Porth Ysgaden and the beach looked rather stony and muddy. Jim and I remember this area for another reason. Neither of us are sure if it happened during our honeymoon or on one of our day trips before we were married, but we had driven out to the car park at Ysgaden, which in those days was very uneven and bumpy. When we were ready to leave, the car wouldn't start and a kind lady gave us a lift to the garage in Morfa Nefyn in her Citroen C5. Jim especially was struck by the smooth drive along the bumpy road compared with our jolting experience in his Ford Escort. We returned to Porth Ysgaden in a tow truck and the car was repaired back at the garage, with Jim vowing that our next car would have to have better suspension and would probably be a Citroen C5. He stood by his word and our green Citroen C5 served us well for many years until one day it refused to move from the side of our friends' caravan in Llannor, and Brian kindly pulled it out of the field with his tractor allowing us all to then be transported home in the RAC rescue truck. I took a photo of it on the back of the truck and used this with an honest description of its broken-down condition to sell it on eBay soon after we got home. I'm guessing it is now restored and still going strong in east Europe somewhere, which is where the highest bidder came from!

The gate from Porth Ysgaden car park led to a boardwalk which crossed a stream, and further along the grassy path another gate led the way to Porth Gwylan farmland. A National Trust notice announced that we were entering a 'Payment for outcomes farm' and explained that this trial project was also being carried out on two other farms in Llŷn and aimed to reward farmers for supporting and enhancing nature. This was being done by a scoring system for different habitats, with increased payments for higher scores to reflect better conditions for nature. I was interested to know how the farmers would be doing this, presuming it would be by planting of certain crops and vegetation. Porth Gwylan is a small hooked shaped bay with a shingle beach and was empty as we passed by along the continuing grassy clifftop. A skylark was singing its heart out above a freshly ploughed field and I was thrilled to be able to see it this time as it hovered in mid-air then quickly plunged down into the field. Large clumps of pink sea thrift blew in the breeze towards the cliff edge and the sea was a beautiful aquamarine colour. We noticed a lot of ants' nests in this area and I wondered if this would earn points and pounds for the farmer.

The path led us down steps to Porth Ychain, a small pebbly cove, fed by a stream, where a family were just leaving. The mother

Finding that one special pebble on Porth Ychain beach.

was carrying her large baby in a back pack and looked tired. We empathised with her and shared our memories with her of carrying chunky one year old sons on our backs when out walking and how they can feel very heavy after a while. We enjoyed a few moments on the beach choosing a pebble for our collection – another new beach for us – and agreed to have our lunch here on the way back. We clambered up the steps at the other side of the beach and the path wound gently around the headland, Penrhyn Melyn, passing fields of grazing dairy cows. We noticed that they all had a painted mark on their buttocks, either red, green or blue and we joked that maybe this identified which of them were skimmed, semi skimmed or full fat milk producers, as the colours matched those of the bottle tops! We finally reached the cliff tops at the start of Penllech beach. We were pleased to have managed this stretch in one day, even if it had been broken into parts because of the mudslides which we could now also see again in the distance. I wondered about the future of the cliff paths and hoped they would continue to be cared for and kept safe for walkers to enjoy in the future.

On our return, we enjoyed our packed lunch on Porth Ychain beach as planned and later watched curlews and oystercatchers flying close to Porth Gwylan, where there was now a family enjoying their picnic. Porth Ysgaden car park was full of vehicles and we noticed a lot of activity on the beach, where the tide had now returned. There were dinghies and divers in the sea and a drone flew ahead filming them. A few days later, a short film was available to watch on YouTube, with a young bearded Yorkshireman, probably the main diver, describing the experience, followed by some stunning aerial views, filmed by his drone camera, across the sea to Porth Ysgaden. He had also added some interesting film of the creatures they had seen underwater on various dives. Unfortunately, he didn't identify the creatures or say which were seen at Ysgaden, but he had said he had hoped they would at least find crab and Goby fish and these did feature in the film. At Porth Ysglaig, people from the campsite were now heading down to the sea with their kayaks and as we reached Porth Towyn a lot of activity was going on there with families setting up windbreaks and some people were kayaking.

Cwt Caffi was very busy now and as I queued to buy a hot drink and a cake for us both, Daloni was busy serving people in the shop area. It felt a real treat to be able to sit together in a café environment again, even if only outside at present. In just over two weeks' time, it was looking likely that the COVID-19 restrictions were going to relax further and allow people to eat and drink indoors in cafés and restaurants, something that most people, including ourselves, were looking forward to. As you'll have noticed, we quite like a nice café!

The sheep leading the way.

Walk 30

Bluebells and Scary, Hairy Flies
Porth Towyn to Porth Bryn Gwydd –
14th May 2021

May had brought quite a lot of rain, which was needed after an unusually dry April. We ignored the dark clouds and light drizzle and trusted our weather app which said it was going to be fine within the hour and set off in the car for Porth Towyn in our waterproofs. Cwt Tatws shop and café hadn't yet opened as we ambled past to head northwards. Keeping a large grassy mound to our left, we followed the path that skirted the farmer's fields, and grazing sheep fled nervously. The rain came down quite heavily but not quite heavy enough to say **Mae hi'n bwrw hen wragedd a ffyn**, (It's raining old women and sticks), which is the Welsh saying, equivalent to the English 'raining cats and dogs.' I love Welsh idioms!

Garn Fadryn to our right was surrounded by mist and we could barely make out the silhouette of Yr Eifl in the distance ahead of us. The undulating path stayed close to the cliff edge for much of the way on this walk, with lots of small bridges or boardwalks enabling us to cross small inlets and eroded areas. A lamb looked at us defiantly as we neared some steps, where it looked very settled and resting, but quickly moved as we got closer. Across a field full of black cows and very young calves, we could see the back of Morawel Cottage where we had stayed when Tom was a baby. I noticed buttercups for the first time this year. There were

Along the boardwalk.

Cwt Tatws at Towyn Bay.

also tiny, low growing purple flowers growing amongst large patches of common silverweed leaves. My nature app identified these later from my photographs as spring squill. The Welsh name for these is the rather lovely **seren y gwanwyn** – spring star. I'd begun to realise that we'd probably left chough territory behind as we hadn't seen them on this walk or the previous two or three, but the gulls continued to be plentiful; I noticed mostly herring gulls and black backed gulls. The path narrowed as we approached a wide sandy and stony beach which is unnamed on modern maps but was close to Plas yn Bieg and according to an old map that I later found, is known as Porth Bieg – probably an OS spelling mistake for **y Big** (pointed headland, or triangular field). Several steps, then a tiny plank bridge, took us down to the beach and we couldn't resist having a moment there. As usual I examined the pebbles and selected one with an attractive purple hue, from amongst the mass of limpet shells, to add to the collection. Further steps led to another field of grazing sheep and ahead we could see a traditional looking park bench. We weren't ready for sitting yet and I was unsure if I would sit so close to the cliff edge these days. We crossed the bridge which spanned a waterfall at Pant Gwyn, which was made prettier by the heavy rain which was persisting. So much for the weather app!

The path widened out again near fields which had been recently sown, with healthy seedlings appearing, but of what I was unable to identify. We dodged many large mole hills and I wondered if the cute and speedy creators of these cause headaches for the local farmers. As we approached Penrhyn Cwmistir, a natural arch

Close to Traeth Cwmistir with Yr Eifl hills in the distance.

caught our attention in the sea below as did the cries of a couple of oystercatchers and curlews as they flew out to further rocky outcrops. The coastguard's lookout tower on Porth Dinllaen headland was just about visible in the mist but Yr Eifl beyond had disappeared totally. We carefully negotiated some muddy steps down to a small stony beach, Traeth Cwmistir. The rain was finally beginning to ease and we propped on our sticks, watching, and listening to, the waves gently lapping over the rocks on the shoreline, before we headed upwards onto the cliff top again.

Electrified fences surrounded the fields ahead and the path followed the fence closely on the inside now. We could see by the cow pats and deep muddy hoof prints, that these fields were regularly inhabited by cattle but luckily not today. The plant life immediately beneath the fence had been destroyed, either by burning or with chemicals. Jim suggested this had probably been done to prevent a power shortage. This created a bright orange path across the fields, which was a bit unsightly but showed us our way very clearly. The sun was beginning to shine and as we looked out to sea, the head of a grey seal bobbed up and down in the calm water. Of course, by the time I got the monocular focussed, it had disappeared altogether, but popped up again to tease us as we continued walking. A little further on we spotted a cormorant enjoying a swim and more oystercatchers sped past, landing on rocks below. A mass of bluebells was growing amongst the grass on the cliff side of the fence. Bluebells in Welsh is **clychau'r gog**, which translates to the cuckoo's bells and poet R. William Parry has written a poem of the same name in which he says that the flowers arrive and leave with the cuckoo. I'd yet to hear the cuckoo in Llŷn this year. Four cormorants appeared to be sunning themselves on a long rocky outcrop, opening their wings out wide, to dry them off after the rain. One of them was a young one, smaller and lighter in colour. On a rock close by a pure white bird landed and seemed to be resting with its head tucked in, making it difficult to identify.

It was a relief to throw off our hoods, be able to see our surroundings more clearly and to finally feel the sun on our faces. A fishing boat was heading out to sea from near Abergeirch (often also written Aber Geirch); perhaps the skipper had been waiting for clearer weather. Just beyond Penrhyn Cwmistir, we could see a grey, stony beach below us, with a rather old, neglected looking fisherman's hut. The path led obliquely to a bridge across a small ford and a long, new looking boardwalk helped us across very uneven ground and past a tiny inlet. Steps then took us down to another small horseshoe shaped inlet where a small stream entered and where we had planned to stop and turn back. Two shelducks landed in the sea there ahead of our arrival. This bay isn't named on the map but I later found out that locals call it Porth Bryn Gwydd. I would love to see signs on all the tiny beaches, giving their local names and perhaps the English translation. I had read recently about a local artist who had created a large decorative finger post, which had been positioned in the Uwchmynydd area, naming many of the small sites in the vicinity, whose original names were almost forgotten.

I had hoped to come across it on our walk but it was probably positioned further inland.

As we arrived on the beach, a couple of a similar age to us were leaving and continuing north. They were the first people we had seen that morning and seemed oblivious to us. We propped on our sticks and ate part of our

Having a moment.

Sea Thrift

lunch whilst watching the brightly coloured ducks with their red beaks swim back and to in the gentle waves, with the smell of seaweed filling our nostrils. The rapid change of weather in Llŷn has become very familiar to us and rarely surprises us anymore. What started out as a wet and cold morning had turned into what felt like a warm summer's day. The sea had transformed from a murky grey to a beautiful bright blue-green. Even an odd butterfly flitted past. I spotted a meadow brown and a small white as we started on our journey back to Towyn. Not too far out at sea from where we were, two speedboats seemed to have appeared from nowhere. They stopped suddenly, close by each other and we realised that they were anglers when the pilot of each boat cast a rod out to sea. Unfortunately, the sun also brought out swarms of large flies, that looked as if they could give a nasty sting and they appeared intermittently for the rest of the walk, which we did at a much faster pace to avoid them! Later I managed to find out that they were hawthorn flies and what appeared to be a horrible, ugly sting dangling down behind them, was in fact their long hairy legs! Their original name was St Mark's fly as they were said to emerge on St Mark's Day, the 25th April. They are apparently harmless to humans but can damage roots of certain crops and plants such as celery, lettuce and roses. The anglers would be keen to get their hands on them as they are said to be very good for fly fishing. When we reached a fly free area, we peeled off some of our layers and stuffed jumpers and scarves into our rucksacks. A flock, or parliament to be correct, of rooks landed in the newly planted field. The white bird we'd spotted earlier, flew across to another rock as we passed by again, revealing a long neck which later allowed me to identify it as a little egret. We sat for a while on the bench that I'd been doubtful of earlier and finished our lunch. I closed my eyes and listened to the gentle burble of the waterfall close by and began to feel very relaxed and sleepy.

On the last short stretch before arriving back at Towyn, a small, very fast, but rather insignificant looking brown bird continually landed on the path not that far ahead of us, before quickly darting off into the distance again. The monocular and bird song app revealed that it was a meadow pipit and not that insignificant at all, but like a small attractive thrush, with a speckled belly. As we reached Towyn, a distant yacht reminded me of some quite romantic photos Jim and I had taken during our honeymoon, when we had sat on the grass on this same headland, waiting for the sun to set. A perfectly timed yacht had sailed past as we took a couple of 'selfies' which were a much more complicated affair then than these days, needing a tripod and a timer switch!

We picked up a locally ground Dwyfor coffee at Caffi Cwt Tatws and strolled down to the beautiful sandy beach, which was empty apart from a young family with a toddler and an elderly couple, perhaps proud grandparents, watching. With our waterproof coats tied around our waists, we plodded along the sand, enjoying our coffee and sharing further memories of this area from the time of our honeymoon and holidays with baby Tom.

Sorry to disturb but we need to pass!

Baby Seals and an Angry Golfer
Porth Bryn Gwydd to Porth Dinllaen – 16th May 2021

Nefyn and Morfa Nefyn Golf Club car park at Porth Dinllaen was our most convenient starting point for this walk and I had phoned the night before to ensure we had permission to park there. We were heading backwards again to reach Porth Bryn Gwydd where we had turned back two days previously. This golf course is huge in size and popularity and spreads itself along the cliff path for quite some distance. We strode out along the concrete path at the edge of the golf course, which was already busy with golfers with their trollies and buggies, despite the ominous looking grey sky. Runners passed by in both directions on what was probably their regular morning route. To our right, not far along the path, we were able to catch glimpses of the sea, the coastguard lookout tower on the promontory and the lifeboat station and slipway. The original RNLI lifeboat station was built in 1864 from stone but in 2014, this was replaced by the current one which now houses the Tamar Class lifeboat John D. Spicer.

An information board, which was new to us, informed us that we were approaching Porth Dinllaen promontory and that in 200 B.C. it had been an iron age fort with a gatehouse and steep ditches on either side. It further explained that several tribal families would have lived here in roundhouses and the fort would have been used for trading animals and goods and for special celebrations but more importantly as a safe haven in times of trouble. It was hard to imagine that now, when the only imaginable danger along this stretch of Llŷn is that of being hit by a stray golf ball! We ignored the familiar path to our right which would have taken us down to the beach and the award-winning Tŷ Coch inn which was named the third best beach bar on earth in 2013. **Tŷ Coch** means red house and it was built in 1823 with red bricks which had been imported from Holland to be used as ballast. Its other claim to fame was that it featured in several scenes in the rather creepy 2004 movie *Half Light* starring Demi Moore. Newspaper cuttings adorn the walls inside of the pub, boasting of this connection.

As we followed the curve of the bay, we got a full view of the beach now and we could see the converted outdoor bar and socially distanced benches at Tŷ Coch. From the following day onwards, this would not be as necessary as there were to be further relaxations of COVID-19 restrictions, allowing people to go into bars and restaurants again and allowing two family households to meet in their own homes. However, this extended bar area will probably continue to be very useful as this pub is extremely popular and likely to be extra busy for the next few months as people made up for lost time. If history had been different, Porth Dinllaen could have been even busier than it is. In the early 1800s, it was said to have been in the running for being transformed into the main ferry port for Ireland, but it was outbid by Caergybi (Holyhead) on Ynys Môn.

Jim and I reminisced about our first experience of Porth Dinllaen many years ago, which also coincided with our first experience of live Welsh singing. We had done a walk along the promontory as we were doing today, but had turned off to scramble past the lifeboat station and onto the beach – an area of path that has more recently been damaged by landslides and had

Porth Dinllaen and the Ty Coch Inn.

171

Approaching Aber Geirch.

to be closed. As we had approached the beach, the beautiful sound of children's voices singing a Welsh sea shanty filled the air and we could see them standing at the top of the steps of the large prominent grey stone house next to the Tŷ Coch, being watched by a small crowd below and filmed by a T.V. crew. We later discovered that it was part of an event arranged by the National Trust to celebrate their purchase of Porth Dinllaen. The song that was being sung, unknown to me then, was *Fflat Huw Puw* (Huw Puw's Boat), an old song which mentions Porth Dinllaen in the lyrics and one that I've heard many renditions of since then, including a reggae version which I particularly enjoy.

We stopped to take in the view from the path above the lifeboat station and I was struck by how close we now seemed to Yr Eifl. The middle and highest of its three peaks, Garn Ganol, which we still intend climbing, was hiding in cloud. A myriad of boats, tied to buoys close to the shore, were bobbing up on down in the calm waters. Jim pointed out an unusual signpost that the bright sun had prevented me from noticing. What a coincidence – the style of colourful writing on the finger post sign was obviously the work of the artist who had created the Uwchmynydd signs I had remembered about on our last walk! I had only been reading about her the day before – Sioned Williams was her name and she traded under the name of Dylunio Swi Design. I hadn't realised that she had also created a coastal sign. The many 'fingers' of the sign directed to various bays and caves such as Aber Geirch and Ogof Dywell. I look forward to seeing more of her signs around the peninsula in the future.

A walker heading in the opposite direction to us, stopped to chat and asked if we'd been here before and on hearing his local accent, I took the opportunity to practice my Welsh, but threw in English translations for Jim to follow the conversation. He wanted to share with us that there were grey seals and pups near the rocks at the end of the promontory, Trwyn Porth Dinllaen. He also told us about how he'd been enjoying walking the coast path during Lockdown, and more fully appreciating his own local surroundings or **milltir sgwâr** (square mile) as it is often called in Welsh. We empathised and explained

Sign at Porth Dinllaen.

that we had also been doing the same back home, whilst missing being able to visit Llŷn. We said **hwyl** (which means 'bye' but literally means sail) and strode eagerly to the edge where we could look out to Carreg Ddu, a tiny island where cormorants and gulls were perched. Lots of grey seal noses appeared and disappeared in the waters around the rock and occasionally we were able to see the full length of the young ones as they frolicked close to the adults.

Coastguard Station, Porth Dinllaen.

We trudged up the grassy mound to the coastguard station and I was amused to see that even here was a 'marker' for the golfers with a square of artificial grass near to the door. Apologies to golfers as I'm sure this marker must have a proper name of which I'm clueless. The views out to Caernarfon Bay were even more stunning from up here. A simple stone bench sited at the side of the station was dedicated to Cledwyn Davies, a 'watcher' and popular local character who had recently died. We followed the path along the western side of the promontory, which then skirted the edge of the golf course, with the cliff edge staying close to our right side. Swallows surprised us intermittently, swooping down low in front of us and we continued to spot seals swimming quite close to land. We passed many small inlets, with the grassy slopes decorated with pretty white sea campion, gorse and bluebells and with warning signs reminding us of the steep drops. As we followed the edge of Borth Wen, a wide, stony beach, we were still in golfing territory. We paused occasionally to allow golfers to take their turn undistracted and to avoid any risk of a golf ball to the head! We could see several golfers, looking like ants in the distance on the headland towards the bay of Abergeirch. Beyond Abergeirch we could make out a large herd of cows dotted about in a field and along the coast path. Our hearts sank and we wondered if we would have to cut our walk short as we didn't want to walk through them especially during calf season, when they would be extra territorial.

We plodded on, wondering what we would do and two young Irish runners ran past and greeted us. The grassy cliff slopes were now covered in white scurvy grass flowers and pink sea thrift. The Welsh name for sea thrift is **clustog Mair**, which then translates to Mary's cushion. As we approached Abergeirch, we were thinking we would be unable to proceed beyond the beach, when we heard the noise of a tractor and plenty of mooing. We couldn't believe our luck as we realised that the farmer was shifting the cows into the fenced field behind the coastal path! We scrambled down the muddy rocky steps onto Abergeirch beach. **Aber** means mouth of a river, so any place name beginning with it, immediately tells you the name of the local river. This was where the river Geirch entered the sea and unfortunately also the long sewage pipe, making it probably the least attractive beach we've seen in Llŷn so far. To add to its grimness there was a carcass of a dolphin washed ashore in the middle of the beach. There is however some interesting history attached to this bay, which in English is sometimes known as Cable Bay. It took this other name from its use as the terminus of a telegraph cable installed between Wales and Ireland in 1886 and if you look closely, you can see the remains of a small hut that housed the machinery. We didn't linger on the beach and soon headed for the wooden bridge which took us across the river. A small boardwalk led the way ahead, but as I stepped off it, the mud almost reached the top of my boot! As I stepped back quickly, we saw the two friendly young runners, confidently running back down the uneven cliff. They advised us to continue the way they had returned as they had also gone across the boardwalk on their way out and got covered in mud as we could see from their legs. We struggled up the slippery, uneven, edge of the cliff which seemed only slightly less muddy than the route we had almost taken. I ignored my legs being scratched by gorse and brambles as I concentrated on trying not to lose my foot hold. We were relieved to reach the kissing gate at the top, which led us onto the wonderfully dry and even field, now empty of cows, where we stopped to recover for a few seconds.

At the other side of the field, a further gate led to an open and undulating grassy path, skirted with carpets of the tiny purple

seren y gwanwyn flowers. This led us past a couple of small inlets, one of which was overlooked by a bench dedicated to a local man. As we walked a little further, we could also see a bench directly underneath this one on the beach below, but we agreed that both looked in very precarious positions being so close to a part of the cliff that had clearly seen recent erosions. Primroses, although now beginning to fade, were numerous and still looked attractive on the grassy cliff slopes. We finally reached Porth Bryn Gwydd where we had turned back two days ago, but this time there was just a solitary shelduck in the sea. It began to rain quite heavily as I followed Jim, who followed several sheep, down the steps to the shore. The stony beach was heavy with seaweed and I noticed an unfamiliar bird with a brown speckled back and orange legs, pecking at the ground. As I looked closer, I noticed that there were about ten of them scurrying along the water's edge, searching with their beaks through the line of seaweed. They allowed me to get quite close to them as they were so distracted finding lunch. I later discovered that they were turnstones and that they were probably looking for sandhoppers, which are small crustaceans which spend the day time buried in the sand.

As we headed back, the rain slowly began to ease off. A young couple approached us from ahead and we checked out the safest place to allow enough distance for them to pass us. Each of our walks have only involved about a handful at most of encounters with other people and during these recent times it had been interesting to see how different people negotiated social distancing along the cliff path. Most people approached warily as we tended to do, respecting the other people's space, but on odd occasions we have been shocked by family or friend groups who have been so busy chatting we have almost been knocked off the path! This couple looked very wary so we stepped back as far as the path allowed, to let them pass. They greeted us and their accents revealed that they were probably German. In an attempt to ease the tension, I laughingly said that as from tomorrow we would be able to hug as restrictions were being relaxed. The young lady smiled, but the man gave me a very stern look and said that he was very unsure about the idea of hugging! I was left amused, but wondering if he had understood me to mean that the two of us could hug, when I meant close family members! Further along we stopped in the cow field to chat to a friendly man from the Black Country, who I almost offended by guessing his accent was from Birmingham. I really need to think more before I speak! We compared bird spotting finds and as he continued on his way, we decided this was a good place to pause a while longer and we propped on our poles for lunch. We watched meadow pipits flitting about between fences and gorse bushes as we ate and contemplated our muddy return.

We grumbled about the lack of decent path as we tackled the steep rocks which were now even more muddy and slippery and we were finally relieved to be back on the lush green, even grass of the golf course. The map and coastal path signs indicate that there is an alternative path across the golf course which avoids having to walk around the promontory. We saw a family setting off to do this from the opposite side, but they were being chastised by a loud Irish golfer who also looked at us menacingly reminding us that this was a private golf course. I replied that this was actually also part of the official coastal path but he maintained his angry stare. The family turned back and we continued for a little while until there were no golfers in sight and quickly crossed like two naughty school children at the narrowest part of the course. Over a coffee and **bara brith** from Porth Dinllaen café, we discussed our next walk which would feel very special for us as it would take us through Nefyn, which holds many memories for us.

Three Herrings and a Brewery
Porth Dinllaen to Pistyll – 11th June 2021

After several continuous hot, dry days at home, we were surprised by the contrast on our return to the caravan, as we were met with steady rain and grey mist. We decided to chance our next walk on our first morning despite the heavy mist continuing to cover the surrounding hills. Our plan was to start in Nefyn, walk back to Porth Dinllaen, then return to Nefyn and if we had enough remaining energy, to continue towards Pistyll.

We parked at the car park called Y Ddôl close to the colourful and recently modernised children's play park. We cut through the park, passing the tennis courts behind the old St Mary's Church, which for many years has been the maritime museum **Amgueddfa Forwol**, advertised to all by its sailing ship weather vane positioned on the top of the tower. Many of the graves in the surrounding graveyard are of Nefyn captains, sailors and ship builders, including some who lost their lives at sea. We have been regular visitors to this fascinating museum for many years. It was founded in 1977 by a group of local volunteers and I can remember in the 1990s wandering around the rather dark and musty church, with Tom as a little boy, admiring the display of interesting artefacts related to the local shipping and fishing industry including pieces retrieved from shipwrecks. Sadly, the museum had to be closed in

Nefyn Maritime Museum.

2000 as it was deemed unsafe but thanks to the hard work of the local community and grants offered from various organisations, the now bright and airy interactive museum reopened its doors to visitors in 2014. At the time of this walk the museum was just beginning to offer pre-booked visits following the relaxation of COVID – 19 restrictions.

Aproaching the quarry and granite ramp above Nefyn .

We turned right off Stryd y Ffynnon, passing some new houses, which now stood where we remembered the old fire station having been. We passed the small white cottage where locals had told us many years earlier that Welsh pop singer Duffy had lived with her family during her childhood and teens. We followed the lane between fields that led to the road Rhodfa'r Môr with its detached, white painted houses, many with hydrangea bushes in their front gardens, which were beginning to bloom. We had walked this way to the beach many times with the boys when they were young and these hydrangeas still remind me especially of Simon, who has had a love for the large flowers of this particular shrub since he was a tiny boy, when he used to call them 'bobos' and liked to kiss them! One of the houses along this road is called Garth and bears a slate plaque stating that Elizabeth Watkin-Jones, who wrote Welsh language children's novels between the 1930s and 1950s, had lived there. Her father had been a Nefyn ship's captain and was killed at sea when she was an infant. Towards the end of the road, we passed the houses that had been affccted by the recent landslide, one of which had lost a large portion of its garden onto the eastern end of Nefyn beach.

We emerged onto Lôn y Traeth, which quickly becomes the steep Lôn Gam, which winds its way down to the sea. This must be our road most travelled in Llŷn. Up and down, we would go with the boys, with beach towels, buckets and spades or part way with ice-creams from the beach café at the lower end of the lane. We followed the coastal path above Lôn y Traeth today, passing the familiar quirky house with the castellated and turreted roof, that we always called the castle, on our left. On our right was a relatively recent addition to the coastal path – an ornate iron fence, made by a blacksmith from Tudweiliog, decorated with anchors and three herrings. Throughout Nefyn, you will see three herrings on various signs, as this is the town's symbol which represents its having been an important herring fishing port. Jim and I remember going into the Three Herrings on Stryd y Ffynnon for a meal whilst on our honeymoon. This pub has been closed for many years and is now a private house, but the sign bearing the three herrings remains on the wall, to show its history. The whole of Porth Nefyn suddenly came into view and a lump came to my throat as it always does when I see the view from anywhere on or near the beach. The old white fishermen's cottages at the west end of the beach and Yr Eifl to the east make it an artist's and photographer's dream. So many happy times we have had here with the boys. We used to rent a beach hut when we stayed in Nefyn for our summer holiday, and at the beginning of the fortnight, this would be filled with buckets, spades, dinghies, body boards and wet suits. The tide table would be consulted to decide if playtime was before or after lunch, a hill walk or maybe a castle visit. We would often return to the beach again in the evening, when it was virtually empty and sit on the beach hut steps or on camping chairs enjoying a hot chocolate made on our tiny camping stove. Sometimes we played boules or bat and ball, before enjoying a salty chip supper, wrapped in newspaper from the chip shop on Stryd Fawr, which was run by Richard and Lis Williams for 30 years. We have missed this chippy since they retired in 2016 and we will always remember Richard as a kind, friendly man with the gruffest voice in Llŷn. The beach huts had now been reinstated in their usual positions after having been redundant in storage during 2020 due to COVID-19. We could see the beach cottage where we had managed to afford an Easter stay once when the boys' school holidays had started earlier, outside of the more expensive peak holiday period. Cars were allowed on the beach when the tide was out but when the tide was in, as it was on our walk today, we had to leave the car at the car park and walk along the coastal path to get to the cottage, which added to the sense of adventure, especially for the boys. We wondered how people now felt living so close to the cliff edge since the mud slide, especially as we passed the back of a beach house with part of the cliff still wedged through a broken window. Another Nefyn beach stay for us had been in the flat above the café many years before, when both were owned by a Yorkshire family. We had heard that it had recently been modernised by Geraint and Gillian Jones, who owned and ran the bakery, Becws Islyn, in Aberdaron, and was now ready to be booked by holiday makers once more. Today workers were still busy transforming the old café that had been empty for many years. We both looked forward to having a cuppa and cake on our favourite beach, as well as stocking up with 'Aberdaron bread,' as we have always referred to the delicious loaves from Becws Islyn. The coastal path passed small wooden gates, some leading to the private gardens of houses backing onto the coastal path and some to other narrow public paths. I felt quite emotional, when we spotted the almost hidden path that we used to walk along to get to and from the beach, when staying at John and Olwen's chalet when the boys were very small. I was soon laughing again as Jim and I remembered when we had to go and ask the occupiers of one of the private houses if we could have our stunt kite back from amongst their horses in the adjoining paddock. It had been caught by a strong gust and taken flight from the beach below.

Benches are plentiful along this stretch of coastal path, inviting walkers to rest awhile and take in the stunning views towards Yr

Nefyn Bay and the mudslide with Yr Eifl hills in the mist.

Happy on the coast path with my favourite view, Nefyn.

Eifl or out towards Porth Dinllaen. The hedgerows were overgrown and sweet smelling with white wispy cow parsley, red campion and purple foxgloves. The sea was calm as it so often is. This isn't the place for surfing as waves are a rarity but ideal for swimming and messing around in dinghies or on body boards. Yr Eifl was almost lost in the mist as we looked back at the recent mudslide which was now gradually dispersing into the sea with each incoming tide. We ignored the stone steps, much trodden by us in the past, which led down to the west end of the beach and where there were now warning signs about the unstable cliffs. We followed the path as it bore right taking us along Nefyn headland. Swallows dove down towards the path ahead of us, as we looked down onto the beach at the tiny fishermen's huts which were also now backed up by earth. A couple of years ago, one of these tiny tin sheds, with only enough room for some fishing equipment, was advertised for sale for £12,000.

We could just make out Porth Dinllaen through the heavy mist and we put on our jackets to protect ourselves from the cool south westerly wind. We were surprised to see fences blocking the usual route and the path now diverting us inland behind some large empty looking detached houses, then winding back closer to the coastal edge again. With Morfa Nefyn village now to our left, we continued until we came to the steps near the Cliffs Hotel, leading us down to the beach. We tend to call this quieter end of the beach 'Morfa Nefyn beach' even though it is part of Porth Dinllaen. We gazed across the beach to the Tŷ Coch inn and the lifeboat station, which were now beginning to emerge from the mist. The short cut through to the National Trust car park from the beach was closed due to what looked like erosion around the steps that normally led up there, so instead, we walked along the main road to get to Caffi Porth Dinllaen. I spotted a sticker on a sign post that I recognised as being one designed by Marian Brosschot, a friendly, young local artist who I've met a few times at events for Welsh learners, as she is also a language tutor. The message on the sticker was in Welsh and said **Hawl i Fyw Adre** which means 'The Right to Live at Home,' a slogan now being used to try and highlight the concern about the increase in second home owners especially around the Morfa Nefyn and Nefyn areas. I admire Marian's work which often involves the creative use of words. We have a print of hers with the shape of the map of Wales made up of the names of towns and villages of Llŷn. Marian, had recently returned from a trip to Patagonia, Argentina, where she had been teaching Welsh to the adults of Y Wladfa. Y Wladfa is a Welsh settlement, mostly along the coast of Chubut Province. In 1865, 150 passengers from various parts of Wales, sailed on the ship Mimosa to Patagonia, hoping to start a new life out there. There are many books available which describe this voyage and the ensuing experiences of these people. Currently in Patagonia, there are thousands of descendants of these original settlers, many of whom speak Welsh and continue their Welsh ancestors' customs. The area where the settlers landed was named Puerto Madryn and this town is now twinned with Nefyn.

We enjoyed a panad at Caffi Porth Dinllaen and shared one of their outdoor sheltered eating areas with a charming local family. I was intrigued to hear the **nain** (grandmother) and **tad** (dad) rapidly switching from Welsh to English with the little girl and then speaking only Welsh to each other. We guessed that the toddler's mother was English and that they were ensuring she was brought up hearing both languages equally.

Our return walk to Nefyn was warmer as the mist was beginning to lift. Within minutes, our jackets were tied around our waists and the bees were humming as they flew by in the sunshine. We diverted off the coastal path and through the centre of Nefyn along Ffordd Dewi Sant, as we wanted to have some lunch in

Nefyn's Tŷ Caffi, a relatively new café near the Spar store on Stryd Fawr. We passed St David's church on the left, with the nineteenth century watch tower known as Nefyn Castle just beyond it. The watchtower is said to be in the exact location of a twelfth century motte and bailey castle. Across the road from the church is the field where various fun days and festivals have been held over the years. One of the most memorable of these was the Bronze Age Beer Festival, organised by Nefyn's craft ale company Cwrw Llŷn in 2014. The company had been established by a co-operative of enterprising locals a few years earlier. The festival was held to celebrate a 3,500-brewing trough found on Porth Neigwl beach, beneath the sand and clay. Each of the beers brewed by the company are named after a historical character or place associated with Wales and especially Llŷn. A beer brewing enactment took place at the festival, with gorse flowers and hops being used in the process. The beer was brewed in a partly buried trough, using traditional methods and was named 'Porth Neigwl.' This craft beer is still sold at many local shops and bars, but is now brewed using slightly more modern methods at the brewery, where you can watch the process taking place on a guided tour.

As the street changed its name to Pen y Bryn, we looked fondly towards what had been our favourite café in Nefyn, Caffi'r Penwaig. This had now been converted into a home for Albi Jones, who, along with his wife Val had been the proprietor of the café. They were such a friendly couple and we'd had lots of chats with them at the popular café, where we'd visited regularly for lunch. Both involved themselves in charitable events and raised a lot of money for local and national causes. In 2012 Albi's charitable efforts were rewarded by his being selected to carry the Olympic torch for part of the Gwynedd section of its journey in May, as it made its way to London where the games were held that year. He even used this as an opportunity to help raise money for charity and accepted donations from his friends and customers for having their photos taken, holding the torch that he had been allowed to keep as a souvenir. On a Nefyn holiday in June that year we all posed with Albi and the torch in the café. In 2017, we noticed that the café was closed and on enquiring were shocked and saddened to hear that Val had died suddenly from pancreatic cancer. We continue to bump into Albi when we are in Nefyn and he always stops for a chat.

At the top of Pen y Bryn, it's difficult to miss a stunning piece of artwork which was created in 2020 by Coastal Painters and Decorators, the company run by Darren Evans, mentioned earlier. A bright blue and white mural depicts Nefyn's fishing and shipping industry and the gable end of the old post office, now the Premier Off License is covered with huge swirling waves, an anchor, three herrings and a sailing ship. As we turned

Darren Evans's Mural in Nefyn.

onto Stryd Fawr, we shortly passed Tafarn yr Heliwr (the hunter's pub) and noticed its newly painted signs that I'd read about recently in the local paper. In 2019 the pub was bought by the residents of Nefyn after standing empty for ten years. In July that year, even though we're not regular pub goers, we were happy to join in with the **Parti ar y Pafin** (pavement party), which was held to raise funds to help with the renovation. Stryd Fawr was alive with craft and food stalls and live music from local bands and I even got the T-Shirt...literally! Quite recently the swing sign was repainted by the local artist Sioned Williams, who had created the colourful fingerpost that we'd seen at Porth Dinllaen on our previous walk. The eye-catching sign depicts a fisherman on one side and a fisherwoman on the other, both with their catch of herring and with a Nefyn scene as background. I was pleased to see that the word hunter had been interpreted in this way, illustrating the important herring fishing industry of Nefyn's past, rather than showing a pompous man on a horse chasing a fox! The pub was finally preparing to reopen.

After lunch, we decided we had the energy to continue on the coastal path, and in fact needed to, in order to walk off our generous meal! We returned to the car to collect our walking poles, leave our jackets and don our sun-hats as the sun was now blazing.

We continued through the play park again but this time followed the path in the direction of the disused steep granite quarry hills, and between Gwylwyr and Carreglefain, which soon loomed in front of us. We tried to remember how many years it had been since we'd climbed the side of Gwylwyr with the boys but we were unsure. Cow parsley lined the path that led through a line of trees which provided us with some welcome shade. The ground was strewn with catkins and the white downy seeds of willow trees, and horses flicked flies away with their tails in the fields beneath the wooded hill, Mynydd Nefyn. It felt like mid-summer with bees and butterflies and an occasional dragonfly winging their way past us as we trudged along.

The path came alongside the grounds of a large house, with a small pine wood and a pond. Cultured plants spilled out onto the path and blended with the wild ones, including gunnera or giant rhubarb leaves, which really are giant! Beyond the garden, the path became overgrown with ferns, foxgloves and nettles. Luckily there were dock leaves not too far away thanks to mother nature and I rubbed these onto my legs to ease the nettle stings. Various butterflies flitted past too quickly to be photographed or identified other than being white or brown. Shortly we came upon a well with a slate sign telling us it was Ffynnon John Morgan. The identity of John Morgan appears to be a bit of a mystery. Local censuses show a couple of possibilities. There was a John Morgan, who was a minister living in Stryd y Ffynnon in Nefyn in 1841 and in 1851 there was a John Morgan, from Ceredigion, who was farming at Tan yr Allt in Nefyn. I'm not sure what a person needed to do in order to get a well dedicated to them, but John Morgan must have made an impression.

A gentle incline soon offered us clear views of Porth Nefyn and eventually just above the tips of foxgloves and ferns we were able to see Porth Dinllaen once again behind a blanket of mist. An old metal gate led the way to the next stretch of path from where we could look down on Aberafon Caravan Park on the cliffs above the east end of Nefyn beach. The grassy path became even and wide, as we passed nearby houses, and looked freshly mown, giving the impression of a long carpet. This quickly became overgrown again as we left the houses behind and I was wishing I had kept hold of the dock leaves as nettles were plentiful again. The peak of the quarry was ahead of us and to our left we looked down on Wern Farm and caravan park, where Caffi Ni (mentioned earlier) is situated, with the sounds of building work as the farmhouse is being extended. The path was now uneven, being made up mostly of granite from the quarry. I concentrated on my foothold, not wanting any more sprained ankles. Ahead of us, we could now see the remnants of the once busy quarry and the impressive man-made granite ramp where stone would have been transported across the road and down to the jetty onto the part of Nefyn beach known as Wern beach. This quarry was opened in the 1830s and was one of several in the area that together were constituted as the Welsh Granite Company and provided setts for road paving to growing British industrial cities including Liverpool and Manchester. The jetty was blown up during WW2 to prevent it being used by enemy ships. Steep steps took us onto the ramp and we propped on our poles to rest. In our virtual silence, I tried to imagine what it must have been like here when the quarry was active with men working long hours in dirty, noisy and sometimes hazardous conditions. In sharp contrast, the slope of the quarry has now been colonised by dainty pink star-shaped stonecrop flowers and the only visible industry is the collection of pollen by the bees.

The downward steps now led us off the ramp and through the shade of a line of sycamore trees. What I thought was a dragonfly flew past and landed on some nearby fern, allowing me to photograph and admire its beautiful colours. It had a long turquoise body with a metallic sheen and blue/brown wings and I was able to identify it in my nature book later as a male damselfly appropriately named beautiful demoiselle.

On the other side of a kissing gate, we were taken by surprise as we stepped onto a neatly tended lawn with trimmed hedges, a border and a Victorian style garden lamp. The path cut straight across the garden of someone's home! As we crept past the house, we were reassured that we weren't trespassers by a hand-crafted wooden fingerpost stating 'llwybr/footpath.' A few steps further and we reached a small wooden gate, with an adjacent sign warning us that 'livestock' were grazing. The livestock indeed were grazing and watching us warily across the gate, with their large cow eyes. We could hear the traffic on the main road beyond and knew that we were very close to our intended end point for the day, so we decided to let them continue without intrusion and turned back towards Nefyn.

Walk 32b

Before heading back to the caravan, we agreed on our next step. Jim drove to where we had originally planned to end this walk which was at a lay-by on the B4417, close to a white house called Tŷ Uchaf, which is almost on the border of Nefyn and Pistyll. We crossed over the road and found the opening to the coastal path which was overgrown with tall grass and wound behind Tŷ Mawr farm. Within a couple of minutes, we reached a gate, which was at the other end of the enclosed area where we had left the cows grazing. Dogs barked loudly from the farm as if unaccustomed to walkers along that stretch of the path. We'd completed our walk except for one small field and felt better not to have been beaten by cows!

Cornflakes, Wild Goats and a Tragic Love Story

Pistyll to Nant Gwrtheyrn – 13th June 2021

Two days later, we were parked at the lay-by again across the road from Tŷ Mawr farm, ready to continue on our journey. The coastal path sign directed us behind the white houses on the main road. A short archway of hawthorn trees, whose blossoms were now giving way to berries, almost hid a kissing gate which led to an open field where recently shorn sheep were happily munching. The summit of Yr Eifl appeared ahead of us and behind us, the sea glimmered turquoise in the sunshine showing off Porth Dinllaen at its best. Cockerels were crowing at the farm to our right, where touring caravans and tents were set up in the adjoining field. Here's my opportunity for an interesting bit of trivia concerning the Welsh language and cockerels. It has been said that in the early 1900s Welsh harpist Nansi Richards was visiting the United States and met Mr John Kellogg, who was looking for marketing ideas for his cereal. She told him that the name Kellogg sounded very like **ceiliog**, the Welsh word for cockerel, and in later years he added the image of a cockerel on the packs of Kellogg's cornflakes and used the Welsh flag colours of red, white and green. Nansi Richards did exist and did visit the United States, but there are some uncertainties about the accuracy of this tale. I'd like to believe it to be true.

As we passed through another gateway, a sign indicated that we head diagonally downwards to the lower end of the field. The headland Penrhyn Glas or Carreg y Llam granite quarry as it became, was now visible, along with the whole Yr Eifl range beyond. The sea was calm with only a little disturbance from a few small pleasure boats and yachts. To the right, on the main road through Pistyll, beyond the campers and grazing horses, we could see the disused chapel, Capel Bethania, which had been in the news earlier in the year. Locals call it Tom Nefyn's chapel, in memory of Tom Williams, who was a local quarry worker and later a minister, evangelist and poet. In May, the chapel sold at auction for £257,000, double its asking price, to a bidder from outside the area.

Pistyll

Locals had been campaigning for it to be saved and renovated for the community as it had been originally built in 1875 by the residents of Pistyll. They were concerned that the chapel would be converted to a second home as planning was already in place for a four-bedroom holiday home on the site. It is sad to see so many empty chapels around Llŷn falling into disrepair and it would be amazing to see them converted into community centres or affordable housing for the locals.

Steps now led down to another kissing gate, and then a rougher grass path, lined with fern and with gorse bushes that were no longer in bloom. Mother nature didn't do a good job today, as there were no dock leaves in sight and we suffered plenty of nettle stings along the way. Remnants of bluebell flowers hid amongst the grass alongside the upwards path and we shortly came to a tarmac lane, with a gate on each side. Signs with handwritten instructions in bold capital letters stressed that the path continued across the lane rather than along it which would have led to private property. Old ploughing equipment in the front garden of a large house on the lane reminded me of my dad. He would have been able to tell me the name and the purpose of each item and describe how they would have been fastened to the horses to then be pulled along in the fields. We clambered over a stone stile and found ourselves at the back of a collection of luxury self- catering cottages known as Nature's Point. They were built on the site of the former very grand looking Plas Pistyll hotel, built by the Goddards, of silver polish fame. Our memories of the hotel were of an empty and derelict shell with a stripped roof, seen from the main road for many years on our journeys into Nefyn.

Across the field, we followed close to the low stone wall behind the cottages, and a wooden gate led to another tarmac lane which took us past further cottages and then out through a gateway, with one remaining stone pillar, the only remnant of the old hotel. We followed the lane as it wound right and then left to St Bueno's church. It was difficult to believe that it had been almost a year since I had sat alone in silence on the wall behind this church on a similarly hot day, remembering my colleague who had died. Finally, with the lifting of restrictions, myself and a few colleagues have been able to plan a meal out to commemorate our time working with this lovely young lady. St Beuno was a missionary in the seventh century who found solitude on the site of the church. It was later said to have been the site of a hospice for pilgrims travelling to Ynys Enlli. The current church mostly dates from the fifteenth century. The actor Rupert Davies, famous for playing the title role in the 1960s television adaptation of Maigret, was buried here in 1976 and his grave can be seen close to the wall near the coastal path, along which we now continued to tread.

The gradually narrowing path led across a rock-strewn field with more sheep grazing. The sun was getting very hot and I was wishing we'd gone inside the church for a rest. We trudged between a mass of ferns from where we heard the regular sound of chirping grasshoppers as we passed by. We were a little concerned to see fresh cow pats along this stretch of the path and hoped that by now that the producers of them had moved to an enclosed field. A gentle incline led towards Penrhyn Glas and we couldn't resist an occasional glance back to admire the view of Porth Pistyll and

St. Beuno's Church, Pystill.

View of Nant Gwrtheyrn.

Penrhyn Bodeilas with nearby Gwylwyr and Carreglefain, quarries, with the bays of Nefyn and Porth Dinllaen in the distance.

As we sauntered on, following the path that skirted Penrhyn Glas, we spotted a couple of goats on the distant slopes to our right. We knew these to be the feral goats that we've seen on our frequent visits to Nant Gwrtheyrn. According to locals they've been living in this area for centuries. During the first COVID-19 lockdown in 2020, the goats crept down into the nearby villages of Trefor and Llithfaen and were seen feasting on the grass on the football fields. Soon after this walk, I read about a research project, which had been commenced by The Game and Wildlife Trust Conservation, commissioned by Nant Gwrtheyrn, to look at the effect of the goats on the area's biodiversity and to try and discover their unique bloodline. I look forward to hearing the findings of the research. As we reached the headland we paused for a while just beyond a bench, where other walkers had beaten us to it and were sitting enjoying their picnic. This was the first time we had approached Nant Gwrtheyrn along the coastal path from this side and we wanted to soak up this stunning view of Yr Eifl and the village. Nestled between the disused quarries with their clearly defined terraces, we could now make out the converted old quarry houses, the recently extended café and the chapel.

Nant Gwrtheyrn means the valley of Vortigern and is steeped in history and legend. Vortigern was a fifth century British ruler who was said to have found refuge from the invading Saxons in the Nant. Some say that he was King Arthur's uncle. In the mid nineteenth century, granite quarries were opened at Nant Gwrtheyrn and provided setts for paving as did the quarries around Nefyn that I mentioned earlier. Terraces of houses were later built for the workers and their families as well as a large house for the manager and a chapel for the Calvinistic Methodists. A village was created known as Porth Nant and the quarrying business was a success, with huge ships loaded regularly with setts which were transported to industrial cities and returned carrying produce for the quarry workers which weren't available to them locally. In the 1930s, there was a reduction in demand for granite for roads and by the time the Second World War broke out, the quarries had closed. By 1959, all the families had left the village and it remained deserted until the early 1970s when a group of hippies calling themselves the New Atlantis Commune, occupied it. Sadly, they caused a lot of damage to the houses and finally left the village in ruins. During the remainder of the 1970s, Carl Clowes, a G.P. who had recently moved from Manchester to the nearby village of Llanaelhaearn, founded a trust and led a campaign which eventually resulted in the development of the Nant into the National Welsh Language and Heritage Centre. The first Welsh lessons were offered by volunteers in 1982 and since then the village has continued to grow and develop. The chapel is now used for weddings as well as being a museum offering information about the area and its history. The renovated houses are available to holiday makers and to learners attending Welsh courses which are offered on a regular basis at the centre. Not long after this walk, a curious green corrugated hut appeared near the chapel and we found out that it was a replica of the old surgery from Llithfaen, where Dr Carl Clowes had been a G.P. It is now open for visitors to learn about his important role in saving Nant Gwrtheyrn. I was lucky enough to meet Dr Clowes, when he was invited as a celebrity guest at the SSIW 10-year birthday party as a celebrity guest and he was very modest about his achievement. Sadly, he passed away in 2022 but will always be remembered for his contribution to the community.

Looking downwards off the tip of Penrhyn Glas, we could see a platform, the remains of the loading jetty at the disused Carreg y Llam quarry. As we continued, we saw a younger couple heading along a lower, alternative path to the beach. We decided it was safer on our ankles to continue along the upper path and to avoid this very rocky section of the beach. However, our chosen path became very narrow and uneven in parts and I tried to focus on my foothold and not on the steepness of the seaward slope to my left. A few stunted and twisted hawthorn trees were dotted along the slopes, showing clearly the prevailing wind direction. We reached a tunnel of beech and oak trees, whose trunks and branches were gnarled and weather beaten, which provided us with some welcome cool shade. The path crossed a shallow stream, which we carefully stepped through, then continued to wind downwards. I wished I had the energy to remove my walking boots and walk through the water barefoot but we trudged onwards and emerged onto a grassy clearing where a curious looking wooden sculpture had been placed. On closer inspection, we could see it was an iguana with lettering carved along its length in Welsh. The words looked like **maint** (size) and **eiliad** (second). We were left puzzled by its meaning. We crept through the space in the long dry-stone wall that sloped down to the sea and the path led us down to some derelict quarry buildings and rusting remains of equipment. Two very keen photographers were taking artistic shots of Penrhyn Glas through a large rusty wheel that must have served many years at the quarry. As they moved on, I copied their idea before we joined the familiar steep path which runs between the village and the beach, one that we have walked many times with the boys and their friends. We headed upwards, with the café in mind rather than downwards towards the beach. After over two hours of walking in the heat, we were feeling ready for a rest and lunch at Caffi Meinir.

The café takes its name from the tragic folk tale of the young lovers Rhys and Meinir who as the story goes grew up in the 1700s on two of the three farms that were in the Nant at the time. Their favourite meeting place was under an old oak tree on the slopes of Yr Eifl. The couple decided to marry and they set a date for their wedding at the church in Clynnog, several miles away. On the morning of the wedding, Meinir hid and the friends of her bridegroom searched for her, as was the custom at the time. Meinir was never found and after months of continued searching, Rhys slowly lost his mind. One stormy night, Rhys was taking shelter

View of Penrhyn Glas from Nant Gwrtheyrn quarry.

beneath the special oak tree after having searched yet again for Meinir. A bolt of lightning struck the tree and split the trunk into two. The splintered tree revealed the skeleton of his bride to be, wearing a wedding dress. Overcome by grief, Rhys collapsed and died beside the tree. Close to the café there is a split tree with engraved metal plaques, telling the sad story of the couple in words and pictures for passers-by to see.

Inside the café, after checking in, using the obligatory COVID-19 'Track and Trace' system on our phones, we were greeted by a familiar face and beautiful smile from the young lady who took our order. It was Elain, our young friend from the farm at Llannor, daughter of Amanda and Brian, whose caravan we used to stay in. We had a little chat to Elain and ordered our food at the till, which wasn't that easy as mask wearing was still compulsory indoors until seated at the table in cafés and pubs. We chose a table inside to shelter from the sun and while we waited for our food, I tried to grasp the meaning of the four-line Welsh poem by Myrddin ap Dafydd, which spoke of the sea, the horizon and of Ireland, which on a crystal-clear day can sometimes be seen from the Nant. One line of this englyn is written on each of the four walls of the café, above the large windows which frames spectacular views of Porth Nant.

On our return walk, we were lucky to see a red kite circling above the sea near Penrhyn Glas, presumably looking for its lunch. Then further along, we spotted a seal's head bobbing up and down in the gentle waves. The sun was very hot with grasshoppers chirping loudly in the ferns, and butterflies were plentiful. We followed a sheep and her lamb along the path for a while until they joined others in a field. As we approached the bench at Penrhyn Glas, we were taken by surprise to see more than a dozen wild goats and kids. They seemed timid and hurried away from us. A solitary curly horned adult goat was crossing a field and gave a pitiful high-pitched cry, which was very different to the deep Billy Goat Gruff sound I had expected to hear. We crossed a field where cows were now grazing at the far side – very brave for us. Unfortunately, a notice at St Bueno's church informed us that it was still closed to the public due to COVID-19, yet another reminder that times weren't yet back to normal.

The next walk was relatively short and our most straightforward so far, as we would be going along a very even, mile long tarmacked road, turning around then walking back again. That sounds easy enough, but there was a bit of a catch, as this is probably the steepest road in Llŷn, along the 'screw hill,' that leads into and out of the valley, Nant Gwrtheyrn. This was going to be a challenge for our knees! The previous evening on Summer Solstice, we had watched a beautiful red sunset behind the summit of Carnguwch, from close to our caravan. We had then hurried off towards Nant Gwrtheyrn and parked at a layby just before the start of the 'screw hill,' where we knew there was an excellent view of Nefyn and Porthdinllaen and the sea. We had wanted to try and catch the sun setting again, but into the sea this time. We had arrived just in time but unfortunately, it was very cloudy so we'd had a very hazy view. Several campervans had been parked on the upper car park and these were still there on the morning of our walk as we drove down into the valley. We presumed people had been camping there overnight for the Solstice.

Jim drove down the steep, winding road to the lower car park behind the two terrace rows of cottages. These quarry cottages were

The beginning of the Screw Hill incline.

Nant Gwrtheyrn Chapel, now a museum.

called Sea View (**Trem y Môr**) and Mountain View (**Trem y Mynydd**). One of the sea facing cottages has been converted into an example of an 1800s quarryman's home for visitors to view. As you leave the car park behind and set off uphill your attention is immediately caught by the beautiful pine forest lining the road ahead and some remaining deserted quarry buildings to your left. The first time we did this walk was at the time when the village was still under development and able-bodied folk wanting to use the café or visit the beach, had had to walk from the upper car park to get there. There had been limited spaces close to the café for anyone with a mobility problem or people working or staying at Nant. We have walked the hill a couple of times since then, when Tom and Simon were school age and their friends were holidaying with us, but an improved and extended car park is now available for all to use.

It was a clear, sunny day, with a slight breeze, which helped to keep us cool as we quickly warmed up with the effort of the steep walk. Birds were singing loudly near the tops of the pine trees, but were too distant for us to see to try and identify. The tarmac of the winding road ahead, glinted in the heat and we enjoyed the shade while we could. We could hear a stream rippling as it ran alongside us, hidden by ferns and brambles just before the road curved sharply to the right. We spotted the springs trickling down the high rockface close to a passing place along the road. We smiled as we remembered a friend of Tom's, when they were about 12, being so in awe of the springs, that he had collected some of the water in his drinking bottle with the intention of keeping it 'forever.' We stopped every so often to allow our legs to recover or to allow an occasional car to pass by. We were soon looking down on the pine forest and beyond that a group of distant derelict farm buildings with adjoining fields divided by dry stone walls and a couple of small white dots that were sheep grazing close by. An elderly man, who we later discovered from friends was called Dewi, was walking down the road towards us. We exchanged greetings and comments about the weather in Welsh, then continued in English for Jim to understand. He told us that he did this walk five times a week, weather permitting, and that he had always lived in the adjacent village of Llithfaen. He mentioned that two of his daughters worked in the Nant, one of them in the café, and he knew our friend Elain – **byd bach** (small world). He enjoyed sharing his knowledge of the valley and its earlier occupants and we enjoyed listening. He told us of the primary school that had been established in the chapel but explained that when children reached the age of eleven, they'd then had to walk the steep road up into Llithfaen to attend secondary school. The road has been altered from the original one and we had seen signs of the old road as we had been walking. The old road had been known as the 'sled road' and had been much steeper and narrower than it was now. Only one car was allowed into the village at once and if someone died, the only way to get the coffin out of the Nant was by horse and sleigh Dewi told us. Not long after this walk, we found a short, 1934 news reel clip on YouTube, called 'Climbing the Unclimbable,' which shows the old road and a car struggling to manage the sharp turns. Dewi laughed as he remembered how the postman used to leave his van at the top of the 'screw hill' and walk down, often accompanied by others on their way to the village. He recalled when the farm used to produce milk and other produce for the quarry families and for

Nant Gwrtheyrn converted quarry houses.

Llithfaen. He shook his head as he told us how the derelict farm buildings were now on sale for £700,000 and he wondered what the fate of the old farm would be. He proudly explained how the stones used for curling in the Winter Olympics had been provided from the quarries here at the Nant, including those used by the female Scottish Team in 2002 who had achieved the first Winter Olympics gold in curling for Britain in 18 years. We thanked Dewi for his interesting conversation and said our goodbyes and he replied, saying that he'd see us in a year's time, which left us puzzled.

We reached the point where the road bends sharply to the left and gives one of the most stunning views of the Nant with a bench strategically placed allowing people to appreciate this. The whole of the village and the bay were visible, with the sea sparkling in the sunshine and Yr Eifl looking majestic beyond. We continued upwards and the path gradually levelled off, much to the relief of my calves! From the road, we could see the next stage of our coastal walk, the pass (Bwlch yr Eifl) leading upwards between two of the Eifl hills – Garn Fôr (the quarry, also known as Mynydd y Gwaith which means quarry mountain) and Garn Ganol (the highest and middle of the hill range – Ganol meaning middle). The smallest and most southerly hill in the Eifl range is called Tre'r Ceiri, and is well worth a visit. We have walked to its summit a couple of times with Tom and Simon, where one of the best examples of a prehistoric hillfort in Europe can be found, in addition to the most stunning views of Llŷn. **Ceiri** comes from the word **cewri** which means giants and **tre** means town so 'Town of the Giants'.

We stopped at the upper car park, which until 2013 was flanked by a beautiful pine forest. We remembered how shocked we had been on our first visit following the felling of the forest and how devastated it looked. The felling had been as a result of the Woodland Project between 2013 and 2016, whose aim had been to get rid of weak and vulnerable pine trees and replace these with native trees. The young trees are slowly growing in their plastic tubes, but remain quite small. I hope to see a native forest developed here within my lifetime. We sat on a stone wall gazing at our next walk directly ahead of us and spotted other walkers following this route. From where we were, it didn't look too steep but we have learnt not to judge from a distance and we had been told that the downwards path leading to Trefor on the other side was very steep.

We discussed our wish to walk to the summit of Garn Ganol one day soon while our legs were able, but decided this should be some time after we had completed the Llŷn coastal path walk.

I took photos of the three standing stones at the car park, which are a fairly recent addition to the area. They are covered in carvings which are meant to resemble stone age art and on a polished slate between them is an engraved poem written by Myrddin ap Dafydd called *Ar Lwybr Chwarel* (On the Quarry Path), a dedication to the quarry workers of the past. A sign near the old gate posts saying it was a 25-minute steep walk down to the café made us smile as we set off back. Another walker made us chuckle as he pointed to the sign and commented to his partner 'yes and 45 minutes back up!' We hadn't got far, when we were surprised to see Dewi on his way back up. As we met up again, he explained that he had forgotten that he had left his washing machine on and he felt he needed to get back to it, so he'd cut his walk short today and had to miss his **panad**. We admired his fitness and he explained that he counted the wooden barrier supports all the way up and stopped at every fifteenth one to catch his breath for 30 seconds. As we said our goodbyes, he left us puzzled again by saying that he would now see us in two years! A slow stroll took us back down to the village where we enjoyed a picnic on the bench overlooking the bay, followed by a **panad** in the café.

*Standing stones in Nant Gwrtheyrn Car Park with
Tre Ceiri hill beyond.*

A Derelict House and Rain, Rain and More Rain

Nant Gwrtheyrn to Bwlch yr Eifl –
23rd June 2021

There was a heavy mist over Yr Eifl as we looked out from our caravan bedroom window and the forecast said there was a chance of rain but we decided to risk it. We parked near the three standing stones in the upper car park at Nant Gwrtheyrn and strode out in the drizzle towards Yr Eifl, heading for Bwlch yr Eifl. The wide, stony path gently inclined between clumps of heather and thistle, interspersed with tall purple foxgloves. Small amounts of heather were just beginning to bloom pink. We were soon looking down at our walk from the previous day – the steep road to Nant Gwrtheyrn village and the pine woods with the sea beyond. There was no sign of Dewi today. A small boat was creating patterns in the otherwise very calm water. The rain started to come down heavier as we neared the quarry hill, Garn Fôr and through the mist we could see parts of the old road and the big rambling farm below and we wondered together about what would become of it when it was sold. Would it return to being a farm or would it become holiday accommodation? We liked the idea of it being owned by the community as a working farm, and providing fresh produce to Caffi Meinir. Tiny white bedstraw flowers were growing along the grass verge on each side of the path which now wound to the right

around Garn Ganol. We could just make out Porth Dinllaen, then Porth Nefyn as we looked back through the rain and mist. Ahead of us a few goats crossed our path and headed up the slopes of Garn Ganol, towards the rest of the herd which appeared to be waiting for them.

Bwlch yr Eifl in the pouring rain.

Looking down at Nant Gwrtheyrn.

There were about thirty of them in total, mostly white coats but with a couple of black coated ones amongst them. Ahead of us in the distance we could make out the large hill Gyrn Goch and the beach at Trefor below. We were surprised to hear the skylarks singing in the rain and then even more surprised to see a couple of choughs flying playfully in the breeze, but they spurred us on.

We took the official coastal path which wound to the right around the base of Garn Fôr, rather than the steeper path up into the quarry. The path became narrower and uneven and ran amongst a mass of scratchy heather. It gradually opened out, as did the view of Trefor, and we could just make out the cars driving along the main Caernarfon to Pwllheli road passing the hills of Gyrn Goch, Gyrn Ddu and Moel Penllechog as we do on our journeys to and from the caravan. As we reached a wooden gate, my phone rang and an electronic voice told me that if I didn't select 'one' I would be risking imprisonment for tax fraud. I replied to the voice in Welsh, using as many rude words as I could think of until the call ended automatically due to lack of cooperation on my part. How dare these scammers intrude on our walk! Another couple approached the gate from the other side and we stood to one side to allow them to pass. They greeted us in Welsh and I

The bleak hills.

responded, then explained that Jim only knew a small amount of Welsh so we continued in English. They were from Mid Wales and were on holiday and walking different sections of the coastal path. They were heading to Nant Gwrtheyrn and were pleased when I told them that the café would be opening shortly as they were wet and tired. We said our goodbyes and continued through the gate where the path began its decline. We decided that we would only continue for a little further and that on our next walk we would work our way up the pass from Trefor until we got to wherever we stopped today. We began to look out for a place to stop that would be easy to identify next time, even though Jim also records our stopping points on his gadget. The path was becoming quite slippery in parts due to the rain, which had become increasingly heavy. Suddenly I found myself on the ground; I'd slipped on a rock and fallen on my bum! My fall had been slightly softened by fern and nothing seemed damaged apart from my pride, so once I was over the shock, Jim helped me up and we continued.

A moss covered low dry-stone wall, that looked like it had been there for centuries, appeared along the grassy path with a couple of ash trees and an oak growing out of it, all looking rather stunted and gnarled. We ducked underneath a large twisted branch that crossed the path, which was now beginning to level out and we were surprised to see a derelict single storey stone cottage in a hollow just beyond the trees. We both agreed that this was the perfect place to stop. As we explored what was now the shell of a building, we wondered about the cottage's history and who had lived here in such a remote spot. There were signs that someone had just begun to do some work on the ruin as they had left some fresh planks of wood, a small cement mixer and the remains of a **panad** in a mug that was now filling up with rain water! We didn't linger as the rain was lashing down now. We knew we would be back soon on our next walk and could have another look on a clearer day.

On our return journey, I focussed on the path and not falling. Our visibility was restricted to within a few feet anyway with the driving rain and the mist. As we eventually reached the car park, there was a small group of sheep standing very still, close to our car, looking as bedraggled as we did. Dewi had made the right decision today!

The quarry hill Garn For.

Chickens and Pizza
Bwlch yr Eifl to Tanygraig – 2nd July 2021

As we set off walking from the car park at Trefor harbour at 8.30 am on this warm Friday morning, the tide was on its way out. I noticed a few vans parked, with men having mugs of tea as if waiting for something to happen. I wondered if they were waiting to go out in one of the small colourful boats, of which there were many lying on the shingly shore. An information board explained that the harbour was created to export stone from Garn Fôr and was also home to a busy fishing fleet in the past. Some commercial fishing continues today. The coastal path took us past the harbour wall; the sea was very calm and still, with only the sound of the gulls on the rocks close by. Pink valerian was growing in large clumps out of the shingle as we went by and a brightly painted sign caught our attention with a cartoon of a hen and the name Bobi. It reminded me of the signs made by Carys Bryn that we'd seen around Llŷn to cheer people up during the pandemic. Behind us in

Approaching Garn For from Trefor.

the distance were Gyrn Goch and Gyrn Ddu with a blanket of cloud covering the summits.

A wide gateway led us to the path which followed the back of the sand dunes, and ahead of us Garn Fôr was clearly visible with its terraces and derelict quarry buildings. Despite a bright blue sky, Garn Ganol, the middle and largest

Exploring the ruined house on Bwlch yr Eifl.

of the hill range, was also partly hidden in cloud. A wooden bridge took us across a stream and we strode out towards a National Trust sign, that told us we were in the area known as **Morfa** which means marshland, and warned of steep cliffs. The coastal path sign directed us through a wooden gate and around a rubble hill. As we started the climb upwards, we realised we had forgotten our walking poles so headed back to the car slightly begrudgingly. It was an opportunity to leave jackets behind and collect our sunglasses – the weather was turning out much nicer than our weather apps had forecast.

As we retrod our steps we were disheartened to notice that there were now cows on the slopes where we had turned back earlier. No cows for us, so we decided to divert slightly and continue left away from the harbour along the tarmac lane with Garn Fôr directly ahead of us. The edges of the lane were amassed with tall sweetly scented cow parsley, with occasional foxgloves and red campion breaking up the waves of white. Another gate led the way past a large white house with a sign in the front garden saying 'Bert's Kitchen Garden, members only,' with a picture of an American style bus. On Googling later, I discovered it was a campsite with a difference. Visitors were invited to use the kitchen garden and pitch their tents or stay in a cottage or a converted American school bus called Otto. The lane then took us past a large car park full of empty local school buses, and onward past Trefor's social club **Y Tŵr** (The Tower) and a car repair garage not yet open for business. We followed the lane past the side of the club and began a gradual incline, with a low stone wall and fields on each side of us. The lane became rougher to walk on and was lined with hedgerows, tall grass and trees. The quarry hill appeared very close to us now. It had a very different look about it from the views we were familiar with from Nefyn beach. Its pale grey, almost white slopes, gleaming in the sunshine, gave the impression of an Alpine hill. Rusting metal fences brought to our attention that the lane was now bridging another one and we could see that we had now met up with the official coast path again. A few stone steps and a small gate to our left led the way through trees to meet it. We strode out quickly along the path as it continued through long grass and ferns, interspersed with pink clover and buttercups, trying to avoid the horseflies that unfortunately preferred human flesh to flowers and bit us both several times. We grumbled and waved our arms around, looking like a couple of windmills, trying to avoid further attack from these nasty stinging beasts as we proceeded uphill! We passed through a modern looking metal gate with stickers on it reminding us that we were also still on the North Wales Pilgrim's Way. I wonder how many pilgrims have been stung on route to Ynys Enlli! The ruined cottage on Bwlch yr Eifl, where we had ended our last walk, was now visible further uphill. We turned right through a metal kissing gate along the granite path, passing the gateway of a farmhouse and were surprised to see another brightly painted sign, but this time with a cartoon chicken called 'Wini'. I later found out on Facebook that the signs had been made by a local school teacher/artist known as Dafydd Trefor. He had hidden four of them around the Trefor area in May 2020 for children to find during Lockdown. We didn't come across the other two – Owi and Elsi!

The path towards Bwlch yr Eifl and one of Dafydd Trefor's signs.

Hawthorn hedges full of green, not yet ripened berries, flanked the steep path, with pink and white blossoming dog roses, bindweed and brambles tangling their way through. The path levelled off as we arrived at a clearing where in the past there had possibly been a house. We felt as if we had stepped back in time as we walked the final short stretch of path leading to the derelict cottage. Uneven stone setts were hidden beneath the thick grass underfoot and surviving sections of dry-stone wall were covered with tall ferns. We wondered who had walked or ridden along this path in years gone by – labourers young and old on their route to work in the quarry more than likely.

We sat on the steps of the cottage and ate our lunch, admiring the view down the slopes and across the fields to the small village of Trefor with its beach and the hills to the east. What an amazing place this must have been to live. As we left the cottage, I said **Da bo chi** (goodbye) with respect to its previous occupants and thanked them for their hospitality, whoever they had been.

The delightful sound of children's laughter drifted towards us as we made our way downhill – it was lunch time at Trefor primary school and they were playing outside. We could see the chapel and the church close by. Close to home, we had been hearing of many children having to isolate at home for ten days due to classmates testing positive for covid. This seemed to be especially since the arrival of a new version of COVID-19, known as the Delta variant, which was first detected in India and was beginning to overtake the Alpha variant. Children throughout the UK were being tested at least twice a week, with instant result 'lateral flow tests'. I was now also using these, as I was gradually beginning to see clients at work face to face in addition to using video consultation. Only that morning I'd had a message from our peninsula friend Amanda who works as a teaching assistant, telling us that she wouldn't be able to visit as she was having to self- isolate while she was waiting for the results of one of the children in school who had possible symptoms of the virus.

We retraced our steps and hurried through the horsefly areas, but got bitten yet again! At the repair garage, workers were now busy fixing a school bus which was up on a ramp and I smiled as I heard Radio Cymru blaring from their radio. Other walkers were making their way towards the quarry path as we reached the car park and the men who'd been drinking tea in their vans were now fishing at the end of the harbour wall. After a quick discussion, we decided we had enough energy to continue further towards

Gyrn Goch, Gyrn Ddu and Moel Penllechog.

Aberdesach and we left our poles in the car as the next stretch was along even main roads. We realised that in fact the remainder of our coastal path walk to Caernarfon, was now going to be without cliffs and hills. Our legs would be glad of this, but we would miss the views that they provide.

There was more of an incline to the road out of Trefor than we had realised but I ignored my grumbling knees and enjoyed the distraction of the colourful scented rose gardens of the private houses we passed. We trudged along the newly built footpath, which took us all the way to the A499 Caernarfon to Pwllheli road. Cows and sheep were grazing in fields on either side of us, but the magnificent hills demanded most of our attention. Yr Eifl to our right and Gyrn Goch, Gyrn Ddu and Moel Penllechog ahead of us looked almost close enough to touch. We enjoyed being able to admire them at a leisurely pace, as usually we are speeding past them in the car on the way to the caravan. We turned left onto the busy and noisy A499 with Yr Eifl now behind us. Very soon after the junction, we saw the coastal path sign directing us to cross the road and a small path took us to a section of the 'old road'. The A499 was upgraded in 2008 and 2009 between Aberdesach and Llanaelhaearn and the remaining parts of the old road intermittently run parallel to the new, and both are used as the official coastal path. It was nice to be sheltered a little from the traffic by the hedgerows, the long grass and masses of ox eye daisies. We soon reached an attractive row of grey stone terraced houses which we've seen so many times on our journeys. The row is called **Tanygraig** which means beneath the rock, but oddly the English name given to them on the road sign is Seaview Terrace. We were surprised to see our regular Friday night pizza van parked at the side of the row. Later that night when we collected our pizza order from the van in Llanaelhaearn, I chatted to the friendly young couple, Mitch and Helena, who run the business and they explained that they live in one of the terraced houses. As the old road is rarely used, we decided that it would be safe to park the car near Tanygraig on our next walk and that we would turn back at this point. We had earned our pizzas!

An Ancient Well and Mythical Tales
Tanygraig to Aberdesach – 4th July 2021

Most of this walk was following the current A499 and the remaining parts of the old road, with the noise of racing traffic to our left and the dramatic hills of Gyrn Goch, Gyrn Ddu and Moel Penllechog for most of the way to our right. One of the guide books we had glanced at had suggested that all of the A499 stretch of the coastal walk could be avoided by taking a taxi, but we decided this would be cheating and we were interested to see this area at a slower pace than usual. The forecast had said light rain all day but it was dry as we set off, but thick clouds were hanging ominously over the hills. The old road was available to us for a few hundred yards beyond Tanygraig with a wide grassy verge shielding us from the traffic at one side with hedgerows and blackthorn trees on the other, with farms and fields at the foot of the hills. Occasional cats' eyes and faded white lines along the road remained as a reminder of the its previous use. Soon after we emerged onto the main road, we came upon a familiar honesty box with eggs for sale. We've tended to arrive at our caravan in the evenings and therefore have been too late to buy the eggs on our way, so we were pleased at the opportunity to try them and decided we'd get some on our return walk. The fields beyond were busy with sheep, geese and goats grazing and the farmhouse was tucked a distance away at the base of Gyrn Ddu. The owners of the farm had a shop in Pwllheli called 'Farmer and his Wife' where they sold eggs, fruit and vegetables and goat produce, including milk soap and hand spun wool. Sadly, on recent visits to the town, we'd noticed it had closed down but we'd heard that business was continuing with a mobile shop.

We were soon back on the old road again and felt like rebels as we walked along the fading centre white line of this now virtually unused road. Jim, who misses nothing, spotted a small concrete building, close to the road but hidden by trees and ivy. I took a photo of the bit of sign that was visible over a doorway that read 'Y STANTON GR...' A Google search enlightened us later that day;

it was Enderby and Stoney Stanton Granite Co. Ltd and this was an old quarry building. Gyrn Ddu had been quarried for granite which was used for setts and the quarries had been called Tyddyn Hywel and Tan y Graig. This made me think that the terraced row of Tanygraig had been built for quarry workers. A further visit to the pizza van sometime later gave me the opportunity to ask Mitch and Helena about the houses and they told me that indeed they were built in the 1800s for the quarry workers. The quarries apparently merged in 1915 to form the company and had produced crushed stone for road surfacing or railway ballast.

The road gently inclined as we reached the sign telling us that we were entering the roadside hamlet of Gyrn Goch and we could see the sea again, with the seaside village of Dinas Dinlle, and Ynys Môn just about visible in the mist. It began to rain lightly and we passed a large converted chapel 'Hen Gapel Seion.' It was good to see one of these beautiful buildings at least being saved from demolition by being converted into a home. We passed an old stone bridge Pont y Felin, which crossed Afon Hen and just before the path returned to the old road, hawk eye Jim spotted an old milestone which was almost hidden by a mass of oxeye daisies. It told us we were halfway between 'Caernarvon' (anglicised spelling) and Pwllheli which were both ten miles away.

The rain began to ease and the sun came out, warming us nicely as we strode on, and several individual runners and cyclists passed both ways and we exchanged greetings. Shortly, we gained a glimpse of the tower of St Beuno's Church at Clynnog Fawr, again a very familiar sight to us on our journeys back and forth to the caravan. Just before we reached the church, we came upon something that we had heard of, but had never got around to finding – St Beuno's Well. I was surprised at its proximity to the road and at its size. It is a

Beuno's Well, Clynnog Fawr.

Clynnog Fawr Church.

large, square, stone-walled well with steps leading to its entry gate and an information board gave us some of its and St Beuno's history. St Beuno, the seventh century saint was said to have brought back seven people from the dead, including his niece Winefride (later St Winefride), after who the famous well at Holywell is named. Since then, and even up to the current time, St Beuno's churches in Clynnog Fawr and Pistyll and the wells have been an important part of the journey of pilgrims along Llŷn. Historically, a dip in the curing waters of St Beuno's well followed by a night on St Beuno's tomb in the chapel attached to the church at Clynnog Fawr was said to cure 'the falling sickness' (epilepsy) in children. Families travelled miles hopeful of a cure. Just the thought of it makes me shiver.

We continued to the church, noticing new homes being built on the edge of the village and passed the garage shop which has many times been a handy stop for us, for last minute provisions on the way to the caravan. Immediately after a row of attractive old cottages on the left, we entered the churchyard through the high stone archway. St Beuno's church seems huge for the size of the parish it has served and continues to serve. Built in the fifteenth century and restored in the mid-nineteenth century, it certainly makes its majestic presence known. We wandered across the graveyard and around the tower making our way to the main entrance, wondering if there could be worshippers inside as it was a Sunday. I was surprised by the large new sign near the door saying '**Croeso** – Welcome' and then even more so by an elderly lady, who appeared in the doorway from inside the church. She thanked us profusely for visiting the church and shared her excitement at it now being open to worshippers and visitors after so long. Since the beginning of the COVID-19 outbreak, many church services in Wales, as in the rest of the UK had been taking place online, being streamed live allowing people to take part from their own homes. Gradually, relaxation of restrictions had been allowing churches to open and people to attend, providing masks were worn, no singing occurred and two metre distancing was maintained. On the 19th June, the Welsh government announced that congregations would be allowed to sing in places of worship providing masks were worn whilst doing so. They can't stop the Welsh from singing for too long! The lady explained that it had been a short 'do it yourself' service that morning as they were having problems getting a minister. I was amused when she told us that the church was opened up each morning by 'Henry' when he let out his chickens, then closed by him in the evening when he brought them back in again. We said goodbye to the lady and made a brief visit inside. The whitewashed walls and numerous windows (though none of them stained glass) offered a bright, airy welcome to visitors and display boards gave interesting accounts of the history of the church and its artefacts. One of the most intriguing artefacts is the pair of nineteenth century dog tongs, used to extract unruly dogs from the church if needed! Our last visit inside the church had been several years ago to watch a chamber concert by performers from the Canolfan Cerdd William Mathias, a music school named after the renowned musician, composer and conductor who was also the founder of the North Wales International Music Festival. There had been no unruly dogs there that evening! As we left the church and headed for the other small gateway, we passed the monument of Ebenezer Thomas (bardic name Eben Fardd), a poet, school teacher and diarist, who lived from 1802 to 1863. He used to also bind books, keep accounts for people and look after the village mail to supplement his income.

His monument is looking rather worn in parts but you can still see engraved Welsh verses on the panels, one by himself and others in tribute to him.

We left the churchyard and meandered on, but soon stopped to look at an old end of terrace cottage on the road leading away uphill north eastwards out of the village. It had a large modern 'Clynnog Fawr Post Office' sign above the door and window, but a very old looking red metal post box built into the leaded window of the cottage, which is now a private residence. The occupiers had placed an information sheet in the window, explaining that the post office had closed in 2006, but that they had wanted to retain some of the old features for the community to enjoy. Next door to this was a large rambling white building. Jim remembered that it had been a pub, and prior to the road improvement, the A499 road had passed close to its beer garden where locals and visitors had flocked to in the summer. I discovered that it had been called 'The New Inn' in the 1800s, then was later known as 'The Newborough Arms' and more recently 'St Beuno's Inn' or 'Y Beuno.' It is a listed building and closed in 2015, when it was then converted into housing.

Walking along part of the old A499 road.

Just before the old road merged with the A499 again, we passed a bed and breakfast called 'Bryn Eisteddfod'. I had remembered our peninsula friend Amanda, telling us that this was owned and run by yet another poet Meirion Macintyre Huws, known locally as Mei Mac. He had been the winner of the 1993 National Eisteddfod Chair and in 2001 was the Welsh language Children's Poet Laureate. Is there anyone in Llŷn who doesn't write poetry? Our legs were beginning to grumble and I was wishing we had rested in the church for a while, but instead we leant on farmers' gates on each side of the A499 admiring the views which were now clearer as the clouds were shifting. Llanddwyn Island, and Newborough Sands and Forest on Ynys Môn looked a stone's throw away.

We plodded on and soon reached the sign for Aberdesach and turned left towards the village, following the short winding roads past an occasional house and ending at the beach car park, where nearby pretty pastel painted holiday bungalows lined the sea front. We sat on one of the benches by the beach and ate our picnic, whilst sharing our sense of bemusement that we had never visited Aberdesach before and it had such a beautiful view of Yr Eifl. I was spoilt for choice for a pebble to add to the collection as this is a very stony beach. It also has one large very special stone, which we could see further along the eastern end of the beach and I learnt about it from the information board near the holiday bungalows. Maen Dylan has connections with the Mabinogion. The Mabinogion are the earliest prose tales of British literature and were compiled in the twelfth and thirteenth centuries from oral traditions. Within these are the Four Branches of the Mabinogi, which are interrelated mythological tales, often told to children in Welsh schools and translated into many languages. Maen Dylan was believed to have been named after Dylan Eil Don (Dylan the second wave or second born), one of the characters in the tale of *Math, Fab Mathonwy* (Math, son of Mathonwy), the Fourth Branch of the Mabinogi. At low tide, Caer Arianrhod reef, said to be the remains of the semi mythical fort, Caer Arianrhod, can be seen about 900 metres west off the mainland and is connected to land by a submerged area of stony ground. Arianrhod was Dylan's mother in the tales and she gave birth to him immediately after stepping over Math's magic wand – that's their story not mine! From infancy, as soon as Dylan touched the sea he could swim like a fish and he continued to live in the sea. There are several references to the surrounding area within the various legends of Y Mabinogi. In the Black Book of Carmarthen *Llyfr Du Caerfyddin*, a thirteenth century Welsh manuscript, thought to be the earliest surviving manuscript written solely in Welsh, it says that the grave of Dylan is in the church of Beuno.

Some of the history of the village was also recounted on the information board. Desach, the name of the river which feeds into the sea here, is said to mean belonging to the tribe of Deisi, which was a Celtic tribe from Ireland. The village had never had a school or chapel but was known for its coal storage. Small ships used to land on the beach at low tide and the coal was unloaded and stored within the walls of the building now known as **Yr Iard** (the yard), which we had passed on our way in. A bench close to the board had a slate sign beneath it, with a dedication to a local Welsh man and had the words of the poet R. Williams Parry *Mae Hiraeth yn y Môr a'r Mynydd Maith* (There's a deep longing in the sea and the distant hills). We have a lampshade in the caravan decorated with an image of mountains, birds and these words as we felt it described how we feel about Llŷn and went well with the name of the caravan.

On our return journey, we stopped for a takeaway coffee at the garage shop, which gave me change to be able to buy some eggs from the honesty box further along the road, which we enjoyed later for tea.

Eggs for sale near Gyrn Ddu.

Llŷn is Officially a Natural Outstanding Beauty!

Aberdesach to Glynllifon Estate – 15th July 2021

Across the summer, we had got into a pattern of going to the caravan on alternate long weekends, spending the other catching up with friends and family, which was now easier to do with the lifting of COVID-19 restrictions. Earlier in the month Prime Minister Boris Johnson had set out the last stage of the 'road map' for lifting restrictions and it was expected that on the 19th July there would be an end to compulsory wearing of masks, social distancing, the rule of six in private homes and the work from home rule. I had begun to work one or two days of my three-day work week at my clinic base, seeing clients face to face, as well as continuing to do reports and admin from home. Jim and I had received both of our vaccinations by now and the boys their first one. The Welsh and Scottish government had introduced different guidelines throughout the pandemic and we were always mindful of this when visiting Llŷn. Flashing information signs along the motorways reminded visitors of this as they travelled to their holiday destinations in Wales. During July, Mark Drakeford, the First Minister of Wales, announced that most of Wales's remaining Covid rules would be lifted from the 7th August, but that face coverings were still to be worn in public places. With our increasing visits, we could see that our coastal walk adventure was likely to be completed before the end of the summer and that we would probably reach Caernarfon sometime in August.

Aberdesach Beach.

As we stepped out of the car at Aberdesach beach car park, we were met with a real sense of the seaside with a cool sea breeze, the fresh smell of seaweed and the cry of seagulls overhead. Poet

R.S. Thomas shared my love of the smell of seaweed and described it as smelling like flowers in a garden when summer visited it. The tide was out and slowly making its way back in as we crossed the turquoise painted metal bridge over the river Desach. The path led past the sea front holiday bungalows and lodges, some with adverts in the windows with contact numbers for booking. I was pleased to see that most had retained their seaside themed Welsh names, such as **Haul a Gwynt** (sunshine and wind) and **Min y Môr** (by the seaside), but suspected they were mostly second homes.

The path gradually became overgrown with grass and brambles, so we clambered down onto the beach, which became increasingly pebbly as we went along. It was lovely to be so close to the sea again after a lot of road walking recently. We passed the large rock, Maen Dylan, and noticed that someone had scratched its name into it. We wondered about Caer Arianrhod reef, but we were unable to see any sign of it when we looked out to sea. Not far along the beach, as we passed low cliffs, we were able to see the white painted chalets and bungalows at Pontllyfni ahead of us. As we reached Pontllyfni, we scrambled up some large rocks onto an open grassy area near to the holiday homes and looked out to sea. The iron age hillfort at Dinas Dinlle looked very close further along the beach and we wondered about continuing our walk that way, but we decided it could be too rocky and a bit risky for dodgy ankles. The clouds were beginning to disperse and further out we were able to see the white lighthouse at Llanddwyn Island on Ynys Môn, glinting in the sunshine.

We passed the caravan park and followed the narrow road out of Pontllyfni. I breathed in the sweet smell of honeysuckle, which intertwined the hedgerows that lined the road, but we soon met up with the hum of the traffic on the A499 and turned left to continue our way along it. The road crossed the river Lllyfni, something we had never noticed when travelling by car and continued through the village with its several houses. An old converted chapel and chapel house caught my eye on the opposite side of the road and the kitchen shop adjoining it looked very familiar. Jim remembered us calling there on one of our journeys over twenty years previously, when it was an antique shop. There were still signs of old bric-a-brac in the window. I love one of the Welsh ways of saying antiques which is often seen on shop signs – **hen bethau**

Cottages along the old A499.

which simply means 'old things.' As we plodded along the A499, the sea appeared and disappeared from view beyond the fields. We crossed the main road to take the old road for a while, and the trees between the two dulled the noise of the traffic. We passed a row of old single storey cottages and thought of their occupiers, who, before the road alteration, must have stepped out of their front door almost straight onto the busy main road.

We were soon alongside the A499 again and shortly passed the boundary sign for Dwyfor as we came out of Pontllyfni. Dwyfor was one of the five local government districts of Gwynedd from 1974 to 1996 and included the whole of Llŷn. It is still in use as an area, governed by an area committee of Gwynedd Council. We crossed the road at the junction, where a right turn takes you to Penygroes and the road follows the long stone side wall of the old Glynllifon Estate, which was originally owned by the Newborough family. We continued past the front wall of the estate, which was colourful with pink valerian growing between the stones. We soon reached our turning back point which was the gateway of Plas Newydd which is a large private hall within the Glynllifon Estate.

Glynllifon Estate Wall.

A large part of Parc Glynllifon has been open to the public for years and its impressive gateway is much further along this wall which extends for about a mile and a half along the A499. Our family tradition when the boys were younger was to visit the park, which included a café, a slate storytelling area and a small play park. But our favourite part was always the mini cave built into a grassy mound with a slate lined tunnel leading to it. A grate in its roof allowed people to peep down at you when you reached the cold, damp centre of the cave, which oddly had parts of dolls and cars embedded into its walls. Close to the car park were three chairs made of curved pipes with tall wooden backs, in graded sizes, that we named the 'Three Bears' Chairs'. We have many photos from over the years of us all sitting on various ones of these and looking back at them, have enjoyed comparing the size of our boys as they were growing up. The mansion, Plas Glynllifon, which dates from the 1800s, has changed hands many times over the years and has recently undergone renovation, after having a short unsuccessful period as a hotel. In addition to being the site for an agricultural college, Glynllifon is also home to the lesser horseshoe bat and is a maternity and hibernation site for about 6% of the UK population, making it a Special Area of Conservation.

Due to the tides, our return journey had to be along the A499 until the junction for Aberdesach, which meant missing out Pontllyfni beach. Not far beyond the junction for the beach, we passed Caen y Morfa Dairy Farm, which had a sign advertising that it was one of the suppliers of milk to South Caernarfonshire Creameries who produce the local Dragon produce. We frequently pass the creamery which is in Chwilog, just a couple of miles from our caravan site and regularly buy the cheeses which are available in most of the local shops. Just before the junction for Aberdesach, was a sign we hadn't previously taken much notice of when passing in the car. A geometric stone sculpture, bearing a plaque with the familiar image of the chough announced that we were now entering into 'Llŷn – Area of Outstanding Natural Beauty.' We didn't need telling this, after admiring the hills of Yr Eifl, Gyrn Goch, Gyrn Ddu and Moel Penllechog for the majority of our return walk. Before returning to the caravan, we had a vital mission to complete – a visit to Nefyn to sample the goods at the recently opened Becws Islyn café and bakery by the beach. We weren't disappointed as we sat and enjoyed coffee and croissants watching the tide rolling in!

Area of Outstanding Natural Beauty sign along the A499.

Walk 39

A Crowded Mountain and a Woman made of Flowers

Glynllifon Estate to Morfa Dinlle –
18th July 2021

Our car thermometer registered 23 degrees as we arrived at the sea front car park at Morfa Dinlle just before 7.30 am. We were in the midst of a heatwave and the following day the Met Office issued the first ever heat warning for the U.K. with temperatures reaching as high as 33 degrees in western areas. Everywhere was asleep and only a few low fluffy clouds were scattered across a clear azure sky as we set off along the road towards Dinas Dinlle less than half a mile away, with the iron age fort dominating our view. This was another 'back to front' walk and our reason on this occasion was so that on our return we could enjoy a dip in the sea to cool off.

As we looked back, the south west shores of Ynys Môn looked a stone's throw away and eastwards the Snowdonia Mountain range looked near enough to walk to. The Welsh words for Snowdonia and Mount Snowdon are Eryri and Yr Wyddfa. As I write this, there are ongoing discussions about a motion brought forward in April 2021 by a Gwynedd County councillor that they both be referred to by their Welsh names only. From now on in this book, I will refer to them by their Welsh names. **Yr Wyddfa** means 'the grave' and there is a legend associated with it. It is said that an ancient Welsh king, named Rhita Gawr, who had a bit of a

Morfa Dinlle

thing about beards, was killed by King Arthur and was buried at the summit. We have travelled to the summit of Yr Wyddfa by train with Tom and Simon a couple of times and Tom and Rhi have climbed it on foot. It has always been popular with walkers and attracted crowds of people in the summer months, but never as many as had been visiting during the pandemic. At the beginning of the Lockdown in March 2020, it was reported that there were so many people on the summit that it was impossible to maintain effective social distancing! In January 2021, the Eryri National Park Authority closed all of its car parks to stop visitors who were breaking COVID-19 lockdown laws, which at that time were banning people from unnecessary travel. I used to think I'd like to walk to the summit of Yr Wyddfa, but now I'm satisfied with walking the hills of Llŷn instead, where the views are as stunning and people are scarcer. We'll continue to admire Yr Wyddfa from a distance, either from our walks or from the living room window of our caravan, when the mist and clouds allow!

We passed the beautiful sandy shoreline at Dinas Dinlle, which is backed by an area of stone and pebble, then strolled by the row of houses which had a variety of Welsh names. We noticed that a brand-new studio café called **Braf**, had replaced one that we had visited in the past and where I had become star struck on noticing Bryn Terfel, the internationally famous opera singer, dining with his family. The other cafés and shops looked unchanged since our regular visits with the boys when they were younger, as did Wendon Apartments where on several occasions we enjoyed a short easter break. The apartments are housed within a large, attractive white four storey building that dominates the beach road and offer stunning views of the sea from the front and Eryri from the back. We were told by the friendly landlady on our visits in the 2000s that it had originally been built as a hotel, as there had been plans for the railway line to be laid close to Dinas Dinlle promenade, but this never materialised.

We followed the road bearing left out of the village, passing a children's play park at the foot of the hillfort. The hillfort is owned by the National Trust and is a Site of Special Scientific Interest due to the glacial sediments which can be seen in the exposed sections in the cliff face. A fifth of the fort has been lost due to erosion and there are fears that within the next 500 years, it will

Heading towards Dinas Dinlle and the hillfort.

be lost completely. It is thought to be Iron Age, but excavations in August 2019 revealed Roman coins and artefacts in addition to a stone-built roundhouse a few metres from the cliff edge. The fort (and subsequently the village) is supposedly named after legendary Mabinogi character Lleu Llaw Gyffes (translates as lion of the steady hand), who was said to have been brought up here, **Din** meaning fort and **Lle** being short for Lleu. He was twin brother to Dylan, son of Arianrhod, nephew of Gwydion, as mentioned earlier and also featured in the *Math, Mab Mathonwy* story. In the story Arianrhod disowned her son and cursed him so he would never possess a name, bear arms or marry. With the help of Gwydion's magic, she was tricked into naming him and bestowing arms upon him. He was also given a beautiful wife, Blodeuwedd, conjured for him out of flowers. Lleu became lord of Gwynedd and Gwydion is said to be buried in Morfa Dinlle. Shortly after this walk, we heard that further excavations were about to take place.

The sun was steadily rising and we were beginning to feel the heat as we passed private houses with their sickly-sweet smelling privet hedges which were now in full bloom. We tried to stay in the shade as much as possible as we strode out along the road. Occasional gaps in the brambly hedgerows alongside farmers' fields revealed horses or sheep grazing and views of Yr Eifl in the distance. Trees lined the road for a while, giving us much appreciated shade and we passed some large houses and farms. Dog roses, meadowsweet, honeysuckle and yellow toadflax grew amongst the brambles and we eventually reached the A499, where a sign at the junction told us Caernarfon was ten miles left and Pwllheli 14 miles right. We turned right and crossed the road, which was surprisingly busy for an early Sunday morning, and continued along the path running between the A499 and the overgrown wall of Glynllifon Estate. As we looked back, we could just make out the gateway to Parc Glynllifon. An archway of trees protected us from the sun and the noise of the traffic, but our homemade fly repellent didn't seem to be working very well and we both got bitten by midges and horseflies. A lot of the old wall was covered in ivy but every so often we got a glimpse of the stones, some of which were

crumbling. A large, modern mock wood double gate looked rather out of place along this ancient wall and was the entry to Mount Pleasant Lodge, another house on the Glynllifon Estate. But a little further along, a much smaller single, iron studded wooden gate looked very old and more in keeping with it,

Plas Newydd Gateway, A499.

possibly an original one from when the wall was built. We finally arrived at the driveway of Plas Newydd with its large gate posts and metal gates which allowed a sneaky peek into the lush lawned grounds of this 'impressive moated Manor House Listed Grade II* occupying a tranquil rural position' as it was described in an estate agent's online sales booklet. We didn't put in an offer!

We trudged back in the increasing heat and Dinas Dinlle was beginning to come alive. People were already swimming or riding their horses in the sea and the cafés were beginning to open up to customers. Thankfully the car park at Morfa Dinlle was still very quiet and I was able to discreetly change into my swimming costume. The sea was very calm and cold, perfect for a swim after our hot walk. I had to keep an eye on the occasional jelly fish that floated by, but otherwise it was heavenly. Jim cooled off by paddling whilst being entertained by the small pleasure flight planes taking off from the nearby airport.

The Sounds of a Curlew and a Concrete Festival

Morfa Dinlle to Y Foryd – 31st July 2021

What a difference two weeks had made. The sky was filled with heavy grey clouds and there was a cool breeze as we set off from the car park at Morfa Dinlle. We had invested in a new pop-up beach tent since our last visit to make changing into swim things easier, but we didn't need it today. I was still buzzing from the night before, when we had been to our first live gig since pre-covid times. It was an outdoor event and the first day of the 'Concrete Festival' **Gŵyl Goncrit**, held in the loading bay of Pontio Arts Centre in Bangor. On our way over from the car park, we had seen the first act, Eve Goodman, who was very familiar to us as we had seen her at several small gigs in Caernarfon. She spotted us and came over to say hello and we all realised that the last time we'd seen her was at her last gig (and ours), before Lockdown in March 2020, which had been part of the Women's Festival. She told us about some of the songs she would be performing later including one called Neurodiversity, which was inspired by a book she had read recently about the difficulties that women with autism are often faced with. She was surprised to hear that I worked with people with autism. Eve was first heard (but not seen) on a

Morfa Dinlle

YouTube video in 2010 at the age of 15 singing her own beautiful arrangement of a traditional Welsh folk song *Dacw Nghariad*. The video has been watched over 1.6 million times and this mystery singer with the unique, clear voice was spoken of often by Welsh learners on the SSIW forum, before she finally emerged and began to give live performances. The setting of the festival sounded cold and hard, but it was nothing of the sort. There was a wonderful, warm atmosphere, with people like ourselves keen to return to enjoying the sounds of the local talent. We were all seated on our own camping chairs with blankets to keep off the night chill and with the obligatory two metres distance between each family group. Seagulls regularly flew across the loading bay and much to the amusement of all, often cried out in perfect time to the music being played. There was an interval in between the second performers Plu and the final act Cowbois Rhos Botwnnog. On our way back from the loo, we were greeted like old friends by Elan, the lead singer of Plu, who was surprised to see us so far from home as she remembered seeing us in Manchester as well as in Llŷn. The evening ended with the lively rocking sounds of the 'Cowbois' as they're often known and some of the audience danced. We tapped our feet and saved our energy for the following morning's walk. Oh yes that's where I was, walking, at Morfa Dinlle...

We followed the old tarmac path, which used to be the main road before erosion enforced the need for a new road behind this. Pretty daisy like sea mayweed was growing amongst the pebbles alongside the path, with sea thrift now browning after the couple of weeks of hot sun. We reached the locked gates for Fort Belan (more about this place later), with its private driveway beyond and we turned right along the main road towards Caernarfon Airport. As we passed this small airport, we reminisced about visits there with the boys or just the two of us, either to see the Air Museum or for a pleasure flight. During our honeymoon, Jim and I had taken a pleasure flight from there and I use the term pleasure a little reluctantly. It was a pleasure for Jim, who loves being in the air, but not so much for me. I loved the amazing views as we flew over Yr Wyddfa, but hated the feeling of my stomach trying to jump out of my mouth every time the plane banked over to allow us a better view. The pilot seemed to do it all the more when he saw the look of horror on my face, until Jim kindly asked him to ease up. Tom has inherited his dad's love of flight; his first passion was hot air balloons from toddlerhood onwards and he has terrified me twice by flying along the mile long, 500-foot high zipline over Penrhyn Quarry. Jim and Tom enjoyed a pleasure flight together across Llŷn in 2013, to celebrate Jim's 60th birthday and Tom's 18th. Three years ago, as another birthday treat, Tom and Jim had a helicopter pleasure flight from Caernarfon Airport across Llŷn, but Simon, Tom's partner Rhi and I kept our feet firmly on the ground at the caravan and waved at them as they flew over, taking photos of them as they took some of us and the surrounding area.

Opposite the airport was a large derelict brick building, where sheep wandered in and out. We presumed it was from WW2 times as we spotted the sign on one of the airport buildings 'RAF Llandwrog 1941 – 1955'. The airport originally opened in 1941 as RAF Llandwrog Base and was mostly used for training gunners, radio operators and navigators. It later also became the home of the RAF Mountain Rescue. One of the four Wales Air Ambulance helicopters is now based at this airport and is easily spotted when on its travels, by its bright yellow colour. The road continued past the remaining airport buildings on our left and fields of grazing cows on our right. Pied wagtails lined the wire fence of the airport, their tails rapidly wagging of course. The first Welsh bird's name I learnt was from our peninsula friend Brian who told us that the

Caernarfon airport at Morfa Dinlle.

pied wagtail was called a **sigl-di-gwt** (shake your bum) – I love the Welsh language! We passed another derelict building, covered with ivy, with swallows darting in and out of the numerous windows.

Cars and cyclists passed us along the road and we arrived at the entry to Morfa Lodge Holiday Park, which had an old rundown building at its gateway that we later found out had been Morfa Calvinistic Methodist Chapel, built in the late 1800s and in use until 1997. A narrowing stone path took us past the side of the park and led us through an archway of trees with a metal kissing gate at the end. We turned right onto the wide, raised grassy path which crossed the marshland, from where the area gets its name; **Morfa** means marshland. The tall grass verges of the path were burnt and yellowed from the recent heatwave. We were now following the edge of the estuary **Y Foryd**. Y Foryd was designated a Site of Special Scientific Interest in 1971 and became a Local Nature Reserve in 1993, because of the birds and other wildlife it attracts. A flock of about 15 honking Canada geese flew high above our heads and then over the airport. We were feeling much warmer, without the sea breeze to cool us down now, as we trudged along the uneven path, avoiding puzzling burrows that were scattered along it and looked too large to have been made by rabbits. At the edge of the estuary, I was excited to see another egret and was thrilled when it decided to fly low to a larger group of them further along the bay, showing off its stunning pure white wings, slender neck and long grey legs.

The path bore left and a wooden bridge took us across the river Carrog, which feeds into the estuary. We continued along the narrowing path between overgrown hedgerows and trees until we reached a wooden gate, beyond which the path opened out. We could see houses ahead and shortly passed a large one which stood out from the others, with its bright red paint work. We strode through a gateway alongside it, following the ivy-covered gable end until we reached a blue painted house immediately before we reached the junction with a B road. A home-made sign pointed back towards **Tai Coch Chatham** (Chatham's red houses) which were holiday cottages. At the junction was a sign for 'Sain,' which is a recording studio situated not too far down the lane ahead of us, but today we needed to turn left and continue along the road. As the road bore right, we could see the tower of 'White Tower

Holiday Park' further ahead, but we took the tarmac lane, which was the coastal path, to the left, with its hedgerows filled with sweet smelling honeysuckle. Rows of caravans on the site peeped above the hedgerow and after a short distance we reached a bungalow on our left which sat on the eastern edge of the estuary. We stopped for a while to watch the birds on the mudflats and we could see the same group of egrets still resting on the opposite side of the bay in the sunshine, occasionally their long orange bills searching in the mud for a treat. Egrets belong to the same family as herons and their Welsh name is creyr bach, which translates as little heron.

The narrow road followed the side of the estuary and we greeted a couple of young walkers, heading in the opposite direction, carrying heavy backpacks and looking rather tired. We wondered if they were walking the coastal path the hard way and wild camping as they went along. Along the hedgerows, bramble flowers were now beginning to give way to blackberries, and sloe berries were looking ripe and ready to pick on the blackthorn bushes. Bales of hay were drying in the hedge-lined farmer's fields beyond. We came upon a bird hide, almost hidden from view by bushes and brambles. We sat inside for a while, watching the salt marshes but not a single bird appeared in view. They had richer pickings in the mud today.

We continued along the road, which was lined with scorched long grass, until we reached Bwthyn y Foryd, a large fort shaped holiday house with a hot tub and stunning views across the estuary. We paused at the edge of Y Foryd again, watching more egrets, black headed and herring gulls, and a pair of swans swimming in the far distance. A few grey birds took flight and I thought I recognised the haunting cry as being that of the curlew. A quick look through the monocular confirmed this, as I could see their long downcurved beaks. We had already decided that this was to be our turning back point.

On our way back, we saw the young hikers again, looking weary and resting on a patch of grass by the roadside and having a picnic. We took a slightly different route back as we had seen an alternative path on our outward walk. We continued straight ahead when we got to the junction near the lane for Sain and not much further along the road, we came upon Blythe Farm Industrial

Estate on the right. We walked through the Estate, passing a garage and a shop selling garden ornaments and antiques, with people busy loading a van with their purchases. The path crossed the river Carrog and immediately after was a high metal gate, which we were surprised to see was locked. We were getting tired and didn't feel like returning the other way and we could see the public footpath directly on the other side. There was a small square gap in the gate and Jim managed to squeeze through it and reassured me that I could get through easily too. I wasn't so sure and had flashbacks from a P.E. lesson in my primary school days. I had put on a bit of puppy fat and we were told to mime the actions of a wild creature, awakening from hibernation from our shelter or nest. Much to my embarrassment, when I'd tried to 'slowly and sleepily' leave my 'nest' (a wooden gym bench), I'd got my bum stuck under it and looked up to see a myriad of faces staring down at me. Like many others, I had put on a few pounds during Lockdown and today I envisaged history repeating itself. Despite my flashback, I gave it a go, and in my own very ungainly fashion, I managed to crawl through the gap, without too much trouble. I was feeling very smug

Crossing the River Carrog at Morfa Dinlle.

at having managed this, until a cyclist came along. He greeted us and stopped at the gate, swung his bike, then himself, around the side of it above the river. He explained that he did this every day to avoid a much longer route home. This path cut between fields of tall grasses with creamy meadowsweet and white yarrow flowers and an abundance of flag irises along the edges, their yellow flowers now long gone.

We soon emerged onto our original path, not far from the airport. As we looked back towards the holiday park, we saw the young couple resting on the grass verge. We wondered if their back packs had become too heavy for them as they didn't look very happy and were doing back stretches. The airport was coming alive, with a small plane and a helicopter taking off, probably with tourists enjoying a pleasure flight. There was a slight hint of blue in the sky but the clouds were still lying heavy on Yr Eifl as we reached the car park.

Not More Cows!

Y Foryd to St Baglan's Church –
1st August 2021

To avoid parking close to housing, we found a safe spot on the main road close to the crossroads signposted for Saron, Dinas and Llandwrog. We then walked back to the previous day's finishing point, south east of the estuary, to complete this short section of the coastal path, before heading in the direction of Caernarfon. As we strode along, a coastguard helicopter flew above our heads and we wondered if it was practising or on a mission. Today was very much like the previous one weather wise, with lots of heavy grey clouds, but with a cooler breeze. The high hedgerows along the road had recently been trimmed back but still allowed very few views beyond. However, these shortly gave way to a sea of tall reeds and Y Foryd came into view. We passed the mudflats, where an old wooden boat was almost buried in the mud. Gulls and egrets were out on the marshland and we could see Yr Eifl in the far distance, with clouds sitting on the summits. We turned around and headed back to the junction where we sat on a bench for a few minutes, trying to identify the mountains in the far distance to the east. We couldn't make out the sharp peak of Yr Wyddfa but using our new mountain peaks identifying apps on our phones, we managed to locate where it was situated and realised it was completely hidden in cloud.

Mudflats at Y Foryd.

We plodded on along the main road through Saron, passing houses and the old Saron Chapel, dated 1901 on the slate plaque above the door. It was a Sunday morning and I thought how different this scene would have been here less than fifty years ago. Villagers would have been scurrying on their way to chapel and chatting to one another, but today it was empty and silent as so many churches and chapels are these days, and even more so since the COVID-19 outbreak. The house next door to the chapel was called **Hen Dŷ Capel** (old chapel house) and looked well maintained and occupied. We passed the playpark, which was deserted. I wondered if this was because of the virus or just a sign of the times, with many children preferring their computers or games consoles to playing outdoors. We passed a small community of houses, some with faded children's pictures of rainbows in the windows, similarly to back home, a reminder that we weren't yet 'out of the woods' as far as COVID-19 was concerned yet. There was recent news of different virus variants and a lot of uncertainty about how things were going to be especially as winter approached. The road narrowed and was lined with tall, dense hedges with an occasional pink foxglove, clumps of blue sheep's bit and yellow meadow peas. We passed the gateway of a large house, Tŷ Cerrig, in its ample grounds, with the river Gwyrfai running through. This river starts in Eryri National Park and ends its journey in Y Foryd, and the tidal channel within the bay flows north into the Menai Straits. We followed the road, which crossed the river via the stone bridge, Pont Faen. At the T-junction shortly after, we turned left,

Y Foryd at Llanfaglan with the political slogan .

rather than continuing straight on to Llanfaglan village. We saw some familiar faces of locals from the day before, on their regular morning walks and the cyclist we'd chatted to passed by and said hello.

Lower hedgerows now allowed views across to Yr Eifl and Dinas Dinlle. Deep pink bell heather and my first sighting of harebells was a

Harebells

reminder that summer was still with us. As we passed the gateway to a farmhouse, we were allowed a view of St Baglan's Church in a field behind and an expanse of the bay further out. We passed a large white house along the lane, with its unimaginative English name 'The White House,' painted on the sign. We joked about it not being a very popular house name these days, after all the trouble President Trump had been causing in the American White House, prior to him finally being usurped by Joe Biden, much to the relief of a large percentage of the world's population. We, and the rest of the world, were still waiting to find out if he would finally be prosecuted for his many misdemeanours including tax evasion.

A little further on the views opened up beautifully, and we could now also see the large hills Gyrn Goch and Gyrn Ddu. We came upon a large concrete sea wall, acting as a barrier along a section of Y Foryd and on the seaward side someone had graffitied 'Cymru is not 4 Sale' with the curved arrow symbol of Cymdeithas Yr Iaith (The Welsh Language Society), yet another sign of the growing concern about the lack of affordable housing in Gwynedd. Several red painted pebbles had been placed close by with the words 'Yes Cymru' written in white. This is the slogan for the non-party-political campaign for an independent Wales. The organisation was formed in 2014 and T-shirts and signs can often be seen with this slogan around many parts of Wales.

We sauntered along the road which was now running alongside Y Foryd estuary, passing the car park and picnic benches, where a large group of cyclists had gathered. I looked ahead to St Baglan's

Church across the fields on the opposite side and was disappointed to see cows surrounding the church. I had been looking forward to having a look around the churchyard and inside the church if it was allowed, as we'd never visited it before. We reached the church gates at the same time as two ladies. The older lady asked if cows were dangerous, as they wanted to take flowers to the graveyard. We shared some of our cow experiences and said that we wouldn't be risking it, but that others feel fine amongst them. The younger lady, who she explained was her daughter, decided to chance it and hurriedly walked across to the churchyard with the bunch of colourful flowers. Her mother stayed with us and explained that the flowers were for her mother and brother. She said they had chosen this spot for her brother to be buried as he had been in the navy and it had a lovely view of the sea. She explained that she was a **Cofi**, the colloquial name for people from Caernarfon. We had a little chat in Welsh about our mutual love of old churches and she described a tiny church in her home town, which was close to the old wall with only a small doorway visible to passers-by. She thought it was the smallest church in Wales and later when we searched for it on Google Maps, the symbol on the door (the only part of the church that was visible to passers-by) suggested it was a Russian Orthodox Church. I was pleased that I'd managed some Welsh chat with her, as Cofis have their own regional dialect and can be tricky to understand, especially by Welsh learners. The younger lady returned unscathed and we said goodbye to her and her mother before heading for the benches to have our packed lunch. I hoped to have a nosy around the church on our next walk, cows permitting.

As we ate our picnic, we looked out across the bay to Fort Belan. This sprawling castellated fort was built in 1775 by Thomas Wynn, who was at that time the M.P. for Caernarfonshire and later became Lord Newborough. Its purpose was to guard Britain's coastline at the time of the American War of Independence, but thankfully it saw no action. It has changed purposes over the years since then and now houses six self-catering cottages, holding up to forty-five people in total. In 1969 Princess Margaret stayed there for the Caernarfon ceremony of the investiture of her nephew Prince Charles when he was given the title of Prince of Wales, an event that doesn't lie comfortably with many Welsh people. Many would like the title to be either scrapped or to see the return of it being given to a native Welshman as was the tradition pre twelfth century. Before heading back, we took turns with the monocular to look at birds further out on the estuary and spotted swans, oystercatchers, Canada geese, egrets and unidentifiable ducks (too far away to see their detail) as well as various types of gulls. What I was most surprised about was the number of crows and rooks happily finding food there amongst the seabirds.

We retrod our steps back to the car and chatted about how our next walk would be the last one of this adventure. At only two miles each way, it should be an easy one, as this one today hadn't felt too strenuous. On our drive home, I put in a request for a detour, as I often do and we parked at the top of the lane near Sain Studio. **Sain** means sound and is said exactly like the English word sign. I'd heard of the place so many times, as many of the singers and musicians we enjoy listening to have recorded here, but I'd never seen the building. The studio was a very short walk from the top of the lane and the first thing I noticed was a brightly painted mural on the side of this small, single storey building, which is hidden away on an industrial estate. The mural was full of portraits of many of the artists who had recorded there, including Cerys Matthews, Bryn Fôn, Plethyn and Elin Fflur and many others I didn't recognise. I felt quite in awe of this rather unassuming place, that had played such an important part in the lives of many great Welsh musicians.

Sain Studios

The Final Walk and a Quiet Celebration

St Baglan's Church to Caernarfon –
13th August 2021

*A celebratory selfie at the end
of our adventure.*

Neither Jim nor I are superstitious, so we found it quite amusing that our last walk happened to be on Friday the thirteenth. Even more amusing was the fact that it was our 42nd walk. Readers of the author Douglas Adams will understand immediately. Jim, Tom and Simon are fans of all things scientific and of science fiction, and Adams's comedy science fiction 'trilogy' (consisting of five books), 'The Hitchhiker's Guide to the Galaxy,' is well known in our house, as is the significance of the number 42. I won't reveal its meaning, in case you haven't read the books, but let's say it was very fitting that our last walk was our 42nd.

We decided to begin in Caernarfon, so that we could finish there for our celebratory lunch. No cheese or egg butties for us today; we were going to live it up! I was even wearing a different dress... and pants! I decided I could manage this straightforward walk of four miles without needing a pee and I doubted there was anywhere secluded enough anyway. We left the car at Cei Llechi car park (the old slate quay), close to the castle, which had often been an extra loo stop on our journeys to Llŷn when the boys were very little. Caernarfon has gradually meant much more to us than a loo stop or a meander around the castle. Galeri especially has been the reason for many of our visits, often for gigs and art exhibitions. In 2019 it was also the venue for a weekend long celebration of ten years of the online course, SSIW, that has meant so much to me on my journey of learning the language. This had involved musical entertainment by local singers, a formal meal and various Welsh language activities around the town of Caernarfon, including a town trail.

As we walked close to the quay at the foot of the castle, the strong sea breeze caused the ropes to rattle on the masts of mooring boats. The bright blue pleasure boat 'Queen of the Sea' sat quietly awaiting the start of her busy day, when she would be taking tourists along the Menai Straits or further on towards Ynys Môn, with the help of Emrys the pilot. Our next stay at the caravan would be the week of our 30th wedding anniversary and we had plans to celebrate this and the end of our journey, with a boat trip being one of our ideas. It was a beautiful clear day in Caernarfon but there were heavy clouds further across Llŷn. A little girl and her grandad were enjoying an early attempt at crabbing off the harbour wall. We crossed Pont yr Aber, over the mouth of the river Seiont where it flows into the Menai Straits (which separates Ynys Môn from mainland Wales), and followed the signs reminding us to 'keep left', to allow two metres social distancing. Since the 7th August, Wales had been at 'Alert Level Zero,' with no legal limits on the number of people who could meet in private homes, public places or at events. All businesses and premises could now also be open. Guidelines were very similar for us at home, but we no longer had to wear masks, whereas in Wales, adults and children over 12 were still required to wear face-coverings in public places, with the exception of hospitality settings such as pubs and cafés, unless requested to do so by the owners.

As we crossed the swing bridge Aber Ferry House was facing us, backed by the woodland Coed Helen. This attractive, Grade II listed building, with a castellated roof, was built in 1822 for the operator of what was known as the Coed Helen ferry, which transported passengers across the river. In 1900, the first swing bridge was built to replace the ferry, and tolls were levied on pedestrians and carriages. This bridge was replaced in 1970 by the current pedestrian bridge, which is made of concrete and steel, and powered with electricity. As you cross, you can still see some of the wooden supports for the original bridge and today we could also see a couple of beautiful swans enjoying the early morning sunshine.

Aber Swing Bridge and the Ferry House.

We strode out along the pavement of Aber Foreshore Road, which skirts the south westerly end of the Menai Straits as it merges with Y Foryd. As we passed the gateway for Coed Helen Park, the road narrowed and the pavement ended so we walked single file for much of the rest of the way. To our right, we had an expansive view of Ynys Môn across the tidal waters of the Straits. The strong smell of seaweed and the cry of gulls made me feel quite invigorated as we sauntered on, watching the sea with the strong sea breeze in our faces. I was glad of my pants! I heard the eerie sound of curlews again and two of them took flight from the shore. Curlew in Welsh is **gylfinir**, which means long beak and its beautiful high-pitched cry is able to conjure up an image of the coast more than anything for me. Two young men were out on the muddy shore collecting mussels, or maybe oysters, in buckets, as the tide slowly worked its way towards them. Oystercatchers chattered away as they plunged their long orange beaks into the mud to catch their prey – probably also mussels or oysters, which are both farmed on the Ynys Môn side of the Straits. A solitary egret was joining them for breakfast, but a large grey heron flew towards it and scared it into flight. This was a treat for us as it was the first time either of us had seen an egret in proper full flight, with its large pure white wings spread fully – what a majestic sight.

We passed the sign for Llanfaglan and meandered past the golf clubhouse, with people beginning to arrive for an early round. Ripening blackberries and rose hips made me think about the changing seasons and there was an autumnal feel to the day. There were plenty of runners and cyclists passing us and I wondered if there had been an increase in these two activities around this area since Lockdown, as there seemed to have been back home. We noticed a private enclosed dry dock opposite the owner's home, then a little further along were several boats on an open dry dock – a grass verge. As the road curved to the left, we got a good view of Fort Belan at the end of the dunes in Morfa Dinlle. Owain, our young peninsula friend had told us recently that weddings were often held here and that he had attended once with his band to entertain the guests. My naturalist app (not naturist as I have been known to call it – yet another of my malaprops!), helped me to identify the tall dandelion like flowers growing in the grass verges as autumn hawkbit, which reinforced my thoughts about summer being on its way out. There was also sea mayweed and white sea campion and a multitude of large clumps of dock leaves and their tall, rather unattractive red-brown flowers.

The field where St Baglan's church is sited came into view, and we could just make out the outline of the church, amidst the groups of trees and the low stone wall which surround it. To my disappointment, scattered within the church grounds were... yes, you've guessed it...cows! There seemed even more than there had been at out last visit and as we got nearer, we could see that they were much closer to the gate and to the path leading to the church.

St Baglan's Church.

I added the church to my mental list of places to revisit, but just as we were about to turn around to walk back to Caernarfon, a tractor appeared and the farmer quickly and skillfully herded the cows into the next field. I couldn't believe our luck! This was the second time this had happened for us on our coastal walks. I was all smiles as we marched across the field to visit the church. The church is owned by the charity Friends of Friendless Churches, who in Wales are funded by Cadw and the Church in Wales, but in England rely on donors and members. We were pleasantly surprised to find the church unlocked and enjoyed the shelter from the breeze as we read the leaflet and looked for its main features. Its oldest feature is a pillar-stone, discovered in 1855, and now built into the interior of the church above the doorway. It has been dated to the fifth or early sixth century and an inscription in Roman capitals dedicates it to one Anatemor, son of Lovernius. The church's patron is Baglan ap Dingad, a sixth century saint associated with Ynys Enlli. The church has been refurbished over the centuries, but the body of it dates from the thirteenth century. We admired the eighteenth-century wooden seating of box pews and benches, some with the year 1737 and 1769 carved into them. The leaflet explained that due to the building of a new church for the parish in 1871, St Baglan's escaped the hands of Victorian restorers, and the seating arrangement (ensuring that every seat faced the pulpit), is one of only two surviving, unaltered in Wales. Anthony Armstrong-Jones, photographer and designer, but more famously known as having been the former husband of the Queen's sister Princess Margaret, was buried in the churchyard in 2017.

With the breeze now behind us, we set off back to Caernarfon and seemed to arrive in half the time it had taken us to do the outward walk! As we approached the swing bridge, we saw the pleasure boat, on its way out towards Ynys Môn, and at my request we stopped for a rare event...a selfie taken with my phone camera. We had taken many photos of our walks but these were usually of the views and perhaps sometimes with the back of one of us in the foreground, but I felt that this moment needed to be marked with a picture of the two of us with Caernarfon in the background. As we crossed the bridge, the sun was now shining and I had a spring in my step, as we smiled and acknowledged to one another that we'd 'done it!'

Caernarfon had woken up in our absence and was buzzing with tourists in the sunshine. Some were looking out from the viewing ledges of the castle across the car park that was heaving with people. Our first stop was the loo then a change of shoes at the car. We then dodged families taking photographs of each other, with the castle in the background. Edward 1 built Caernarfon castle, the town walls and Harlech castle, between the late thirteenth century and early fourteenth century, following the war between England and Wales. Prior to this, Edward and his army had defeated the Welsh in 1283 and they marched through northern Wales capturing Welsh castles. These included Dolwyddelan castle, which was built by Llywelyn the Great when he was King of Gwynedd, and Dolbadarn castle which was built by Dafydd ap Gruffudd, who was Llywelyn's grandson and also brother of Llywelyn ap Gruffudd, the last sovereign prince of Wales. The exterior of Caernarfon castle was mostly completed but many of the building plans remained incomplete and none of the interior buildings remain. It has seen many battles throughout the centuries up until the English Civil War in the mid-seventeenth century, after which it was then neglected until the nineteenth century when the state funded repairs. It is currently cared for by Cadw and is a huge attraction for visitors to the area.

When we saw the crowds, we were wondering if we should have booked a table somewhere for lunch. We crossed the square, Y Maes, but the small café there that we are fond of was very busy. We continued along Stryd y Plas and passed Palas Print bookshop, where I love to browse and from where we have often picked up gig tickets. The street, which is possibly the Welshest street in Wales and lined with small local businesses, was buzzing and all of its cafés were heaving with people. A fairly recent addition to the street is Llety Arall, a community owned business offering accommodation and promising a taste of local culture, ideal for Welsh learners. We continued along **Stryd Pedwar a Chwech** (four and six street) and passed the Black Boy Inn, which was built in the sixteenth century and is one of the oldest inns in North Wales. The street is said to have got its name from the price that sailors were reputed to have paid for a room, a bottle of gin and a woman for the night at this inn or any other in the Northgate area as this was the red-light district many years ago! I had a pub lunch at the Black

Boy not too long ago, with other Welsh learners as part of the SSIW tenth birthday celebrations and can vouch that it is now a highly respectable establishment! We wandered out of the centre along Balaclava Road, towards Doc Fictoria, where we came across a new café called **Tŷ Winsh** (winch house), which was housed in a small, old, single storey stone building, that we remembered being used for art workshops and displays not too long ago. We decided to give the place a try as there were plenty of tables available. At the doorway, the hand sanitiser and notice asking people to wear masks were reminders of the continuing concern about the virus. A friendly Welsh lady guided us to our seats as we admired the café interior, which was freshly painted white and had a nautical theme. We ordered a Welsh vegetarian breakfast with Glamorgan sausages **selsig Morgannwg**, made with leeks and cheese. I chatted in Welsh with the lady who took our order, asking her how business had been for the café and she explained that they had opened just before the initial Lockdown in March 2020, so it had been difficult, but that in the last few weeks it had been very busy. I told her that this meal was to celebrate the end of our coastal path walk. She applauded us with the wonderful Welsh word for congratulations – **Llongyfarchiadau** – it rolls off the tongue after a few practices! As we waited for our food, I wondered about the original purpose of the building and imagined goods having been transported via a winch to and from the dock, which is not too far behind it. I asked the different lady who brought our food, and who Jim and I thought looked familiar, but she was uncertain. She proudly told us that our tomatoes had been grown in her greenhouse and we tucked into our meal, which was delicious. After a celebratory cake each, we paid our bill and I chatted in Welsh to the familiar looking lady at the till. I told her that we both thought that she looked familiar, but we couldn't work out where we may have seen her before. As we said our goodbyes and left, I realised that instead of saying that she looked familiar, I'd said that she looked likely! From her response, she'd clearly picked up the meaning of my sentence and was being polite in not mentioning my mistake. It seems I'm a master at malaprops in Welsh as well as English now. I later examined an online map from the late 1800s which showed some kind of track leading from the back of the café building to the dock, along which I presume the winching took place. I contacted

Caernarfon archives via email to ask what they knew of Tŷ Winsh and received a very quick and helpful response. They explained that directly behind the building was the Patent Slip, which was built in 1830 and sloped down to the Menai Straits. It was used for ship building and renovation and local people were paid to help haul ships up the slope onto the slipway before the introduction of mechanical winches. The slipway continued to be used for Doc Fictoria, which was constructed in the later 1800s and can still be seen being used for boat repairs today.

On the way back to the caravan, we called at Parc Glynllifon and sat outside the Black Cat Café, eating an ice-cream and listening to a young girl playing traditional Welsh folk songs (as well as a bit of Ed Sheeran) on the harp in the afternoon sunshine. We couldn't resist a quick sit and photo shoot on the 'three bears' chairs' (mentioned earlier) on our way back to the car.

That evening, we had another treat by visiting friends Amanda, Brian, Elain and Owain at their farmhouse for the first time we had been able to since the initial lockdown in March 2020. For the first time ever, I had to say no to Amanda's amazing selection of homemade cakes as I was still stuffed from our earlier treats. She showed us her copy of the *Curo'r Corona'n Coginio* recipe book, recently produced by Merched y Wawr containing many of the shared recipes from the Facebook page including one of hers – **Bisgedi Anti Elin** (Auntie Elin's biscuits). That night, we sent messages to Tom and Simon, to share the good news that we had finished the coastal path walk and they were just as pleased as we were. Although neither of them had joined us on any of these walks due to their own commitments, we'd thought of them both on each and every one and laughed and cried at so many memories that flooded back as we revisited special family places. We're sure that they will have many more journeys and adventures of their own in the future and I hope that the Llŷn coastal path will continue to be safe and available in case they decide to literally follow in our footsteps one day.

The walk had been a challenge for us at times but a huge amount of fun too and we both felt a great sense of achievement. Over the course of our 42 walks, almost 200 miles in total (100 each way), I had learnt even more about the culture and the people of this beautiful part of Wales and I had also increased my Welsh vocabulary, especially with nature related words such as **gwyddfid** (honeysuckle). Yes, I know I mentioned it a lot, but it smells and looks so good! We will continue to put one foot in front of the other for as long as our legs will take them and we will never be short of places to discover in Llŷn.

What Next? Be' Nesa?

As I write this, October is almost upon us and the shops are stocking Christmas stuff! We, like most people, hope for a healthy and happy future ahead of us. COVID-19 looks like it's here to stay, but with vaccinations and continuing research, it will hopefully be controlled in the same way as flu, and people will be able to go about their normal activities. Last week, I got on a bus for the first time since March 2020, attended my first face to face meet up with fellow Welsh learners in Manchester city centre and enjoyed a look around the art gallery. It felt wonderful. I'm looking ahead optimistically to 2022 and anticipating the return of lots of enjoyable events and activities in Llŷn, including live gigs, festivals and sitting around the fire in the roundhouse at Felin Uchaf, being enchanted by Dafydd's storytelling sessions once more. Neuadd Dwyfor, the library, cinema and theatre in Pwllheli is currently closed for renovation so I'm looking forward to the reopening and being able to watch films, plays and shows there again, which are regularly offered in Welsh and in English.The local Welsh language newspapers are now back in the shops and I noticed that Llŷn's September edition had reintroduced the events column, Y Dyddiadur. It had only three events listed, but it's a start. Yr Heliwr community pub in Nefyn has reopened after its renovation, and is welcoming locals and visitors back once again. Pwllheli has now got a new traditional Welsh café, close to the beach. The derelict beachside café mentioned in the Pwllheli to Penrhos walk, has finally taken on a new lease of life and reopened as Caffi Largo at the end of June. It took its name from a poem, by the Pwllheli poet Sir Albert Evans-Jones CBE, more commonly known by his bardic name Cynan. Cynan was born in 1895 in Penlan Street and a slate plaque can be seen on the front of the house which is currently the business premises for Strain and Company Solicitors. In the poem, Largo is a sailor who captures a mermaid, and along one wall of the café, Darren Evans has created yet another stunning mural which depicts the story. The café is a great place for Welsh learners to immerse themselves in the language as the staff are all Welsh speaking as are the majority of customers, and popular Welsh music can usually be heard playing in the background. There is exiting news about the new community garden café at Felin Uchaf, which is due to open next year, with fresh ingredients being provided from the organic garden. We were honoured to contribute a small amount to the Crowdfunding campaign that was set up to help to support this, and in return there will be a slate tile, carved with **teulu Brandwood** (Brandwood family) on the wall around the outside of the café, amongst those of other contributors. Two other new businesses began to take shape following the pandemic, both of which I am yet to visit. The old Caernarfon Harbour Office building and some adjoining derelict buildings are being transformed into a site which will house 19 workspaces for local artisan and craft manufacturers as well as some self-catering accommodation. As I write this, some craft shops are hoping to open there before the end of 2021 and the site is now named Cei Llechi (slate quay). At the other end of the peninsula is Plas Carmel, a community project which is restoring and reviving Capel Carmel and the old shop, Siop Plas, in Anelog, to create a cultural site. Their café is almost ready to open! Unfortunately, the Pwllheli Welsh learner conversation group, that I attended whenever I was able, has not reconvened since the COVID-19 outbreak and sadly the café 'Gwalia,' where it was held each Saturday has had to close. Only the bakery at the front remains but is still worth a visit for delicious locally baked goods or Welsh Lady preserves.

There is optimism that the Welsh language is going to remain and grow throughout Wales, as well as throughout many other parts of the world. During the COVID-19 Lockdowns, it was reported that thousands of people had used their free time to learn Welsh. In 2020, Duolingo, the world's most popular language app, announced in its report that Welsh was the fastest growing language in the UK, with a 44% increase in learners. It also reported a huge interest from many other parts of the world. I'm hopeful that the Welsh government's aim of 'Cymraeg 2050' will be reached. I will always be indebted to SSIW for giving me this beautiful language. Deservedly they are going from strength to strength, and continuing to offer a plethora of resources for learners of all levels. More signs have appeared on our route towards the caravan, asking in Welsh and English for the selling of houses as second homes to be capped, with concern especially about Morfa Nefyn and Nefyn. There is news that the primary school in Abersoch will be closed by the end of the year, due to the small number of children now attending. This is seen by some as being directly related to the fact that 39% of homes in Abersoch are now second homes. The appeal of Llŷn to us and to many other visitors is its uniqueness as a place that has retained so much of its Welsh culture and especially the language. It would be very sad to see this disappear in the future. It would be great to see an increased awareness of the Welsh language and indeed other minority languages used in the UK, such as Gaelic and Cornish. Welsh could be incorporated into the National Curriculum for languages in schools throughout the UK outside of Wales, with some lessons on the history and culture of Wales thrown in. I wonder how many children are aware that Tolkien was a scholar of the Welsh language and used it for the foundation of Sindarin, one of the Elvish languages he created for Lord of the Rings. Tolkien had a lifelong love of **Cymraeg** and is quoted as having said 'Welsh is of this soil, this island, the senior language of the men of Britain; and Welsh is beautiful'. If children received just a few lessons on the Welsh alphabet, they would at least be able to pronounce the names of the places in Wales that they were visiting on holiday or at the weekends.

During our final few coastal path walks, our conversation often turned to ideas of what to do once we had completed them. We both agreed that we would like to do some more hill walks, perhaps starting with Garn Ganol, the tallest of Llŷn's hills. We have done many of the hills in Llŷn with the boys, but not this one. The day after our final coastal walk, I'd gone into Pwllheli to call at the book shop Llen Llŷn. I bought a copy of the Merched y Wawr cookery book and another book that filled my mind with anticipation and excitement – *Walking the Llŷn Hills* by Des Marshall. This very interesting book catalogues the hills of Llŷn in order of height and gives maps and suggested routes. 'Just what we needed,' I thought. The dilemma we are now faced with is whether to start with the lowest or the highest of the hills. If we start with the lowest, we can gradually prepare our knees for the highest, but of course as the heights of the hills increase, so do our years! Something to consider, but not for too long!

Appendix

afon – river

bach/fach – small

bryn – hill

cadair/gadair – chair

caer – fort

capel – chapel

carn/garn – a cairn (burial mound) and often used as part of the name of
a hill with a cairn on the summit such as Garn Ganol

carreg – rock

castell – castle

cefn – back

cegin/gegin – kitchen

cei – quay

coed/goed – tree

cychod – boats

ddol – meadow

doc – dock

fawr – large

ffordd – road

ffynnon – well

Eryri – Snowdonia

gwylan – seagull

hafan – haven

llan – parish

llyn – lake (notice there is no accent as in Llŷn)

lôn – lane

maen – stone

maes – field or area

moel- hill with a bare summit

môr – sea

mynydd – mountain, but sometimes used for larger hills

nant – valley

newydd – new

ogof – cave

penrhyn – headland or promontory

plas – hall

pont – bridge

porth – harbour or gateway

rhes – terrace

stryd – street

swnt – sound

traeth – beach

trwyn – nose

tŷ – house

ynys – island

Ynys Enlli – Bardsey Island, the island off the tip of Llŷn

Ynys Môn – Anglesey

Yr Eifl – a range of three hills in Llŷn

Yr Wyddfa – Mount Snowdon

Shops, Cafes and Other Small Businesses or Artists Mentioned in the Book

Most of these also have websites and Facebook pages.

Becws Islyn bakery and café – Aberdaron, LL53 8BE

Becws Islyn bakery and café – The Beach, Nefyn LL53 6ED

Browsers Bookshop – 73 High St, Porthmadog LL49 9EU

Cadwaladers café and ice-cream shop – Castle Street, Cricieth, LL52 0DP

Caffi Largo – Embankment Road, Pwllheli LL53 5AB

Caffi Ni, Nefyn – Wern Caravan Park, Pistyll, Gwynedd, LL53 6LW

Caffi Porthdinllaen – Golf Road, Morfa Nefyn, Pwllheli, Ll53 6BE

Caffi Porthor – The Beach, Porthor, LL53 8LH

Caffi Tŷ Winsh – Balaclava Road, Caernarfon, LL55 1SR

Caffi Tŷ Newydd – Tŷ Newydd Farm, Uwchmynydd, LL53 8BY

Cei Llechi – Caernarfon, LL55 2PB

Coastal Painters and Decorators (Darren Evans) – 07580 406928 and see Facebook

Cwrw Llŷn brewery, shop and bar – 1 Parc Eithin, Ffordd Dewi Sant, Nefyn LL53 6EG

Cwt Tatws shop and café – Towyn, Tudweiliog, LL53 8PD

Dwyfor Coffee – Parc Dwyfor, Nefyn, LL53 6EG

Dylan's Restaurant, Cricieth – Maes y Môr, Cricieth, LL52 0HU

Felin Uchaf – Rhoshirwaun, LL53 8HS

Galeri Caernarfon – Doc Victoria, Caernarfon, LL55 1SQ

Glasu icecream shop – 3-4 Mitre Terrace, Pwllheli, LL53 5HE

Gwalia bakery – 82 High Street, Pwllheli, LL53 5RR

HM Catering (pizza van) – order online – https://hmcatering.f4food.net/table

Hefin Underwood Monumental Masons, New Street, Pwllheli, LL53 5HT

Llen Llŷn book and music shop – 5-6 Mitre Terrace, Pwllheli, LL53 5HE

Llety Arall – 9 Stryd y Plas, Caernarfon, LL55 1RR

Llŷn Maritime Museum – Old St Mary's Church, Stryd y Llan, Nefyn, LL53 6LB

Menai Cruises – Queen of the Sea – Caernarfon Harbour Trust, Slate Quay, Caernarfon LL55 2PB

Nant Gwrtheyrn National Welsh Language and Heritage Centre – Llithfaen, LL53 6NL

Neuadd Dwyfor library, cinema and theatre – 19 Penlan Street, Pwllheli, LL53 5DE

Oriel y Môr Tonnau art gallery shop – 21 Penlan Street, Pwllheli, LL53 5DE

Palas Print bookshop – 10 Stryd y Plas, Caernarfon, LL55 1RR

Parc Glynllifon and the **Black Cat Café** – Clynnog Road, Caernarfon, LL54 5DY

Plas Carmel – café and visitor centre – Anelog, Aberdaron, Pwllheli, LL53 8LL

Plas Glyn y Weddw art gallery and café – Llanbedrog, LL53 7TT

Pontio Arts Centre – Bangor University, Deiniol Rd, Bangor LL57 2TQ

Sain Recording Studio – Canolfan Sain, Llandwrog, Caernarfon, Gwynedd, LL54 5TG

Saysomethingin.com – Online Welsh language courses – www.saysomethingin.com

Siop Shop – Welsh café in Manchester – 53 Tib Street, Manchester M4 1LS

Tafarn y Fic community pub – Llithfaen, LL53 6PA

Treddafydd Organic Farm – treddafyddorganic.co.uk

Tŷ Coffi café – 47 Ffordd Gwenllian, Nefyn, LL53 6ND

Tyddyn Sachau garden centre and café – Y Ffôr, LL53 6UB

Welsh Lady Preserves – Bryn, Y Ffôr, LL53 6RL (also available in many local shops)

Yr Heliwr community pub – Y Groes, Nefyn, LL53 6HH

Ynys Enlli/Bardsey Island Boat Trips, Colin Evans – 07971 769 895

Artists, Musicians and Writers Mentioned in the Book

Most of the current artists, musicians and authors can be found on Facebook or Twitter.

To purchase art work, books or music by any of the below, try shops Oriel y Môr Tonnau, Llen Llŷn in Pwllheli, Browsers Bookshop in Porthmadog and Palas Print in Caernarfon (see addresses above)

Al Lewis – singer (pop/folk)

Alys Williams – singer (pop/folk/jazz)

Bendith – musical band (pop/folk/indie) – collaboration between band Plu and singer Carwyn Ellis

Bob Delyn a'r Ebillion – musical band (folk/rock) – lead singer is Twm Morys

Bryn Terfel – singer (bass-baritone opera and concert)

Calan – musical band (folk)

Carwyn Ellis – singer (alternative/indie)

Carys Bryn – artist

Catatonia – musical band (alternative rock)

Catrin Finch – harpist

Ceiriog/ John Ceiriog Hughes – poet (1832 – 1887)

Cerys Matthews – singer (pop/rock/folk)

Christine Evans - poet

Cian Parry Owen – artist

Cowbois Rhos Botwnnog – musical band (folk/country/rock)

Cynan/ Sir Albert Evans-Jones – poet (1895 – 1970)

Dafydd Owen/Dafydd y Garreg Wen – harpist (1711 – 1741)

Dewi 'Pws' Morris – actor/singer

D J Williams – one of 'The Three' – writer (1885 – 1970)

Duffy – singer (pop)

Dylunio Swi Designs – artist – see Etsy Shop SiopSwi and Facebook page

Eben Fardd/Ebenezer Thomas – poet (1802 – 1863)

Ellis Owen – poet (1789 – 1868)

Eve Goodman – singer (folk)

Glain Rhys – singer (pop/musical theatre)

Gwenan Gibbard – singer and harpist (folk)

Gwilym Bowen Rhys – singer (folk)

Gwyneth Glyn – singer and poet
Jan Morris – writer (1926 – 2020)
Kate Roberts – writer (1891 – 1985)
Lewis Valentine - one of 'The Three' – writer (1893 – 1986)
Lleuwen Steffan – singer (various styles including folk, jazz and hymns in Welsh and Breton)
Lowri Evans - singer (Americana/Roots/pop/folk) often in collaboration with Lee Mason and/or others
Mabsant – musical band (folk)
Manon Steffan Ros – writer and singer (folk - with two-piece band Blodau Gwylltion)
Marian Brosschot - artist - see Marian Brosschot Celf/Art- Facebook page
Meic Stephens – poet and editor (1938 – 2018)
Meinir Gwilym – singer (pop/folk)
Meirion Macintyre Huws - poet
Mildred Elsi Eldridge – artist (1909 – 1991)
Miriam Jones - woodturner – www.miriamjones.co.uk
Myrddin ap Dafydd - writer
Nansi Richards – harpist (1888 – 1979)
Pedair – musical band (folk/indie) - collaboration between Gwyneth Glyn, Meinir Gwilym, Gwenan Gibbard and Siân James
Plu - musical band (folk/indie) - collaboration between Gwilym Bowen Rhys and his sisters Elan and Marged
R S Thomas – poet (1913 – 2000)
R William Parry – poet (1884 – 1956)
Saunders Lewis - one of 'The Three' – writer (1893 – 1985)
Tess/Therese Urbanska - artist – see Etsy Shop 'TeskaArt' and Facebook page 'teska'
Sera – singer (folk/Americana/indie)
Siân James – singer and harpist (folk)
Tapestri – musical band (Americana/Roots) – collaboration between Lowri Evans and Sera
Twm Morys – poet and singer
Y Bandana – musical band (alternative rock) – lead singer Gwilym Bowen Rhys